i SPINACH

by
Burgundy Luticia Olivier

A "Green Toque" Publication

Copies of this book may be obtained by mail or by visiting our website:

The "i love SPINACH" COOKBOOK
P.O. Box 61952   Lafayette, LA 70596
www.ilovespinach.com

Author
Burgundy Luticia Olivier

Cover Art and Recipe Sketches
Ann Vilar DuBois

Web Design and Development
Al Olivier
Karen Willingham

First Printing—August 2000

ISBN: 0-9677273-0-8

Library of Congress Card Cataloging Number 00-190390

Printed in the USA by

WIMMER
The Wimmer Companies
Memphis
1-800-548-2537

"A Labor of Love"

How It All Began...

Spinach...Who would have thought that my interest in such an unimposing leafy green would turn into a hobby of recipe collecting? Perhaps "hobby" is too mild a word..."passion" sounds more like it.

When I was a young schoolgirl back in the 60's, it seemed as if every time the school maintenance crew cut the grass on the playground, the cafeteria ladies served spinach in the lunchroom. Oh yuk! Often times while daydreaming in class, I would be snapped back to reality by the mechanical buzzing of the lawnmowers...and sure enough, I knew my lunchtime fate had been sealed.

My passion for spinach began in 1972 at my favorite *restaurant du jour.* After much persuasion by a dining companion, I was coerced into ordering Oysters Rockefeller as an appetizer. The thought of actually eating an oyster was sobering enough, but to cover it with spinach, well the very mention of it brought back less than fond memories. However, I soon realized from that first bite that I was "in love."

Thousands of Spinach Recipes?

Somehow in my passion, I forgot to keep track of just how many recipes were in my collection. A few years ago I started digging them out of desk drawers, file cabinets, old handbags, coat pockets, and those stuffed between the pages of cookbooks. I filled several boxes and started the sorting process.

I would buy cookbooks just to read through the spinach recipes. Friends would send newspaper clippings my way along with recipes cut from food packages. I even found hand-scribbled notes everywhere with elusive origins. One day I found a recipe with "special keepsake" written on it, yet I had forgotten for which special sake it was being kept! Recipes started pouring in from all over the United States and several foreign countries like England, Australia, Germany, Italy, Greece and Africa. How so many people learned of my passion and collection still remains a mystery to this day.

One thing I know for sure: the versatility of this nutritious and delicious vegetable is beyond comparison. There are thousands of ways to enjoy spinach, and the "best of the best" have been painstakingly selected from my vast archives and presented to you in this Collector's Edition *"i love SPINACH"* Cookbook.

"No man is an island." (And no woman, for that matter.)

Since this is my first major self-publishing endeavor, I've been thrust into the wearing of many hats... author, editor, proofreader, chef, researcher, investigator, layout designer, etc. It quickly became apparent that I needed support and guidance. After 28 years of dreaming about this cookbook, I look back and reflect on my deepest gratitude and indebtedness to those people that made the difference in making my dream a reality.

First, my husband, Al: "Sweetie, I knew you were my destiny from the instant I laid eyes on you. Throughout the years you have shown me the patience of unconditional love. Thank

(continued)

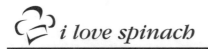

"A Labor of Love" (continued)

you for your countless hours of assisting with recipe selections, testing and tasting for months on end, technical expertise, vast computer knowledge and even proofreading. You stood by me during trying times and cheered me on to the finish line. I've always known that had I not found you, I would still be looking for love. You are my love and my life. Forever."

Ardith Bradshaw (my publishing consultant): for her patience, understanding and impressive knowledge of journalism. (Did I mention she was patient?)

Charlie and Ruth Olivier (my in-laws): for all their heart-felt prayers of support, for believing in this cookbook, and especially for believing in me. "If anyone ever doubts that there are angels walking among us, they have only to knock on your front door and see who answers."

Kim Spence (ASBDC), for her guidance, incredible insights and assistance in business matters; My dear friends at TKL (kitchenlink.com), for their encouragement, suggestions, secret recipes and sense of humor; Karen Willingham (Web Developer), for the long hours and Internet expertise devoted to our website (ilovespinach.com); Myrtle Luticia Meyer, for teaching me so much about cooking...and even more about life.

Ann DuBois (an artist and a life saver)...her professional and exhaustive work on this cookbook has truly been an uplifting experience for me. She has helped meet deadlines and idea changes tirelessly and with good humor. She has brought my visions to canvas. "Thank you Annie, for your talents, your diligence, your energy, and your friendship."

Special thanks to all of you for reading this cookbook. I feel like you have invited me into your homes, into your kitchens and into your hearts.

And most importantly, to Almighty God...through triumphs and adversities, (and even self-doubt), God has shown me grace, love, and the will to stay focused. He has been my strength, my inspiration and my guiding light.

The Cajun people in south Louisiana have a saying, "Lache Pas La Patate" (lahsh pah lah pah-taht), literally translated into "Don't let go of the potato", meaning "Don't give up." The *"i love SPINACH"* Cookbook is the result of *not giving up,* truly making it the fruit of my labor..."a labor of love."

—**Burgundy L. Olivier**

About the Artist:

Louisiana is proud of its own **Ann Vilar DuBois,** a very talented artist with a degree in Art Education. Ann has also studied Advertising Design at the University of Southwestern Louisiana—now University of Louisiana at Lafayette.

Ann lives with her husband, André, a financial advisor, and their three sons in Lafayette, Louisiana. After teaching high school art for 12 years and working at various advertising agencies, Ann began to do freelance work, specializing in illustrations and children's portraits.

She owns and operates **A. DuBois Designs,** producing and marketing her own studio illustrations, greetings cards and original artwork, as well as graphic designs. Visit our website (www.ilovespinach.com) to find out how to contact Annie.

TABLE OF CONTENTS

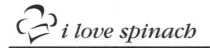 *i love spinach*

SPINACH FACTS and COOKING SUGGESTIONS

NUTRITIONAL INFORMATION

- Spinach is a good source of vitamins A and C.
- It is also a good source of minerals, iron, carotene and potassium.
- Eating foods containing vitamin C, such as tomatoes or fruit, may help your body absorb more of the iron that is in spinach.
- Spinach is low in calories; 20 calories for ¾ cup raw spinach, 20 calories for ⅓ cup cooked spinach, and 30 calories for ½ cup canned spinach.

PLANTING AND HARVESTING SPINACH

- Spinach is a member of the goosefoot family, along with Swiss chard and beets.
- Spinach is a cool season crop.
- Spinach requires a soil pH of 6.0 to 6.5 and will not grow well if pH is below 6.0.
- Spinach is shallow rooted.
- Spinach may be harvested until seedstalk forms.

HOW TO SHOP AND CARE FOR FRESH SPINACH

- Look for fresh-looking, bright green spinach with crisp leaves and thin stalks.
- Avoid yellow, soggy or wilted leaves.
- Peak seasons to buy fresh spinach are Spring and early Summer.
- Fresh spinach is available year-round.
- There are 3 main varieties of spinach: flat leaves; leaves that are crinkled (semi-savoyed); and those heavily savoyed (which trap more dirt and sandy grit).
- Trapped moisture in plastic bags can cause fresh spinach to spoil quickly.
- Spinach, which is usually quite gritty or sandy, must be thoroughly washed and rinsed before eating.

HOW TO COOK SPINACH

- To properly and thoroughly clean fresh spinach, swish it around in a sink or large bowl of water; lift out. Place in colander to drain. Change out water and repeat process twice more, lifting spinach out of water, rather than draining off water.

(continued)

Spinach Facts and Cooking Suggestions (continued)

- To remove the stems from spinach leaves, fold leaves in half lengthwise, grasping the bottom of the stem and tearing toward the tip of the leaf.
- One pound of unwashed fresh spinach will yield about three-fourths cup of cooked spinach, which is equal to about two servings.
- Cooked spinach will collapse, or wilt, to a fraction of its original size. This is due to the fact that it is mostly water.
- To cook fresh spinach in a microwave after thoroughly washing, place it in a heat-resistant, glass casserole dish. Cook, tightly covered, 3 to 5 minutes; stir halfway through cooking time. Drain excess moisture and season to taste.
- Never cook spinach in an aluminum pot; use a stainless steel saucepan or glass cookware.
- Steam spinach for simplicity; blanch spinach for delicacy.
- Freshly steamed or boiled spinach should be wrung out to remove the excess water. Grab a fistful and squeeze dry.
- The best time to steam spinach is immediately after washing. The water droplets clinging to the leaves (along with the natural moisture in the spinach) supply all that is needed to provide liquid for cooking.
- Drain cooked spinach in a colander, but do not rinse in cold water to refresh.
- To prepare for the freezer, clean and stem fresh spinach; blanch 2 minutes in boiling water; drain; cool; pack into airtight freezer containers. (Date and label before freezing.)

OBTAINING OPTIMUM RESULTS FROM THESE RECIPES

- Thoroughly read through the ingredients list and directions before starting.
- Set out all the ingredients called for in the recipe, along with mixing bowls, baking pans and pots, measuring cups, mixing spoons, small appliances, etc.
- Keep your work surface (and hands) clean at all times.
- Plan your selection of recipes during peak seasons for featured food items.
- Reduce preparation time when you're in a hurry by purchasing items such as pre-washed spinach, chopped onions, shredded cheese, skinless chicken breasts, etc.
- Frozen chopped spinach is often better if it is re-chopped after defrosting, preferably in a food processor.
- If an item is not available at your local supermarket, check with gourmet shops, International food stores, or a kitchen shop.

(continued)

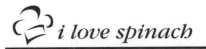

Spinach Facts and Cooking Suggestions (continued)

- Many recipes contain ingredients that may be substituted or eliminated without compromising the overall integrity of the end result. (Example: Salt may be completely eliminated for those on low-sodium diets; nuts may be left out; herbs may be interchanged; alcohol may be eliminated, etc.)
- If a recipe calls for "packaged, frozen chopped spinach, thawed and squeezed dry," it is best when squeezed by hand. Soggy spinach will drastically and adversely affect your end result.
- Fresh spinach that has been cooked may be substituted in any recipe calling for frozen chopped spinach.
- When recipes give a range of cooking times, always set timer on stove for the shortest amount of time, and check food often to avoid over-cooking.

USE PREMIUM INGREDIENTS

- "Quality in" equals "quality out." High quality ingredients used in a recipe will produce the highest quality results.
- Fresh butter is recommended (over margarine.)
- Freshly ground pepper is recommended (over packaged black pepper.)
- Freshly grated Parmesan cheese is recommended (over packaged.)
- Hungarian paprika is recommended. It has a more refined taste.
- Always use fresh eggs. (The recipes in this book were tested with large eggs.)
- Extra virgin olive oil was used in our recipes (rather than regular olive oil.)
- When using fresh herbs, use three times as much as dried herbs.
- Fresh dill is highly recommended; dried dill is a poor substitute but will suffice.
- Freshly squeezed lemon juice is recommended (over bottled lemon juice.)
- Temperature, humidity and high altitudes may affect cooking times and end results.

Hors d'Oeuvres
and
Soups

i love spinach

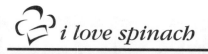
i love spinach

Hors d'Oeuvres & Soups

MARBLED SPINACH

I'm often asked which spinach recipe is my favorite, and although I would be hard pressed to narrow it to just one single recipe, Marbled Spinach is definitely near the top of the list!

8	sun-dried tomato halves, finely chopped	2	(8 ½-ounce) boxes corn muffin mix
1	cup water (very hot)	1	cup cottage cheese
½	pound butter, melted (2 sticks)	1	small onion, peeled and chopped in food processor
1	package (10-ounce) frozen chopped spinach, thawed and squeezed dry	¼	cup toasted pine nuts Vegetable cooking spray
4	eggs, beaten		

Place sun-dried tomato pieces in a small bowl and cover with hot water. Allow to soak 15 minutes to soften and plump. Preheat oven to 325°F. Combine butter, spinach and eggs in a large mixing bowl, mixing well. Add corn muffin mix and cottage cheese, stirring until thoroughly blended. Add onion, pine nuts and drained tomato pieces. Spray bottom and sides of a rectangle baking pan; pour batter into pan. Bake for 45 minutes or until knife inserted near center comes out clean. Remove from oven and cut into 2-inch squares.

Variations: (You may omit the sun-dried tomatoes and pine nuts, and add one or more of the following.)

8	slices bacon, cooked crisp and crumbled	½	cup chopped mushrooms
		¼	cup walnuts or pecans
1	cup whole kernel corn, drained	1	teaspoon minced jalapeño

PINWHEELS

While attending a formal wedding reception a few years ago, I had the pleasure of being served spinach pinwheels that were fabulous. Although I didn't get their secret recipe, this one comes pretty close.

1 ½ cups all-purpose flour	6 tablespoons shredded cheddar cheese
Salt	
Freshly ground pepper	1 package (10-ounce) frozen chopped spinach, thawed and squeezed dry
½ teaspoon baking powder	
4 tablespoons cold butter	
¼ cup vegetable shortening	¼ teaspoon granulated garlic
2 eggs	1 package (3 ½-ounce) sliced pepperoni, minced
Water	

Preheat oven to 350°F. Combine flour, salt, pepper and baking powder in a large mixing bowl. Cut in butter and shortening until dough looks crumbly. Add 1 egg and just enough water to form a soft dough. Divide dough into four portions. Mix remaining egg and cheese in medium bowl. Add spinach, garlic, salt, pepper and pepperoni; mix thoroughly. Roll dough onto floured surface. Spread spinach mixture on top of dough; roll jelly-roll fashion. Bake on cooking sheet 30 minutes. Cut into slices and serve.

SPINACH BALLS

Spinach Balls and I go way back to the early days of collecting recipes, which means I've been making them over 25 years. Adjust the seasonings and ingredients in this recipe to suit your personal taste because it's pretty hard to mess up a batch.

2 (10-ounce) packages frozen chopped spinach, cooked and squeezed dry	½ cup plus 2 tablespoons butter, softened
	¼ cup chopped water chestnuts
2 cups herbed bread stuffing mix	6 eggs, lightly beaten
1 medium onion, minced (¾ cup)	½ teaspoon dried thyme
1 cup freshly grated Parmesan cheese	½ teaspoon granulated garlic
	Salt and freshly ground pepper
	Tabasco (optional)

Preheat oven to 350°F. Combine spinach and stuffing mix; blend thoroughly. Add onion, Parmesan cheese and butter; blend. Stir in water chestnuts; add eggs, one at a time, working into mixture until well blended. Season with thyme, garlic, salt, pepper, and Tabasco. Shape into 1-inch balls, arrange on baking sheet, and bake 15 to 20 minutes. Spinach Balls may be frozen before baking.

SPINACH MEDALLIONS WITH MUSTARD SAUCE

Incorporating many of my favorite "spinach companions," this recipe is the end result of experimenting on my husband. And you know what? He didn't mind one bit!

4	sun-dried tomato halves, diced	6	eggs, lightly beaten
1	small onion, minced (½ cup)	¼	pound plus 2 tablespoons butter, melted (1 ¼ sticks)
1	package (6-ounce) prepared stuffing mix (including herb packet)	2	(10-ounce) packages frozen chopped spinach, thawed and squeezed dry
¼	cup pine nuts		Salt and freshly ground pepper
2	tablespoons chopped fresh parsley		Mustard Sauce (recipe follows)
1	cup freshly grated Parmesan cheese		

Preheat oven to 350°F. Soak tomato pieces in hot water to soften and plump; drain. In a large mixing bowl, combine onion, stuffing mix, pine nuts, parsley and Parmesan cheese. Add eggs, butter, spinach and sun-dried tomato pieces; stir to blend thoroughly. Season with salt and pepper. Shape into small medallions, about 2 inches in diameter. Place medallions on a large baking sheet and bake 15 to 20 minutes, or until cooked through. Serve with mustard sauce drizzled on top.

MUSTARD SAUCE FOR SPINACH MEDALLIONS

⅓	cup dry mustard	½	cup sugar
½	cup vinegar	1	egg yolk, lightly beaten

Combine mustard and vinegar in top of a double boiler. Add sugar and stir. Beat in egg yolk and simmer over medium-low heat until thickened. Drizzle over Spinach Medallions.

SPINACH BROWNIES

The look on your face must be priceless right about now...if indeed you are thinking that there's chocolate in this recipe! These are called "brownies" simply because they are baked in a pan and cut into squares, just like brownies.

1 cup all-purpose flour	1 medium onion, minced (¾ cup)
1 teaspoon baking powder	1 pound cheddar cheese,
1 teaspoon salt	shredded (4 cups)
2 eggs, well beaten	1 package (10-ounce) frozen
1 cup milk	chopped spinach, thawed
4 tablespoons butter, melted	and squeezed dry
(½ stick)	

Preheat oven to 350°F. In a large mixing bowl, sift together flour, baking powder and salt. Add eggs and stir until thoroughly combined. Add milk, butter and onion, stirring well after each addition. Fold in cheese and spinach, and stir until evenly distributed. Pour mixture into a large, greased baking pan; bake 30 to 35 minutes or until knife inserted near center comes out clean. Cut into squares and serve.

EASY GREEK SPINACH SQUARES

The best way to describe this recipe would be to say it's a cousin to spinach soufflé. Okay, maybe a distant cousin, but related just the same, and just as captivating.

6 eggs	1 package (10-ounce) frozen
½ cup crumbled feta cheese	chopped spinach, thawed
Dash of salt	and squeezed dry
Dash of ground nutmeg	Vegetable cooking spray

Preheat oven to 350°F. Beat eggs in a large mixing bowl. Stir in cheese, salt and nutmeg. Add spinach and stir until thoroughly blended. Spray a square baking pan and pour mixture in. Bake 30 minutes or until knife inserted near center comes out clean. Cut into squares and serve.

CHICKEN PINWHEELS WITH SPINACH AND BLUE CHEESE

For a succulent finger food sure to please the most discriminating taste, prepare a batch of these pinwheels. Tender chicken breasts are rolled around a moist spinach filling and then steamed. They'll be the first things missing from the buffet table.

1 teaspoon peanut oil	1 tablespoon toasted pine nuts
1 small onion, minced (½ cup)	(chopped walnuts or pecans
1 package (10-ounce) frozen	may be used)
chopped spinach, thawed	Salt and freshly ground pepper
and squeezed dry	4 skinless, boneless chicken
1 teaspoon fresh lemon juice	breast halves, pounded to
2 ounces blue cheese, crumbled	¼-inch thickness
	Hungarian paprika

Heat oil in wok; add onion and stir-fry 30 seconds. Add spinach; stir-fry 1 minute. Transfer spinach mixture into a medium bowl; allow to cool slightly. Stir lemon juice, blue cheese and pine nuts into spinach mixture. Season with salt and pepper. Spread each chicken breast with spinach mixture. Roll up jelly-roll fashion; secure with wooden picks. Place chicken rolls in a single layer in a shallow steaming dish. Place dish on steaming rack in wok; position rack over simmering water. Cover wok and steam until meat is firm, about 20 minutes. Remove from wok and cool slightly. Sprinkle with paprika. Slice each roll crosswise into thin slices.

FRIED SPINACH FRITTERS

A dear old friend of mine used to make the best carrot fritters I've ever tasted. She loved my spinach fritters made with spinach soufflé and Swiss cheese, from her very first bite. So, we exchanged recipes.

¾ cup unbleached all-purpose
   flour
1 teaspoon baking powder
¼ teaspoon salt
¼ teaspoon onion powder
   Dash of white pepper
1 package (12-ounce) frozen
   spinach soufflé, thawed

1 egg, lightly beaten
2 ounces Swiss cheese, finely
   shredded (½ cup)
¼ cup fine dry breadcrumbs
   Vegetable oil or canola oil for
   frying
   Freshly grated Parmesan
   cheese

Combine flour, baking powder, salt, and onion powder. Sift into a small mixing bowl; add white pepper and stir. In a medium mixing bowl, combine spinach soufflé and egg. Add flour mixture to spinach mixture; stir until thoroughly combined. Fold in Swiss cheese and breadcrumbs. Place mixture in refrigerator until well-chilled. To cook, heat vegetable oil in a large skillet. Carefully drop chilled fritter mixture, about the size of a golf ball, into the hot oil and fry 2 minutes. Drain on paper towels to absorb oil. Remove to serving platter while still hot and sprinkle with Parmesan cheese. Serve immediately.

Savory Florentine Cheesecake

Start your next dinner party with this delicious appetizer. Cut cheesecake into thin wedges and serve with toasted baguette slices. Accompanied with light cocktails or a fine wine, this recipe exudes stylish elegance.

Vegetable cooking spray
2 cups dry bread crumbs (preferably homemade)
¼ pound butter, melted (1 stick)
3 (8-ounce) packages cream cheese, softened
¼ cup whipping cream
1 teaspoon Dijon mustard
½ teaspoon salt
4 eggs

1 package (10-ounce) frozen chopped spinach, cooked and squeezed dry
4 ounces Gruyere cheese, shredded (1 cup)
¼ cup freshly grated Parmesan cheese
4 scallions, minced
Pinch of Hungarian paprika
Pinch of cayenne

Preheat oven to 350°F. Coat inside of large springform pan with cooking spray. Mix the bread crumbs and butter; press into bottom and sides of pan. Bake until very lightly browned, about 10 minutes; set aside. In a large mixing bowl, combine cream cheese, whipping cream, mustard and salt, beating until smooth. Add eggs, one at a time, beating after each addition. Add the spinach, Gruyere cheese, Parmesan cheese, scallions, paprika, and cayenne. Beat on low speed of electric mixer until thoroughly blended. Pour the mixture into the prepared crust and bake 1 hour, or until center is set and lightly browned. Cool on rack for 15 minutes before cutting into wedges. Cheesecake is best when removed from refrigerator 30 minutes before serving, making it easier to spread on toasted bread slices.

Bagel Sandwich Spread

For easy and delicious finger sandwiches, spread this spinach, cheese and bacon filling on lightly toasted, split bagels. Cut into four pieces, and skewer each with a decorative wooden pick. Arrange mini-sandwiches on a serving platter and set out for guests to enjoy.

Vegetable cooking spray
1 package (10-ounce) frozen chopped spinach, thawed and squeezed dry
16 ounces Monterey Jack cheese with jalapeños, shredded (4 cups)
½ (11-ounce) can cheddar cheese soup (full strength)

4 ounces cream cheese, softened
6 slices lean bacon, cooked crisp and crumbled
½ teaspoon Greek seasoning
Pinch of onion powder
Tabasco
2 tablespoons diced pimientos, drained (optional)
Hungarian paprika (optional)

Coat inside of a microwave-safe, square baking dish with cooking spray. In a large mixing bowl, combine spinach, Monterey Jack cheese, cheddar cheese soup and cream cheese. Fold bacon pieces into mixture. Season with Greek seasoning, onion powder and Tabasco. Pour mixture into baking dish. Cook on HIGH in microwave 2 minutes. Reduce power to MEDIUM, and microwave 5 to 8 minutes, stirring frequently. Remove from microwave and sprinkle with optional pimientos and paprika. Use as filling for bagel sandwiches or spread on crackers.

MUSHROOMS STUFFED WITH SPINACH SOUFFLÉ

Stuffed mushrooms are the perfect accompaniment to grilled vegetable kabobs, an assortment of imported cheeses, and a chilled glass of chardonnay wine.

12	jumbo mushrooms (about 2 inches in diameter)	2	tablespoons dry bread crumbs
4	tablespoons butter, melted (½ stick)	3	tablespoons freshly grated Parmesan cheese
1	tablespoon dehydrated onion flakes, crushed (plumped in water)	2	slices lean bacon, cooked crisp and crumbled
		1	package (12-ounce) frozen spinach soufflé, thawed

Preheat oven to 400°F. Wash mushrooms and pat dry. Remove stems and finely chop; set aside. Dip mushroom caps in melted butter; arrange caps in square baking pan. Combine chopped stems, onion, bread crumbs, 2 tablespoons of the Parmesan cheese, bacon pieces and spinach soufflé in a mixing bowl. Fill mushroom caps with spinach mixture. Sprinkle remaining Parmesan cheese over stuffed mushrooms. Bake, uncovered, 20 minutes.

FLORENTINE CRESCENT APPETIZERS

I bring these spinach, cheese and bacon-stuffed crescents to holiday gatherings more than any other appetizer. In fact, I'm beginning to think that's why I get invited in the first place! It almost seems like a small crowd is standing at the food table just waiting for these to arrive.

1	package (10-ounce) frozen chopped spinach, thawed and squeezed dry	4	slices lean bacon, cooked crisp and crumbled
8	ounces Velveeta cheese, cut into small cubes		Dash of salt
			Tabasco (optional)
¼	cup dry bread crumbs	2	(8-ounce) cans refrigerated crescent dinner rolls

Preheat oven to 375°F. Combine spinach, cheese, bread crumbs and bacon pieces in a medium saucepan. Season with salt and Tabasco. Cook over low heat until cheese melts, stirring constantly. Unroll crescent dough and separate into 16 triangles. Cut each triangle in half lengthwise. Spread each triangle with a little spinach mixture and roll up, starting at the wide end. Place on greased baking sheet and bake 11 to 13 minutes, or until golden brown.

STRIPED CHEESE WITH SPINACH FILLING

Someone once asked if I could tell how good a spinach recipe was by simply looking at it. I answered, "More times than not, Yes." The ingredients in this recipe assured me that this one was going to be spectacular, and sure enough, it was.

White Layer

8 ounces cream cheese, softened	4 tablespoons butter, softened (½ stick)
	1 tablespoon milk

Green Layer

1 cup frozen chopped spinach, thawed and squeezed dry	¼ cup light vegetable oil
1 cup lightly packed parsley (stems removed)	1 garlic clove, mashed
¼ cup chopped nuts (walnuts, pecans or whole pine nuts work well)	1 teaspoon dried basil
	1 cup freshly grated Parmesan cheese
	French bread, cut into ½-inch slices (toasted, if desired)

Line a small 3-cup capacity loaf pan with plastic wrap. To prepare white layer, combine cream cheese and butter in a small mixing bowl; beat until smooth. Add milk and continue to beat; set aside. To prepare green layer, combine spinach, parsley, nuts, oil, garlic and basil in food processor; cover and blend until almost smooth. Add Parmesan cheese and blend. Spread one-third of cream cheese mixture in bottom of loaf pan, spreading all the way to sides. Top with one-half of spinach mixture, pressing down to spread evenly. Repeat layering, ending with white layer on top. Cover snugly with plastic wrap and refrigerate overnight or several hours; can be made up to four days ahead. To serve, invert, carefully remove plastic wrap, and slice. Arrange slices on platter with sliced French bread.

PECAN-CRUSTED SPINACH AND ARTICHOKE DIP

It's hard to imagine improving on a spinach and artichoke dip,
unless of course you add pecans as a topping.

8	ounces cream cheese, softened	½	cup freshly grated Parmesan cheese
½	cup mayonnaise	1	small onion, minced (½ cup)
2	(9-ounce) packages frozen creamed spinach, defrosted	⅛	teaspoon cayenne
1	can (14-ounce) artichokes, drained and coarsely chopped	⅓	cup crushed herb stuffing or soft bread crumbs
		½	cup finely chopped pecans

Preheat the oven to 400°F. Combine cream cheese and mayonnaise in a large mixing bowl; add spinach, artichokes, Parmesan cheese, onion and cayenne. Place in a 2-quart baking dish. Combine herb stuffing and pecans; sprinkle over dip mixture. Bake 20 to 25 minutes, or until hot and lightly browned on top. Serve with thick potato chips, crackers or melba toast.

WARM SPINACH DIP

Entertaining dignitaries? This recipe produces a rich and
succulent dip and would be ideal when every detail is important.

2	tablespoons butter	½	cup whipping cream
2	tablespoons extra virgin olive oil	1	package (10-ounce) ready-to-use fresh spinach leaves
2	medium onions, chopped (1 ½ cups)	1	cup freshly grated Parmesan cheese
6	garlic cloves, minced	¼	cup sour cream
2	tablespoons all-purpose flour	½	teaspoon cayenne
½	cup chicken stock (preferably homemade)		Salt and freshly ground pepper
			Baguette slices, toasted

Melt the butter and oil in a heavy saucepan over medium heat. Add onion and sauté until tender, 6 to 8 minutes. Add garlic and cook another 3 minutes. Add flour; stir well and cook 2 minutes. Gradually whisk in chicken stock and cream; bring to a boil, whisking constantly. Cook until mixture thickens, stirring frequently, about 2 minutes. Remove from heat. Stir in spinach, Parmesan cheese, sour cream and cayenne. Season with salt and pepper. Transfer dip to a chafing dish or serving bowl. Serve warm with toasted baguette slices.

SPINACH DIP IN A BREAD BOWL

The first time I saw dip served in a hollowed-out bread loaf, I thought that was the most ingenious thing I had seen in years. Smaller round loaves may be used for more intimate gatherings.

2   cups sour cream
1   envelope (1-ounce) ranch
       salad dressing mix
1   package (10-ounce) frozen
       chopped spinach, thawed
       and squeezed dry
½   small onion, chopped (¼ cup)

¾   teaspoon dried basil
½   teaspoon dried oregano
1   loaf round bread
       Softened butter (for rubbing on
       inside of bread bowl)
       Crudités (raw assorted
       vegetables)

Combine sour cream, salad dressing mix, spinach, onion, basil and oregano in a bowl. Chill for at least 1 hour. Cut a slice off the top of the round bread; set it aside. Hollow out the inside of the bread, leaving a thick shell to form the bowl. Using a small plastic bag over your hand, dip your fingers in the butter and coat inside of bread bowl. This helps prevent the dip from soaking into the bread bowl lining. Cut the slice from the top of the loaf, as well as the bread from the inside of the bowl, into bite-size pieces. Fill the bread bowl with dip and set on a serving platter. Arrange the bread pieces and vegetables around the bread bowl.

HOT SPINACH DIP

When cold appetizers just don't seem to be enough, try this hot spinach dip. It is guaranteed to warm you on chilly days.

8   ounces cream cheese,
       softened
½   cup milk
2   tablespoons butter
2   teaspoons chicken-flavored
       instant bouillon

⅛   teaspoon ground nutmeg
1   package (10-ounce) frozen
       chopped spinach, thawed
       and squeezed dry
1   tablespoon fresh lemon juice
       Melba toast rounds

In medium-sized saucepan, combine cream cheese, milk, butter, bouillon and nutmeg. Mix well and cook over low heat, stirring until thickened, about 10 minutes. Stir in spinach and heat through. Remove from heat and add lemon juice. Serve hot in a chafing dish along with melba toast.

ARTICHOKE-SPINACH DIP

I'm not sure who first introduced spinach and artichokes to each other, but they certainly stumbled onto something captivating and delectable!

1   package (10-ounce) frozen chopped spinach, thawed and squeezed dry
½   cup freshly grated Parmesan cheese
3   ounces mozzarella cheese, shredded (¾ cup)
1   cup mayonnaise
1   jar (6-ounce) marinated artichoke hearts, drained and chopped
1   small garlic clove, minced Salt and freshly ground pepper
1   tablespoon chopped fresh parsley

Preheat the oven to 350°F. Combine spinach and Parmesan cheese; add mozzarella and mayonnaise. When well blended, fold in artichoke hearts and garlic; season to taste with salt, pepper and chopped parsley. Bake 15 to 20 minutes. Serve hot with pita bread, white corn chips, or party rye.

Double Recipe

OYSTERS ROCKEFELLER DIP

*Stylish elegance amidst a symphony of refined
flavors sets this dip apart from the rest.*

1	cup minced celery	½	teaspoon sugar
¼	pound butter (1 stick)	1	ounce Pernod or Herbsaint
2	bunches of scallions, chopped		Salt and freshly ground pepper
1	bunch flat-leaf parsley, minced (stems removed)	2	teaspoons fresh lemon juice
3	garlic cloves, minced	½	teaspoon MSG (optional)
1	package (10-ounce) frozen chopped spinach, thawed and squeezed dry	6	anchovy fillets, mashed, or 2 tablespoons anchovy paste
	Pinch of thyme	6	dozen oysters, drained (reserve liquid)
1 ½	tablespoons Worcestershire sauce		Seasoned bread crumbs

Sauté celery in butter until limp. Add scallions, parsley, garlic and spinach. Simmer 15 to 20 minutes. Add thyme, Worcestershire sauce, sugar, Pernod, salt, pepper, lemon juice, MSG, and anchovies. Mix well. Purée mixture, a little at a time, in a blender or food processor, using reserved oyster liquid to thin, making mixture easier to blend. Return mixture to saucepan. Sauté oysters in large skillet until edges curl; allow to cool. Coarsely chop oysters and add to blended sauce mixture. Heat 5 minutes. Add bread crumbs until proper dipping consistency. Transfer to chaffing dish and keep warm. Serve as a dip with cocktail crackers.

EASY SPINACH DIP

*A young girl about ten years old gave this recipe to me. She said it was her
favorite dip and asked if I would consider it for my cookbook. Well dear, here it is!*

1	package (10-ounce) frozen chopped spinach, thawed and squeezed dry	½	cup mayonnaise
		½	teaspoon cayenne
			Dash of salt
1	garlic clove, pressed		

Combine spinach, garlic and mayonnaise in a small bowl. Season with cayenne and salt. Cover and refrigerate several hours for optimum flavor. Serve with tortilla chips.

SWEET POTATO AND SPINACH SOUP

Fresh, tender spinach leaves are finely chopped and used as a topping for this soup. It is an elegant way to serve sweet potatoes, and is seasoned by highly prized Cajun tasso. If you don't have tasso, smoked sausage can be substituted, although it will alter the taste somewhat. Serve the soup piping hot so that the spinach "wilts" as it is stirred by each dining guest.

¼	pound butter (1 stick)	3	sweet potatoes, peeled and diced into ¼-inch pieces (3 cups)
1	large yellow onion, chopped (1 cup)		Salt
2	garlic cloves, minced	1	quart heavy cream
½	red bell pepper, seeded and chopped (¼ cup)	½	cup minced fresh parsley, stems removed
1	stalk celery, minced (½ cup)	¼	cup snipped fresh chives
4	ounces tasso, cut into tiny pieces		White pepper
1	cup all-purpose flour	1	bag fresh baby spinach, finely chopped into ¼-inch pieces
1	gallon premium chicken stock (preferably homemade)		

Melt butter in a large heavy saucepan or soup pot. Add onion and sauté until tender. Add garlic, bell pepper, and celery, cooking until soft. Add tasso and cook 5 minutes, stirring frequently. If using smoked sausage, additional cooking time will be required. Add flour by spoonfuls. Stir after each addition to fully incorporate flour into vegetable mixture, forming a pale roux. Gradually add chicken stock a little at a time so as not to reduce the temperature of the pot ingredients. Add sweet potatoes and bring to a full boil. Season with salt. Reduce heat and simmer 45 minutes, or until sweet potatoes are tender. Add heavy cream, parsley and chives. Adjust seasoning and add white pepper. Serve very hot in individual serving bowls. Mound fresh spinach on top of each serving.

SPINACH AND OYSTER SOUP

A favorite get-away of mine is to rent a log cabin deep in the heart of the Ozark Mountains and take early morning drives through the scenic countryside. One day I came upon a farmhouse with an old cowhide-seat chair next to its mailbox. On the chair was a stack of egg cartons filled with fresh country eggs. It also had a light blue canning jar with a rusty lid and a few quarters in it. The hand-written sign read, "Fresh Eggs $1 a dozen and for Fresh Cream come up to the barn and holler." Whenever I prepare this recipe I wish I had some of that fresh cream.

1	quart whole milk	2	teaspoons salt
1	quart half-and-half		Freshly ground pepper
1	pint shucked oysters (reserve liquid)		Freshly grated Parmesan cheese
10	ounces fresh spinach leaves, thoroughly washed		

Gently bring milk and half-and-half to a boil in a heavy saucepan. Put the oysters and their liquor in a separate sauté pan and poach about 3 minutes. Place spinach over the oysters and cook until the spinach is wilted. Process spinach and oysters in a food processor, or electric blender; add the hot milk mixture. Season with salt and pepper. Ladle into warmed soup bowls and serve with hot dinner rolls. Provide a shaker of Parmesan cheese for guests to sprinkle on their soup, if desired.

CLEAR SPINACH SOUP

A wonderful soup, without milk, cream or cheese.

1	quart water	1	scallion, chopped
½	pound lean ground beef	1	garlic clove, pressed
½	pound fresh spinach leaves, washed, stems removed	1	teaspoon soy sauce
			Salt and freshly ground pepper

Bring water to a boil in a Dutch oven. Add the ground beef and bring to a second boil. Cook 15 minutes at medium-high heat; skim off froth. Add spinach, scallion, garlic, soy sauce, salt and pepper. Lower heat and simmer 20 minutes. Serve immediately.

FISH AND SPINACH CHOWDER

While attending a convention in Utah many years ago,
I was served a spinach and fish chowder very similar to this one.

1	cup water
1	small onion, chopped (½ cup)
1	medium red potato, cut into ½-inch cubes
1	package (10-ounce) frozen chopped spinach
2	tablespoons butter
3	tablespoons all-purpose flour
½	teaspoon salt

Freshly ground pepper
¼ teaspoon ground nutmeg
3 cups low-fat milk
1 tablespoon Worcestershire sauce
1 pound lean fish fillets, cut into 1-inch pieces
Lemon wedges

Bring water, onion, potato and frozen spinach to a boil in a Dutch oven; reduce heat. Cover and simmer 5 minutes, breaking up spinach as it cooks. Continue to simmer until potato is crisp-tender; drain. Reserve vegetables. Heat butter in Dutch oven over medium heat. Stir in flour, salt, pepper and nutmeg; remove from heat. Stir in milk and Worcestershire sauce. Bring to a boil over medium heat, stirring constantly. Boil and stir 1 minute longer. Add fish and reserved vegetables; stir gently. Cover and simmer 10 minutes, stirring occasionally, until fish flakes easily with fork. Serve with freshly ground pepper and lemon wedges.

SPINACH SOUP WITH DEVILED EGGS

Deviled eggs bob around like little buoys in a sea of spinach soup. This is a wonderful recipe for a banquet, or perhaps a great way to use all those Easter eggs.

2 quarts chicken stock
    (preferably homemade)
2 (10-ounce) packages frozen
    chopped spinach, thawed
    and squeezed dry
3 tablespoons butter
2 tablespoons all-purpose flour

Salt
White pepper
Dash of ground nutmeg
3 eggs, boiled and halved
    lengthwise
Mayonnaise
Dash of Hungarian paprika

Bring chicken stock to a boil in a large Dutch oven. Add spinach and simmer, uncovered, 8 minutes. Pour entire contents into a sieve set over a large bowl. Press down hard with the back of a serving spoon to release juices. Chop the spinach or process in a food processor. Melt butter in the saucepan. Remove saucepan from heat and add flour, stirring constantly, until a white roux forms. Slowly add the stock, using a wire whisk to blend. Return saucepan to heat and bring to a boil, stirring constantly. Add spinach; season with salt, pepper and nutmeg. Simmer on low heat 5 minutes, stirring occasionally. Meanwhile, prepare the deviled eggs by removing the yolk from the egg white and mashing yolk with a small amount of mayonnaise in a small bowl. Salt and white pepper may be added to yolk mixture, if desired. Spoon deviled yolk mixture into egg white halves and sprinkle with paprika. Ladle spinach soup into individual soup bowls and float a deviled egg in each. Serve immediately.

POTATO AND SPINACH SOUP

Hearty and plentiful, this soup will satisfy even the hungriest of guests. After ladling soup into serving bowls or mugs, you might want to top with croutons or float popcorn on top.

2	tablespoons butter	1	teaspoon salt
1	small onion, chopped (½ cup)		White pepper
2	cups water	12	ounces evaporated milk (or
3	potatoes (each about the size		half-and-half)
	of your fist), cut into ½-inch	1	teaspoon Worcestershire
	cubes		sauce
1	package (10-ounce) frozen	8	ounces cheddar or Swiss
	chopped spinach, cooked		cheese, shredded (2 cups)
	per package instructions		

Melt butter in a large saucepan; sauté onion until tender. Add water, potatoes, spinach, salt and pepper. Cook over medium heat until potatoes are tender, but not mushy, about 20 minutes. Add evaporated milk and Worcestershire sauce. Increase heat and bring soup to near boiling point. Lower heat immediately to lowest setting, stir in cheese and serve immediately.

DRY MIX FOR CREAM OF SPINACH SOUP

Back-packers really enjoy this dry soup mix for both its convenience and flavor. It's mixed with cold water, and brought to a boil for a thick and creamy meal. That's all there is to it!

2	cups instant nonfat dry milk	3	tablespoons instant chicken
	powder		bouillon granules
½	cup plus 2 tablespoons	1	teaspoon dried marjoram
	cornstarch	1	teaspoon dried parsley flakes
½	cup instant mashed potato	1	teaspoon onion powder
	flakes	⅛	teaspoon white pepper
¼	cup dehydrated spinach flakes		

In the container of an electric blender, combine milk powder, cornstarch, potato flakes, dehydrated spinach flakes and chicken granules. Process until spinach flakes are finely chopped. Add marjoram, parsley, onion powder and white pepper; pulse to blend. Store dry mix in an airtight container. To prepare a single serving of soup, start with 1 ½ cups cold water to ⅓ cup dry soup mix. Bring to a boil in a small saucepan, or cook on HIGH in a microwave 2 to 3 minutes.

SUN-DRIED TOMATO AND SPINACH SOUP

Sun-dried tomatoes offer an intense yet splendid
flavor when coupled with spinach in this robust soup.

1	package (3-ounce) sun-dried tomatoes	1	stalk celery, diced
2	cups boiling water	½	small onion, minced (¼ cup)
4	cups fresh spinach leaves, washed, stems removed	4	slices lean bacon, cooked crisp and crumbled
			Salt and freshly ground pepper
1	can (14.5-ounce) chicken broth, or 2 cups homemade	1	pint half-and-half

Cut sun-dried tomatoes with kitchen scissors or sharp knife into ¼-inch pieces. Place in bowl and cover with boiling water. When cool, drain and set aside; reserve liquid. Pour ½ cup of the reserved liquid in a saucepan. Add spinach and cook 5 minutes; remove spinach and chop. Add chicken broth, celery, onion, tomato pieces and remaining reserved liquid to saucepan and cook 15 to 20 minutes. Put spinach back into pot with other ingredients, along with bacon; season with salt and pepper. When ready to serve, stir in half-and-half and heat; do not allow to come to a boil. Serve immediately.

CREAMY SPINACH SOUP WITH PEARS

A delightful surprise awaits you as you bite into the
flavor of fresh pears in this unimposing soup.

1	package (10-ounce) frozen chopped spinach	2	cups chicken stock (preferably homemade)
1	pear, peeled, cored and cut into ½-inch cubes	1 ½	cups half-and-half
		1	teaspoon ground cumin

Cook spinach in microwave according to package instructions; do not drain. Purée spinach and its juice in a food processor. Transfer the spinach purée into a medium nonreactive saucepan. Stir in the diced pear, chicken broth, half-and-half and ground cumin. Cook over medium heat 8 to 10 minutes. Serve immediately.

BUTTERMILK SPINACH SOUP

"Mouth-watering, scrumptious and appetizing"
are words that best describe this exquisite soup.

1	package (10-ounce) frozen chopped spinach	2	tablespoons grated lemon zest
4	cups cold or room-temperature chicken stock (recipe follows)	2	tablespoons cornstarch
		2	cups buttermilk
			Salt
			White pepper

Combine spinach and 2 cups of the chicken stock in a large saucepan. Bring to boil and use spoon to break spinach apart. Transfer mixture to an electric blender container; add 1 tablespoon of the lemon zest and purée until smooth. Combine remaining 2 cups chicken broth with corn starch, stirring until dissolved. Pour into saucepan; add spinach mixture. Bring to a boil on high heat, stirring constantly. Remove from heat, add buttermilk and pour into serving bowls or mugs. Sprinkle with remaining lemon zest; season with salt and pepper. Serve immediately.

CHICKEN STOCK

It's hard to beat a good homemade chicken stock. This recipe produces a rich-tasting stock that has less salt than canned stocks, and is more economical. Prepare plenty on a rainy day, because this freezes very well.

3	pounds chicken parts (wings, backs, necks, gizzards, hearts and/or carcasses)	2	celery stalks with leaves, coarsely chopped
2	onions, unpeeled, quartered	½	cup fresh parsley
4	quarts cold water	¾	teaspoon dried thyme
2	carrots, cut into 1-inch pieces	2	bay leaves
		10	peppercorns

Combine the chicken pieces and onion in a large stock pot. Cover and cook over medium heat until lightly browned. Add water and stir; bring to a boil. Reduce heat and skim off froth that rises to the surface. Add carrots, celery, parsley, thyme, bay leaves and peppercorns. Simmer on very low heat for 3 hours. Pour the stock through a strainer set over a large bowl; discard vegetables. When stock cools, remove the layer of fat that will have set on the surface. Store chicken broth in glass canning jars in refrigerator up to a week, or freeze up to six months.

VEGETABLE BROTH

I can pretty much say without reservation that I have never made vegetable broth the same way twice. Use the foods you have on hand and develop your own personal style and taste. Adjust the seasonings, substitute vegetables, or try dry sherry instead of wine. If you save the liquid from steamed vegetables, it may be used instead of the water called for in this recipe. Label and freeze unused portions for future use.

4	stalks celery, chopped or sliced	3	large parsley sprigs
2	small onions, unpeeled, quartered	2	quarts water
		1	cup dry white wine
2	carrots, coarsely chopped	1	teaspoon dried basil
2	leeks, sliced	1	teaspoon dried thyme
1	garlic clove, cut in half	2	bay leaves
4	mushrooms, quartered		Zest of one-half lemon
1	ripe tomato, quartered		Salt and freshly ground pepper

Combine all ingredients in a large saucepan and bring to a rolling boil. Cover and simmer 1 hour over low heat. Cool slightly and pour through colander set over a large bowl. Squeeze out liquid; discard vegetables. Store vegetable broth in glass canning jars in refrigerator up to 5 days, or freeze up to six months.

CHICKEN AND WILD RICE SOUP

If the truth be known, wild rice isn't actually a rice. Instead, it's a long-grained marsh grass. Be sure to clean wild rice before cooking it. The easiest method would be to place the rice in a bowl and fill it with cold water. Swish it around a couple of times and allow to stand a few minutes. The debris will then float to the surface and can be poured off with the water. Wild rice is also known as Indian rice.

2	teaspoons extra virgin olive oil	6	cups chicken stock (preferably
¼	cup dry sherry		homemade—see page 31)
1	small onion, chopped (½ cup)	½	teaspoon dried marjoram
½	cup minced celery	½	teaspoon dried thyme
½	cup diced carrot		Pinch of ground ginger
½	cup chopped fresh spinach		Pinch of cumin
	leaves		Freshly ground pepper
2	cups cooked and diced	2	tablespoons low-sodium soy
	chicken		sauce
1	cup wild rice, uncooked		

Heat olive oil and sherry in a large stock pot over medium-high heat. Sauté onion until tender. Add celery, carrot and spinach and continue cooking 5 minutes, stirring occasionally. Add diced chicken, wild rice, chicken stock, marjoram, thyme, ginger and cumin; bring to a boil. Lower heat, cover and simmer until rice is tender, about 30 minutes. Season with pepper and soy sauce just before serving.

ALMOND-DILL CHILLED SPINACH SOUP

An excellent chilled soup! Serve this "tribute to fine dining" at your next Garden Club meeting.

2 ¼ cups evaporated milk, chilled	1 teaspoon lemon-pepper seasoning
1 tablespoon dehydrated onion flakes	8 ounces plain nonfat yogurt
1 package (10-ounce) frozen chopped spinach, thawed, undrained	3 tablespoons toasted slivered almonds
2 teaspoons chopped fresh dill	Fresh dill sprigs

Pour ¼ cup of the cold evaporated milk in a small bowl. Add the onion flakes and allow to stand 10 minutes to soften and plump. Meanwhile, pour 1 cup of the evaporated milk in blender container. Add half the spinach, dill and lemon-pepper seasoning. Cover and blend until nearly smooth. Add a little more spinach, cover and blend again. Pour mixture in a mixing bowl; set aside. Combine remaining spinach, remaining evaporated milk, milk-soaked onions, and the yogurt in the blender container, and process until nearly smooth. Return contents of bowl into blender container. Stir to blend; cover and chill until serving time. Ladle into bowls and top with almonds and fresh dill.

BLUE CHEESE AND SPINACH SOUP

When a friend of mine turned 40, she was given a "Got the Blues?" party. Everything on the buffet table was "blue." The tablecloth, flowers, plates, napkins, glasses...everything. Even the food was colored blue, or had something blue in it.

3 tablespoons butter	1 package (10-ounce) frozen chopped spinach, thawed
1 large onion, chopped (1 cup)	½ cup heavy cream
½ cup all-purpose flour	Salt
1 ½ quarts chicken stock (preferably homemade)	Pinch of cayenne
2 cups milk	½ pound bacon, cooked crisp and crumbled
4 ounces blue cheese, crumbled	

Melt butter in large saucepan; add onion and sauté until tender. Add flour and stir to blend. Add chicken stock; bring to a boil. Stir, using a wire whisk to prevent flour from forming clumps. Add milk and reduce heat; cook 5 minutes. Add blue cheese and stir until melted. Add spinach and cook 3 minutes, or until heated through. Add cream and bring just to a boil; turn off heat and stir. Season with salt and cayenne. Soup may be puréed in blender when cooled, a little at a time, until smooth. Heat soup before serving; sprinkle crumbled bacon on top.

CARROT AND SPINACH CREAMED SOUPS

This recipe makes a lovely presentation. Each soup is prepared separately, then poured into the same bowl. By slowly pouring the soups at opposite sides of the bowl, they meet in the middle yet remain unmixed until stirred by guests. I like to drizzle a little heavy cream on top, and whirl into a spiral pattern using a wooden pick.

Carrot Cream Soup

1 ½ pounds carrots, sliced (3 cups)	½ cup chicken stock
1 medium onion, chopped (¾ cup)	1 cup heavy cream
	½ teaspoon curry powder
2 tablespoons unsalted butter	Salt and white pepper

Spinach Cream Soup

2 (10-ounce) packages fresh spinach leaves, washed, stems removed	1 ½ cups chicken stock
	1 cup heavy cream
1 large onion, chopped (1 cup)	¼ teaspoon ground mace
2 tablespoons unsalted butter	Salt and white pepper

To prepare Carrot Cream Soup: Using a small saucepan, cook carrots in enough water to cover. Bring to a boil; reduce heat and cover. Cook until carrots are tender, 10 to 12 minutes. While carrots are cooking, sauté onion in butter in large saucepan until tender, stirring often. Drain carrots, reserving 1 cup of cooking water. Purée carrots in a food processor, along with onion and half of cooking water until smooth. In the same large saucepan used for the onions, combine puréed vegetables, chicken stock, remaining ½ cup cooking water, heavy cream and curry powder. Season with salt and white pepper. Stir to blend. Bring to slow simmer; stir often.

To prepare Spinach Cream Soup: Rinse spinach thoroughly to remove any dirt or sand. Cook spinach in a medium-size Dutch oven, using only the water clinging to the leaves over high heat until steam forms. Reduce heat, cover and simmer 5 minutes, or until tender. While spinach is cooking, sauté onion in butter in a large saucepan until tender, stirring often. Drain spinach. Purée spinach in a food processor, along with onion, until smooth. In the same large saucepan used for the onions, combine puréed vegetables, chicken stock, heavy cream and mace. Season with salt and white pepper. Stir to blend. Bring to slow simmer; stir often.

To serve: Using a ladle in each hand, slowly pour Carrot Soup and Spinach Soup simultaneously into opposite sides of each soup bowl. Pour slowly so that the soups remain separated in the bowl. Garnish with fresh herbs or croutons.

CREAM OF SPINACH SOUP IN BREAD BOWLS

Edible bread bowls create an impressive presentation for your dining guests.

Soup

¼	pound butter (1 stick)	1	teaspoon onion powder
1	medium onion, chopped		Cayenne
	(¾ cup)	2	(10-ounce) packages frozen
3	tablespoons all-purpose flour		chopped spinach, thawed
4	cups chicken stock (preferably	8	ounces Swiss cheese,
	homemade)		shredded (2 cups)
3	cups skim milk		Roasted red bell pepper strips
½	cup white wine		for garnish (optional)

Bread bowls

8	round bread loaves, about 5" in diameter	Softened butter

To prepare soup, melt butter in heavy saucepan; add onion and sauté until tender. Add flour; stir and simmer 6 minutes. Add chicken stock. Gradually add milk, stirring constantly. Add wine, onion powder and cayenne. Stir in spinach and heat 10 minutes. Add cheese a little at a time. Cook and stir until cheese is melted. Ladle into prepared bread bowls, top with optional roasted pepper strips and serve immediately. To prepare bread bowls, use sharp serrated bread knife to cut top off bread; set top piece aside. Carefully remove the soft inside of bread rounds, forming a hollow bowl, being careful not to poke holes in bread bowl. Using a plastic glove or plastic sandwich bag over your hand, dip fingers in softened butter and lightly coat inside of bread bowl. This will help to keep the soup from soaking through the bread. Gently replace top of bread just before serving.

CREAMY GARLIC AND SPINACH SOUP

Calling all Garlic Lovers! This soup is definitely for you!

1	large bunch spinach, thoroughly washed, stems removed	1	large onion, chopped (1 cup)
		8	garlic cloves, minced
		¼	cup all-purpose flour
1	quart chicken stock (preferably homemade)	½	cup light cream
		½	cup heavy cream
2	large carrots, grated		Salt and freshly ground pepper
¼	pound butter (1 stick)		Sour cream (optional)

Chop spinach leaves into bite-size pieces. Combine spinach, chicken stock and carrots in soup pot. Cook until carrots are tender; remove from heat. Melt butter in large skillet; sauté onion until tender. Lower heat and add garlic, cooking gently so as not to brown garlic. Add flour and cook 10 minutes, stirring constantly. Pour contents of skillet into soup pot with spinach mixture and stir well. Purée soup in blender, a small amount at a time; return soup to pot. Add light cream and heavy cream. Season with salt and pepper. Heat soup, but do not allow soup to come to a boil. Ladle into individual serving bowls and top with dollop of sour cream, if desired.

DIET SOUP

Whenever I see "diet soup", I think of a bar of homemade soap I saw one time at a festival...it was labeled "Diet Soap." The vendor said she always sells out of that soap first! This soup recipe is also a crowd pleaser because it's so delicious, even without the rich cream.

	Vegetable cooking spray	1	can (14-ounce) stewed tomatoes, undrained
1	medium onion, chopped (¾ cup)	2	cups chicken stock (preferably homemade)
1	garlic clove, minced		
1	leek, white part only, sliced	1	can (12-ounce) vegetable juice cocktail
1	bell pepper, chopped		
8	ounces fresh mushrooms, sliced	1	tablespoon chili powder
		1	teaspoon Hungarian paprika
1	package (10-ounce) frozen chopped spinach, thawed	½	teaspoon dried oregano
		2	bay leaves
			Cayenne

Spray inside bottom of soup pot with cooking spray. Sauté onion until tender. Add garlic, leek and bell pepper; sauté 10 minutes, or until bell pepper is tender. Add mushrooms and spinach; stir until well blended. Add tomatoes, stock, vegetable juice cocktail, chili powder, paprika, oregano, bay leaves and cayenne; bring to a boil. Reduce heat and simmer 30 minutes. Adjust seasonings.

Salads,
Dressings
and
Sauces

i love spinach

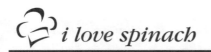
i love spinach

SALADS, DRESSINGS & SAUCES

HERBED SPINACH SALAD WITH TOMATO SOUP DRESSING

Delightfully refreshing, this salad would go well at a garden party. Use your pretty lace tablecloths, decorated with bundles of fresh herbs and flowers from your garden.

Salad

1 pound fresh spinach leaves	1 teaspoon fresh snipped chives
8 sprigs fresh lemon thyme	¼ cup crumbled blue cheese
½ cup fresh chive blossoms (8 to 10 blossoms)	¾ cup canned French-fried onion rings

Dressing

½ (10 ¾-ounce) can condensed tomato soup (full strength)	⅓ cup sugar, more or less to taste
¼ cup extra virgin olive oil	Pinch of salt
⅓ cup white wine vinegar	½ teaspoon dry mustard
	Dash of Hungarian paprika

Thoroughly wash spinach; remove large stems. Tear into bite-size pieces and keep in refrigerator until ready to serve salad. Remove thyme leaves by pulling stems between the tines of a fork; discard stems. When ready to serve salad, sprinkle chive blossoms on top of spinach. Add cheese and onion rings just before adding the dressing; toss well. To prepare the dressing, mix tomato soup, olive oil, vinegar, sugar, salt, dry mustard and paprika in a bowl. Use an electric mixer or wire whisk to thoroughly blend oil into tomato soup. Pour over spinach salad and toss salad to coat.

BAKED HERBES DE PROVENCE CHÈVRE AND SPINACH SALAD

Herbes de Provence is an assortment of the most commonly used herbs in the hills of southern France. Ingredients may be found at health food stores and specialty gourmet cooking shops. Chèvre is French for "goat." This cheese is a pure white goat's milk cheese with a pleasing tart flavor. Served with baguettes and freshly whipped herb butter, this recipe might transcend you to a quaint little sidewalk bistro in France.

2 (6-ounce) rounds of chèvre cheese	1 tablespoon herbes de Provence (recipe follows)
¼ cup extra virgin olive oil	1 large bunch fresh spinach, stems removed
½ cup dry bread crumbs, unseasoned	1 bunch watercress

Dressing

½ cup extra virgin olive oil	1 ½ teaspoons herbes de Provence
3 tablespoons balsamic vinegar	Pinch of salt
2 teaspoons Dijon mustard	White pepper
2 garlic cloves, minced	1 red bell pepper, julienned

Prepare chèvre cheese by slicing each round into thirds, producing 6 slices. Thoroughly coat each slice with olive oil. Combine the bread crumbs and herbes de Provence and press this mixture on both sides of the slices. Cover and refrigerate 1 hour. Wash spinach and watercress; dry and refrigerate until ready to serve. Prepare dressing by combining olive oil, vinegar, mustard, garlic, herbes de Provence, salt and pepper; set aside. Preheat oven to 400°F. To cook chèvre, place breaded cheese rounds on a baking sheet and place in oven until warm and softened. Combine the spinach and watercress and divide among serving plates. Place a warm cheese slice in the center of each bed of greens and garnish with bell pepper strips.

HERBES DE PROVENCE

¼	cup dried thyme	2	tablespoons dried basil leaves
2	tablespoons dried marjoram	1	tablespoon dried rosemary
2	tablespoons dried lavender flowers	1	tablespoon dried savory
		1	tablespoon dried fennel

Combine thyme, marjoram, lavender, basil, rosemary, savory and fennel in a spice grinder to blend. Chop by pulsing a few times.

BRIE AND WALNUT SPINACH SALAD

Salad for two? Enjoy this lovely salad with someone dear to you, perhaps while sitting under a large shade tree.

¼	cup extra virgin olive oil	1	small red onion, thinly sliced
1 ½	tablespoons white wine vinegar	6	ounces Brie cheese, diced (room temperature)
	Salt and freshly ground pepper	¼	cup coarsely chopped walnuts, toasted
1	pound fresh spinach leaves, thoroughly washed and torn into bite-size pieces	4	French bread toast points

Pour olive oil and vinegar in a small bowl; whisk to blend. Season with salt and pepper. Combine spinach, onion and half of the cheese in a large salad bowl. Preheat broiler. Place remaining Brie on toast points and place under broiler for 1 minute. Toss salad with dressing until well coated. Divide salad between two serving plates, top with walnuts and serve with toast points.

CHUNKY ROQUEFORT DRESSING AND SPINACH SALAD

*The Roquefort dressing provides just the right flavors
to complement fresh spinach and mushrooms.*

Dressing

2 tablespoons white wine
   vinegar
1 teaspoon Dijon mustard
1 small garlic clove, minced

   Freshly ground pepper
⅓ cup extra virgin olive oil
2 ounces Roquefort cheese,
   crumbled (¼ cup)

Salad

1 bag (10-ounce) fresh spinach,
   thoroughly washed, stems
   removed
½ cup sliced fresh mushrooms

1 small red onion, thinly sliced
1 ripe tomato, cut into ½-inch
   pieces
   Croutons, if desired

In a blender container, combine vinegar, mustard, garlic, and pepper; pulse twice. Turn motor to lowest speed and slowly add olive oil. Replace top and pulse until well blended. Add cheese and pulse twice; do not over-work. To prepare salad, tear spinach leaves into bite-size pieces. Combine spinach, mushrooms, onion and tomato in a large salad bowl. Pour dressing over salad and toss gently to coat. Serve with croutons.

CREOLE SPINACH SALAD

A chapon is a piece of dry French bread that has been rubbed with garlic or garlic-flavored olive oil. It is used to rub the inside of a salad bowl, leaving just a hint of garlic to enhance a green salad.

1 chapon	4 scallions, minced
1 pound fresh spinach, thoroughly washed and patted very dry	1 tablespoon Creole mustard
	Salt and freshly ground pepper
6 slices lean bacon	½ pound fresh mushrooms, thinly sliced
¼ cup extra virgin olive oil	2 eggs, boiled and chopped
2 tablespoons light vegetable oil	¼ cup freshly grated Parmesan cheese
4 drops Tabasco	

Rub inside of a large salad bowl with chapon. Put prepared spinach leaves in bowl and toss around. Remove chapon. Fry bacon in heavy skillet until crisp. Remove from skillet and crumble when cool enough to handle. Discard bacon drippings, or save for future use. Pour olive oil and vegetable oil into skillet, along with Tabasco and scallions. Sauté 3 minutes. Add mustard and stir. Pour skillet contents over spinach and mix thoroughly. Season with salt and pepper. Sprinkle with mushrooms, bacon pieces, egg, and Parmesan cheese. Toss and serve.

OVERNIGHT LAYERED SALAD

Have you ever noticed how some hostesses seem to be so organized and relaxed when their guests arrived? I believe their secret is to planning ahead. With this make-ahead layered salad, you too will have time to enjoy your guests.

1 pound fresh spinach, washed, stems removed, and torn into bite-size pieces	1 small bunch scallions, cut into ¼-inch pieces
6 eggs, boiled and sliced	1 cup mayonnaise
12 slices lean bacon, cooked crisp and crumbled	1 cup sour cream
	4 ounces Swiss cheese, shredded (1 cup)
1 box (10-ounce) frozen sweet peas, thawed but not cooked	

Arrange spinach in bottom of a large, straight-sided, clear glass bowl; pat down. Arrange layer of egg slices on top. Sprinkle bacon pieces on top of egg. Spoon peas on top of bacon. Sprinkle scallions on top of peas. In a small bowl, combine mayonnaise and sour cream. Spoon mixture over scallions, carefully spreading all the way to touch the walls of the bowl. Sprinkle Swiss cheese over mayonnaise mixture. Cover bowl with plastic wrap, forming a tight seal. Refrigerate several hours or overnight.

CURRIED CORN SALAD

Curry powders vary dramatically, depending on the region and style of the cook. It is actually a blend of many spices, herbs and seeds. Among the most common ingredients are: cardamom, cinnamon, coriander, fennel seed, chiles, cloves, cumin, fenugreek, nutmeg, mace, cayenne, black pepper, poppy seeds, saffron, tamarind, sesame seeds, and the ingredient that gives curried dishes that signature color, turmeric. Curry powder is also available in the spice section of grocery stores and specialty markets.

Dressing

2 tablespoons cider vinegar	2 teaspoons prepared mustard
2 teaspoons curry powder	Tabasco (optional)

Salad

2 cups canned corn (without liquid)	1 small cucumber, peeled, seeded and coarsely chopped
¼ cup diced red bell pepper	1 bunch fresh spinach, thoroughly washed, stems removed
¼ cup diced green bell pepper	
2 scallions, chopped	

Prepare dressing by combining vinegar, curry powder, mustard and optional Tabasco. Allow flavors to marry for 1 hour or longer. Put corn in a large salad bowl. Add bell pepper, scallions and cucumber; toss to mix. Add spinach leaves and continue tossing. To serve, drizzle dressing on top and toss again.

GREEK SALAD

Undoubtedly the most difficult task of publishing this book, has been the selection of the recipes. After more than a quarter of a century of collecting spinach recipes, deciding which ones would go into my first cookbook proved challenging. At one point I narrowed it down to two thousand recipes. It was then I knew that getting that number down would be tough. One taste of this salad and you will know why it was selected.

2	bunches spinach, thoroughly washed, stems removed, and patted dry
1	small red onion, thinly sliced
1	small cucumber, peeled, seeded and thinly sliced
½	cup sliced radishes (optional)
4	ounces feta cheese, crumbled
1	teaspoon Dijon mustard
2	tablespoons chopped fresh parsley
1	scallion, sliced into ¼-inch pieces
1	tablespoon fresh lemon juice
1	small garlic clove, minced
2	tablespoons extra virgin olive oil
¼	cup toasted pine nuts
¼	cup Kalamata olives

Tear spinach into bite-size pieces and place in large salad bowl. Add onion, cucumber, optional radishes, and half of the feta cheese. In a blender, put remaining feta cheese, mustard, parsley, scallion, lemon juice, garlic and olive oil; purée. Pour over salad. Sprinkle with pine nuts and olives.

CASHEW SPINACH SALAD WITH POPPY SEED DRESSING

Included are three recipes for poppy seed dressings. Be adventuresome by swapping out ingredients to create your own signature dressing.

Salad

8	slices lean bacon
1	bunch fresh spinach, washed, stems removed and torn into bite-size pieces
½	head lettuce, washed and torn into bite-size pieces
½	cup cashew pieces
2	ounces mozzarella cheese, shredded (½ cup)
	Poppy Seed Dressing (recipes follow)

Chop bacon into small pieces and cook until crisp. Drain bacon pieces on paper towel. Place spinach and lettuce in salad bowl. Add cashew pieces, mozzarella cheese and crumbled bacon; toss to blend. Serve with choice of poppy seed dressings.

47

BASIC POPPY SEED DRESSING

⅔ cup light vegetable oil
⅓ cup sugar
⅓ cup red wine vinegar
¼ teaspoon dry mustard

2 teaspoons finely grated red onion
1 tablespoon poppy seeds

Combine oil, sugar and wine vinegar in blender container; blend until smooth. Add mustard, onion and poppy; blend until smooth. Refrigerate until needed.

LEMON POPPY SEED DRESSING

2 tablespoons frozen lemonade concentrate, thawed (full strength)

¼ cup mayonnaise
½ teaspoon sugar
1 teaspoon poppy seeds

Combine lemonade concentrate, mayonnaise, sugar and poppy seeds; blend well. Refrigerate until needed.

HONEY MUSTARD POPPY SEED DRESSING

2 cups mayonnaise
¼ cup Dijon mustard
½ cup prepared yellow mustard
½ cup honey
½ teaspoon fresh tarragon, crushed

Juice of half a lemon
Dash of salt
Dash of red wine vinegar
White pepper

Combine mayonnaise with Dijon and yellow mustards. Stir in honey; blend until smooth. Add tarragon, lemon juice, salt, red wine vinegar and white pepper. Stir until thoroughly blended. Refrigerate until needed.

TOASTED HAZELNUT AND MARINATED MUSHROOM SALAD

*The mushrooms in this recipe should be marinated a day
or two in advance and are well worth the wait.*

Marinated Mushrooms

¼ cup hazelnut-flavored oil, or extra virgin olive oil

1 tablespoon balsamic vinegar Salt and freshly ground pepper

½ pound fresh button mushrooms, sliced ¼-inch thick

Salad

¼ cup coarsely chopped toasted hazelnuts

8 cups spinach leaves, washed and torn into bite-size pieces

To prepare marinated mushrooms, pour oil and vinegar in a mixing bowl. Using a wire whisk, rapidly blend until thoroughly combined. Season with salt and pepper. Add the mushrooms and toss gently to coat. Cover with plastic wrap and refrigerate overnight, or up to two days. To toast hazelnuts, discard shells and place nuts on a baking sheet. Roast for up to 30 minutes at 275°F, or until the skins crack. Place hazelnuts between two hand towels and rub to remove skins, or remove skins with hands. Chop hazelnuts in a food processor or nut grinder. Put the spinach in a large salad bowl and sprinkle chopped hazelnuts. Add the mushrooms, with their marinade, and toss. Season with salt and pepper, if desired.

CHIFFONADE SPINACH WITH TOASTED ALMOND SLIVERS AND CREAMY VINAIGRETTE

To create an eye-pleasing luncheon salad, cut fresh spinach leaves into thin strips, or chiffonades, and mound on salad plates. The almond slivers are broiled and then lightly dusted with powdered sugar.

1	bunch fresh spinach, thoroughly washed and patted dry	½	cup blanched, slivered almonds
		2	tablespoons powdered sugar

Creamy Vinaigrette

1	fresh egg yolk		Salt and freshly ground pepper
1	tablespoon fresh lemon juice	¾	cup peanut oil
½	teaspoon Dijon mustard	¼	cup red wine vinegar

Preheat broiler. Chiffonade spinach leaves and keep in refrigerator until serving time. Lay almond slivers in a single layer on a baking sheet. Place under broiler and toast for 1 minute, or until a light gold color. Remove from oven and immediately dust with powdered sugar. To prepare vinaigrette, combine egg yolk, lemon juice, mustard, salt and pepper in blender container; blend thoroughly. With motor still running on blender, add up to half of the oil and half of the vinegar, blending until emulsified. Gradually add remaining oil and vinegar until all is incorporated. Refrigerate until serving time. To serve salad, mound spinach strips onto salad plates, sprinkle almonds on top, and drizzle with vinaigrette.

BLUE-APPLE SPINACH SALAD

*Blue cheese, apples and walnuts provide a pleasant variety
of both textures and flavors in this spinach salad.*

Dressing

⅓ cup extra virgin olive oil

¼ cup white wine vinegar

1 tablespoon prepared mustard

1 teaspoon sugar

Salad

1 bag (10-ounce) fresh spinach leaves, washed, patted dry and stems removed

1 head yellow-tipped Belgian endive, washed, patted dry and trimmed

2 Red Delicious apples, cored and thinly sliced

¼ cup coarsely chopped walnuts, toasted

4 ounces blue cheese, crumbled

To prepare dressing, combine olive oil, white wine vinegar, mustard and sugar in glass jar. Cover tightly and shake vigorously until well blended. Set aside until time to serve salad. Using a sharp knife, cut spinach leaves into thin strips. Trim endive by removing bottom part. To serve, spoon dressing in the center of serving plates. Place a small mound of shredded spinach on top. Arrange endive around one side of spinach, forming a fan. Sprinkle walnuts and blue cheese on top.

MARDI GRAS SPINACH SALAD

My in-laws have been married over 50 years and they still teach dancing! It's such a thrill to see folks that raised seven children still so young at heart. We enjoy watching their dance clubs participating in "Fat Tuesday" parades while wearing the Mardi Gras colors, namely green, gold and purple. The green color in this recipe (spinach), represents "faith"; the gold color (mandarin oranges), represents "power", and the purple color (red onions), represents "justice."

Dressing

¼ cup white wine vinegar
¼ cup sugar
¼ teaspoon dry mustard
¼ teaspoon salt

½ teaspoon dehydrated onion flakes
   Dash of Hungarian paprika
1 egg, lightly beaten
¼ cup vegetable oil

Salad

6 cups torn spinach leaves
2 cups torn romaine leaves
2 cups torn iceberg lettuce leaves

1 can (11-ounce) mandarin orange segments, drained
1 small red onion, thinly sliced
½ cup sliced almonds, toasted

To prepare dressing, combine vinegar, sugar, dry mustard, salt, onion flakes, paprika and egg in a small saucepan; bring to a boil. Boil 1 minute; reduce heat. Add vegetable oil gradually, stirring to blend smoothly. Allow to cool; chill until serving time. To assemble salad, place the spinach, romaine and iceberg lettuce in a large bowl and toss. Add mandarin oranges and onion rings; tossing to mix. Pour dressing on top of salad and continue to toss. Sprinkle almonds on top and serve.

CHICKEN-AND-GRAPES SPINACH SALAD WITH HONEY-WALNUT DRESSING

Succulent chicken, crisp apples, tender spinach and plump grapes provide the "canvas" on which this honey and walnut dressing can create its masterpiece.

Dressing

½ cup vegetable oil
3 tablespoons tarragon white wine vinegar
3 tablespoons honey
2 tablespoon chopped walnuts (toasted)

1 tablespoon fresh lemon juice
1 teaspoon Creole mustard, or whole grain mustard
White pepper

Salad

1 large Red Delicious apple
1 ½ cups acidulated water, or lemon-lime carbonated beverage
1 bag (10-ounce) fresh baby spinach

4 skinless, boneless chicken breast halves, cooked and sliced
½ cup coarsely chopped walnut
½ small red onion, sliced into thin rings
1 cup red seedless grapes

To prepare dressing, combine oil, tarragon vinegar, honey, walnuts, lemon juice and mustard in a mixing bowl. Beat briskly with a wire whisk until blended. Season with white pepper, whisk again, and set aside. To prepare salad, core and thinly slice apple. Put apple slices in a shallow bowl and cover with acidulated water to prevent browning. Meanwhile, divide baby spinach among serving plates. Place chicken slices on top. Arrange apple slices on the salad; sprinkle with walnuts, onion rings and grapes. Drizzle dressing on top of salads and serve immediately.

STRAWBERRY SPINACH SALAD

There's just something about fresh spinach salad and juicy strawberries tossed together on a salad plate. What a nice touch this would lend to an Easter Sunday meal.

1   bunch spinach leaves, stems removed, washed and torn into bite-size pieces

1   pint fresh strawberries, stems removed, cut in half

Dressing

½   cup sugar
2   tablespoons toasted sesame seeds
1   tablespoon poppy seeds
2   teaspoons minced sweet onion

¼   teaspoon White Wine Worcestershire sauce
¼   teaspoon Hungarian paprika
½   cup light vegetable oil
¼   cup balsamic vinegar

Toss spinach and strawberries in large salad bowl. Divide among serving plates. To prepare dressing, put sugar, sesame seeds, poppy seeds, onion, Worcestershire sauce, and paprika in blender container; pulse to blend. With motor running on low speed, slowly add oil and vinegar; blend until smooth and thickened. Pour dressing over salad and serve immediately.

FRUITED SPINACH SALAD WITH DRIED-CHERRY VINAIGRETTE

To experience the full flavor of the vinaigrette called for in this recipe, dried-cherry vinegar must be used. If you can't find a bottle at your local kitchen shop, try the recipe included.

Dried-Cherry Vinegar

1	cup dried cherries	2	cups white wine vinegar

Vinaigrette

3	tablespoons dried-cherry vinegar	¼	teaspoon salt
¼	cup vegetable oil		Freshly ground pepper

Salad

6	cups spinach leaves, stems removed, washed and torn into bite-size pieces	1	apple, cored and thinly sliced (kept in acidulated water until needed)
1	cup dried cherries	1	orange, peeled and cut into sections
		¼	cup salted cashews

To prepare vinegar, put dried cherries in a quart-size canning jar; add white wine vinegar. Cover and steep for 2 days at room temperature. After 2 days, heat to almost boiling stage. Pour through a strainer lined with cheesecloth. Allow to cool; store in tightly sealed container. To prepare vinaigrette, whisk together dried-cherry vinegar, vegetable oil, salt and pepper. To prepare the salad, toss the spinach in a large salad bowl with the dried cherries, apple, orange and cashews. Drizzle vinaigrette on top and toss again. Serve immediately.

BLUEBERRY SPINACH SALAD WITH GINGER-HONEY DRESSING

For the past several years, I've picked my own blueberries at a remote little place in the country called "Blueberry Hill." Every June I eagerly mark my calendar, phone a bunch of friends, grab my old straw hat, and set out for a day in the warm sun.

Dressing

3	tablespoons honey		1	tablespoon light vegetable oil
2	tablespoons fresh lime juice		½	teaspoon freshly grated
1	tablespoon seasoned rice			gingerroot
	vinegar			

Salad

6   cups fresh spinach leaves, washed and torn into bite-size pieces
1   cup fresh blueberries
3   kiwi, peeled and sliced (about 1 cup)

¼   cup coarsely chopped pecans, toasted
2   ounces Gouda cheese, julienned

To prepare dressing, combine honey, lime juice, rice vinegar, vegetable oil and gingerroot in a glass jar with a tight-fitting lid. Shake vigorously to blend. To prepare salad, put spinach in a large salad bowl and toss with blueberries, kiwi, pecans and Gouda cheese. Pour dressing over salad and serve immediately.

FRUIT BASKET SPINACH SALAD WITH HONEY-YOGURT DRESSING

The next time you receive a lovely fruit basket, try this recipe. Add your own choices of fruit and be creative. And when you "give" a fruit basket to a friend in the hospital or perhaps as a house-warming gift, include a copy of this cookbook. Your thoughtfulness will be long remembered.

Dressing

½ cup nonfat plain yogurt

2 tablespoons honey (more to taste)

½ teaspoon lime zest (minced extra-fine)

Salad

6 cups spinach leaves, washed, stems removed and torn into bite-size pieces

1 apple, cored and coarsely chopped (kept in acidulated water until needed)

1 pear, cored and coarsely chopped

½ cup red seedless grapes, cut in half

Roasted sunflower seeds for garnish (optional)

To prepare dressing, combine yogurt, honey and lime zest in a small bowl; stir to blend. To prepare salad, toss spinach in a large salad bowl along with apple, pear and grapes. Sprinkle sunflower seeds on top, if desired. Drizzle Honey-Yogurt Dressing on top and serve immediately.

RASPBERRY AND CHICKEN SPINACH SALAD

When my husband and I were discussing our wedding cake with the head pastry chef at Anjo's Bakery, we both said "raspberry" when asked what our favorite filling was. Although this salad isn't nearly as decadent as that scrumptious cake, you will appreciate the raspberries just the same.

Dressing

½   cup raspberry vinegar
¼   cup salad oil (not olive oil)
2   tablespoons honey

1   teaspoon orange zest
     Salt and freshly ground pepper

Salad

     Vegetable cooking spray
6   skinless, boneless chicken
       breast halves
½   cup orange juice

2   pounds fresh spinach leaves,
       thoroughly washed and
       stems removed
2   cups fresh raspberries

To prepare dressing, combine raspberry vinegar, salad oil, honey and orange zest in a screw-top jar; shake well. Season with salt and pepper and shake again; refrigerate until time to serve. To prepare chicken, lightly spray nonstick skillet with cooking spray. Cut chicken into ½-inch slices and place in skillet. Slowly cook over medium heat until meat is no longer pink, turning once. Pour orange juice over chicken and continue cooking until nearly all of the liquid evaporates. Allow chicken to cool slightly. Tear spinach leaves into bite-size pieces and place in large salad bowl. Add chicken strips and toss. Pour dressing on top and sprinkle with fresh raspberries; serve immediately.

HERBAL-HONEY CHICKEN SALAD

Tender marinated chicken tops a bed of steamed spinach,
accented by sautéed garlic, leeks and mushrooms.

½	cup mayonnaise	1	cup thinly sliced leeks (white and green parts only)
2	tablespoons honey		
1	tablespoon fresh lemon juice	1	small garlic clove, minced
1	teaspoon dried tarragon	1	cup sliced mushrooms
4	skinless, boneless chicken breast halves	1	pound fresh spinach leaves, washed and torn into bite-size pieces
1	tablespoon butter		White pepper

Combine mayonnaise, honey, lemon juice and tarragon in a plastic, gallon-size zippered bag. Add chicken breasts and marinate in refrigerator several hours. To prepare chicken, preheat broiler. Remove chicken from bag, reserving marinade. Arrange chicken pieces on greased rack of broiler pan. Broil 10 to 12 minutes on each side or until tender. Brush chicken occasionally with reserved marinade. Cut chicken into bite-size chunks; set aside and keep warm. Melt butter in heavy skillet. Add leeks, garlic and mushrooms, cooking until tender. Add spinach and season with pepper. Cover skillet and cook until spinach starts to wilt, 3 to 5 minutes. To serve, spoon spinach mixture onto plates, and top with chicken.

59

CRAWFISH DRESSING AND SPINACH SALAD

When crawfish season is upon us, we never run out of ways to prepare them. After all the crawfish boils, the étouffées and the crawfish lasagne dinners, try this salad. It is absolutely the best crawfish salad I have ever tasted.

½   cup vegetable oil
1   small onion, chopped (½ cup)
2   garlic cloves, minced
1   teaspoon Dijon mustard (more
    to taste)
¼   cup rice wine vinegar
    Dash of cayenne
    Salt and freshly ground pepper

8   ounces crawfish tail meat,
    deveined
1   bunch fresh spinach, washed,
    patted dry and torn into
    1-inch pieces
1   fresh tomato, coarsely
    chopped
½   cup sliced fresh mushrooms
    Lemon wedges

Heat oil in saucepan; add onion and sauté until tender. Add garlic and cook 3 minutes. Whisk in mustard, wine vinegar and cayenne. Season with salt and pepper. Fold in crawfish tail meat and cook until warmed through. Place spinach in a large bowl and cover with crawfish dressing; toss to coat. Serve on salad plates; garnish with tomato, mushrooms and lemon wedges.

ARTICHOKE AND TOMATO PASTA SALAD

Radiatore is pasta that resembles "little radiators."
They have a short, chunky shape with rippled edges.

Pasta Salad

6	ounces radiatore pasta, cooked (about 3 cups)	1	medium tomato, chopped
2	cups shredded spinach leaves	2	ounces feta cheese, crumbled

Artichoke Sauce

1	can (14-ounce) artichoke hearts, drained	1	tablespoon water
1	tablespoon extra virgin olive oil	½	teaspoon dried basil
		¼	teaspoon dried oregano
1	tablespoon fresh lemon juice	1	garlic clove, minced
			Freshly ground pepper

To prepare the pasta salad, combine cooked pasta, spinach and tomato in a large salad bowl; set aside. To prepare the sauce, combine 2 of the artichoke hearts, olive oil, lemon juice, water, basil, oregano, garlic and pepper in a food processor; process until smooth. Chop the remaining artichoke hearts and add them to the pasta mixture. Pour puréed artichoke mixture over pasta mixture and toss. Cover salad bowl with plastic wrap and refrigerate 2 hours. To serve, toss pasta salad and sprinkle feta cheese on top.

i love spinach

FRUIT AND SPINACH PASTA SALAD

When selecting a pasta for this recipe, why not visit a gourmet shop
and opt for a fun shape you haven't tried before?

Dressing

⅓   cup sugar
½   teaspoon salt
½   teaspoon Dijon mustard (more,
        if desired)

1   tablespoon white wine vinegar
3   tablespoons light vegetable oil
¼   cup fresh orange juice
2   teaspoons poppy seeds

Salad

1   pound elbow macaroni (or
        other medium-size pasta)
3   cups shredded spinach leaves
2   cups coarsely chopped canned
        peaches, drained

2   cups sliced fresh strawberries
8   slices lean bacon, cooked
        crisp and crumbled

To prepare dressing, combine sugar, salt, mustard and vinegar in an electric blender; blend until smooth. Slowly add vegetable oil, orange juice and poppy seeds; blend until smooth. To prepare salad, cook pasta al dente, drain and rinse in cold water. Drain again. Combine pasta, spinach and peaches in a large salad bowl. Pour dressing over pasta mixture and toss gently to coat. Add strawberries and bacon pieces; toss. Serve immediately.

VEGGIE PASTA SALAD WITH HERB DRESSING

California mixed vegetables are a combination of broccoli, carrots and cauliflower.

Salad

1	package (8-ounce) cheese-stuffed tortellini	8	ounces fresh mushrooms, thinly sliced
8	ounces spinach fettuccine	1	zucchini, thinly sliced
1	box (6-ounce) frozen snow peas, thawed and drained	1	can (6-ounce) whole pitted ripe olives, drained
2	(16-ounce) packages frozen California mixed vegetables, thawed and drained	1	cup freshly grated Parmesan cheese
1	can (14-ounce) artichoke hearts, drained and quartered	2	cups cherry tomatoes

Dressing

1	egg yolk	1	teaspoon dried basil
2	tablespoons fresh lemon juice	1	teaspoon garlic powder
1	tablespoon Dijon mustard	1	teaspoon sugar
1	tablespoon red wine vinegar	1	teaspoon salt
1	cup light vegetable oil		Freshly ground pepper
½	cup extra virgin olive oil		Dash of cayenne
½	teaspoon dried thyme		Finely grated zest of 1 orange

To prepare salad, cook tortellini and fettuccine according to package instructions, drain, rinse in cold water and drain again. Set aside. Combine snow peas, mixed vegetables, artichoke, mushrooms, zucchini and olives in a large salad bowl. Add 2 tablespoons of the Parmesan cheese to the pastas and toss gently. Combine the pastas, vegetable mixture, and dressing, tossing gently. Cover salad and chill for several hours or overnight. Before serving, add tomatoes and remaining Parmesan cheese; toss again. To prepare the dressing, process the egg yolk, lemon juice, mustard and vinegar in a food processor for 30 seconds. While machine is still running, slowly pour vegetable oil and olive oil in a thin, steady stream, forming a light mayonnaise. Add thyme, basil, garlic powder, sugar, salt, pepper, cayenne and orange zest. Blend in food processor; pour over salad.

SUN-DRIED TOMATO VINAIGRETTE

It takes seventeen pounds of fresh tomatoes to produce one pound of dried. That should give you some indication of how flavorful they are. If a recipe calls for a hot liquid, use that liquid to plump the dried tomatoes if at all possible.

¼	cup finely chopped sun-dried tomatoes (not oil-packed)	1	tablespoon balsamic vinegar
½	cup hot water	1	scallion, minced
½	cup vegetable oil		Freshly ground pepper

Put tomatoes in a small bowl and cover with hot water. Allow to stand 15 minutes to plump; drain off liquid. In a small mixing bowl, combine oil, vinegar, scallion and pepper; stir to blend. Add plumped tomatoes. To serve, shake or stir vinaigrette and pour over spinach salad.

RASPBERRY CREAM DRESSING WITH SPINACH SALAD

Don't have fresh raspberries? That's no problem with this recipe...it calls for frozen raspberries.

Dressing

1	package (10-ounce) frozen raspberries, thawed	2	tablespoons sherry wine vinegar
6	tablespoons vegetable oil		Dash of salt
¼	cup heavy cream		

Salad

6	cups fresh spinach, washed, stems removed, and torn into bite-size pieces	2	kiwi, peeled and sliced
		1	small red onion, peeled and thinly sliced
1	can (11-ounce) mandarin orange segments, drained		

To prepare dressing, purée raspberries in a blender until smooth. Pour into a wire-mesh strainer and press with back of spoon to extract liquid; discard seeds. Combine raspberry purée, oil, heavy cream, wine vinegar and salt, whisking until smooth. Refrigerate until needed. To prepare salad, combine spinach, mandarin oranges, kiwi and onion in a large salad bowl. Serve chilled with Raspberry Cream Dressing.

DIPPING SAUCE FOR SHRIMP

Here's a delightful change for seafood lovers. This spinach sauce is great served with boiled shrimp, cherry tomatoes and lemon wedges. Arrange on a bed of lettuce and serve dipping sauce in small bowl.

⅔	cup mayonnaise	2	tablespoons water
⅔	cup sour cream	½	teaspoon dried tarragon
½	cup snipped parsley	¼	teaspoon garlic salt
½	cup frozen chopped spinach,		White pepper
	thawed and squeezed dry		Dash of Tabasco (optional)
2	tablespoons fresh lemon juice		

In a blender container, combine mayonnaise, sour cream, parsley, and spinach; blend. Add lemon juice, water, tarragon, garlic salt, white pepper, and optional Tabasco. Cover and blend until smooth. Refrigerate until serving time.

ROCKEFELLER SAUCE

Rockefeller Sauce is a highly versatile sauce.
Serve cold with boiled shrimp, or toss with hot cooked pasta.

6	ounces butter (1 ½ sticks)	1	tablespoon ketchup
¾	cup minced celery	1	tablespoon anchovy paste
3	scallions, minced		Tabasco
1	pound fresh spinach, washed		Freshly ground pepper
	and stems removed	¼	cup Cognac
1	cup lightly packed watercress,		
	stems removed		

Melt ½ stick of butter in a heavy skillet. Sauté celery and scallions until tender. Add spinach and watercress, stir, and cook 3 minutes. Remove skillet from heat. Place spinach mixture in a food processor and process until smooth. Stir in ketchup, anchovy paste, Tabasco and pepper. Add Cognac and stir until well blended. Add remaining stick of butter, 1 tablespoon at a time, and process until smooth. Transfer mixture to glass bowl or jar, cover, and refrigerate 2 hours to allow flavors to marry. Serve sauce on top of cold, boiled shrimp or stir into hot cooked pasta.

BASIC GREEN SAUCE

A tomatillo is a fruit that resembles a small, green tomato in shape and size, yet its skin is thin like parchment. The flavor of a tomatillo hints of lemon, apple and herbs. They are available in specialty produce markets and are popular in Mexican and Southwest cooking.

½	cup vegetable oil	1	can (4-ounce) green chiles, drained and chopped
1	large onion, chopped (1 cup)		
1	bag (10-ounce) fresh spinach leaves, chopped	2	small garlic cloves, crushed
		1	tablespoon dried oregano
½	pound tomatillos, husks removed, washed and coarsely chopped	1	cup low-fat chicken broth
		2	cups sour cream

Heat oil in saucepan; sauté onions until tender. Add spinach, tomatillos, chiles, garlic and oregano. Cover and cook for 5 minutes over medium heat, stirring occasionally. Transfer mixture to blender container and process until smooth, about 1 minute. Return mixture to saucepan and add broth; stir to blend. Bring mixture to a boil and immediately reduce heat to a simmer. Cook, uncovered, for 10 minutes. Remove from heat and stir in sour cream. Transfer to serving bowl. Refrigerate any unused sauce. Sauce may be used as a dip, or a sauce to pour over vegetables or meats.

Casseroles
and
Side Dishes

i love spinach

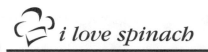 *i love spinach*

CASSEROLES & SIDE DISHES

CREAMY SPINACH CASSEROLE

Sour cream is the key to this family favorite.

2	(10-ounce) packages frozen chopped spinach, cooked and squeezed dry	2	tablespoons bacon bits
8	ounces sour cream	1	teaspoon garlic salt
½	cup freshly grated Parmesan cheese	1	teaspoon dried basil
		¼	cup buttered bread crumbs

Preheat oven to 350°F. Spread spinach in the bottom of a greased casserole dish. Stir in sour cream, Parmesan cheese, bacon bits, garlic salt and basil. Top with bread crumbs and bake 25 to 30 minutes.

SPINACH CUSTARD

Every time I see this recipe, I'm tempted to sneak into the kitchen and prepare it.

2	(10-ounce) packages frozen chopped spinach	¼	cup biscuit baking mix
¼	teaspoon garlic salt	4	eggs, beaten
	Freshly ground pepper	1	cup milk
6	ounces sharp processed American cheese, shredded (1 ½ cups, divided)	1	tablespoon butter

Cook spinach in microwave according to package instructions; squeeze out moisture. Combine spinach, garlic salt, pepper, 1 cup of the cheese and the baking mix. Stir in eggs and milk; blend thoroughly. Melt butter in a casserole dish in microwave, tilting dish to evenly coat the bottom. Pour spinach mixture into casserole dish and cover. Cook in microwave for 3 minutes; stir and microwave another 3 minutes. Continue cooking and stirring until spinach mixture is very hot. Top with remaining cheese; cook in microwave 30 seconds, or until cheese is melted.

BLACK BEAN, CORN AND SPINACH CASSEROLE

Do you ever have a little bit of "this", and a little bit of "that" hanging around your kitchen? Try using those leftovers to create this "poor man's dish."

1 tablespoon extra virgin olive oil	Freshly ground pepper
1 large onion, chopped (1 cup)	2 cups fresh spinach, washed, stems removed and chopped
1 cup chopped tomato	Vegetable cooking spray
1 ½ cups corn kernels, fresh or frozen	2 cups crushed baked tortilla chips
1 can (15-ounce) black beans, drained	8 ounces cheddar cheese, finely grated (2 cups)
2 tablespoons fresh lime juice	2 cups salsa (red)
1 teaspoon salt	

Preheat oven to 350°F. Heat oil in large saucepan and sauté onion until soft, about 8 minutes. Stir in tomato, corn, black beans, lime juice, salt and pepper; sauté 10 minutes. Meanwhile, in another saucepan, blanch the spinach in boiling water for 3 minutes, until just wilted and still bright green. Drain immediately and set aside. Coat casserole dish with cooking spray. Spread half of the crushed tortilla chips on the bottom. Spoon the corn mixture over the tortilla chips and sprinkle with two-thirds of the cheddar cheese. Arrange the spinach evenly on top of cheese; spoon on half the salsa. Finish with remaining tortilla chips and top with remaining salsa and cheese. Bake 35 to 45 minutes, or until cheese is bubbly and starting to turn brown.

WILD RICE AND SPINACH CASSEROLE

This recipe came from Edisto Island, South Carolina and is absolutely scrumptious! I buy the white and wild rice mix in a little orange box in the rice section of my local grocery store.

1	package (6-ounce) white and wild rice		Salt
	Water		White pepper
1	can (14 ½-ounce) beef broth	1	pound fresh button mushrooms, sliced
2	(10-ounce) packages frozen chopped spinach, cooked and squeezed dry	3	tablespoons butter
		1	can (14 ½-ounce) diced tomatoes, drained
8	ounces cream cheese, softened		Vegetable cooking spray
		4	slices lean bacon

Cook rice according to package instructions, using equal amounts of water and beef broth; set aside. Preheat oven to 350°F. Combine spinach with cream cheese; season with salt and white pepper; set aside. Sauté mushrooms in butter until tender, cooking until most of the moisture has evaporated; add tomatoes. Coat a casserole dish with cooking spray and layer half the rice in the bottom. Top with a layer of half the spinach mixture, and half the mushroom mixture. Repeat layers. Place bacon on top and cover with foil. Bake 40 minutes. Remove foil and place under broiler until bacon is crisp.

HERBED SPINACH WITH RICE AND CHEDDAR CHEESE

Got a crowd to feed? This recipe makes a large and hearty casserole.

2	(10-ounce) packages frozen chopped spinach, cooked and squeezed dry	4	tablespoons butter, melted (½ stick)
2	cups cooked rice	½	small onion, chopped (¼ cup)
1	pound cheddar cheese, shredded (4 cups)	1	teaspoon salt
4	eggs, lightly beaten	1	teaspoon Worcestershire sauce
⅔	cup milk	½	teaspoon ground dried thyme
			Vegetable cooking spray

Preheat oven to 350°F. Combine spinach and rice in large bowl. Fold in cheddar cheese; set aside. In a small bowl, mix together eggs, milk, butter, onion, salt, Worcestershire sauce and thyme; blend with wire whisk. Combine spinach mixture with egg mixture. Coat a large casserole dish with cooking spray. Pour spinach mixture into baking dish and cover with lid or foil. Bake 20 to 25 minutes. Remove from oven, uncover, and bake 5 minutes.

BROWN RICE AND SPINACH

I got this recipe from a friend that claims she has never eaten white rice in her life.

2	pounds fresh spinach, thoroughly washed	2	eggs, lightly beaten
1	tablespoon extra virgin olive oil	1	cup freshly grated Parmesan cheese
1	large onion, minced (1 cup)		Salt
1	garlic clove, minced	4	cups cooked brown rice
		1	tablespoon butter

Preheat oven to 375°F. Remove coarse stems from spinach leaves and discard; set spinach leaves aside. Heat olive oil in large skillet or saucepan; sauté onion until tender. Add garlic and cook 3 minutes. Add the spinach leaves and cover tightly. Cook 3 minutes over moderate heat. Uncover, stir and cook another 5 minutes; remove from heat and allow to cool. Stir in eggs and half of the Parmesan cheese; season with salt. Spread the rice in the bottom of a large baking dish. Spoon spinach mixture evenly on top of rice. Sprinkle with remaining Parmesan cheese and dot with butter. Bake 20 minutes.

GREEK CASSEROLE

*Just combine all the ingredients, pour into
a casserole dish and bake. Easy, easy, easy.*

4	cups cooked brown rice	1	medium onion, chopped
1	cup cooked garbanzo beans		(¾ cup)
8	ounces feta cheese, crumbled	1	tablespoon extra virgin olive
	into tiny pieces		oil
1	package (10-ounce) frozen	1	teaspoon dried oregano
	chopped spinach, thawed		Salt and freshly ground pepper
	and squeezed dry		Vegetable cooking spray
3	egg whites, lightly beaten		

Preheat oven to 350°F. In a large mixing bowl, stir together rice, garbanzo beans and feta cheese. Add spinach. Blend in egg whites, onion, olive oil and oregano. Season with salt and pepper. Coat casserole dish with cooking spray. Spoon spinach mixture into baking dish and bake 50 to 60 minutes.

ARTICHOKE AND SPINACH CROWD PLEASER

*Lots of spinach, cream cheese, artichokes and water chestnuts
are a perfect combination in this casserole dish.*

4	(10-ounce) packages frozen	1	can (8-ounce) sliced water
	chopped spinach, cooked		chestnuts, drained and
	and squeezed dry		coarsely chopped
¼	pound butter, melted (1 stick)	1 ½	teaspoons onion powder
16	ounces cream cheese,		Salt and freshly ground pepper
	softened	⅓	cup freshly grated Parmesan
1	can (7 ¾-ounce) artichoke		cheese
	hearts, drained and		Vegetable cooking spray
	quartered		

Preheat oven to 350°F. In a large mixing bowl, combine spinach, melted butter and cream cheese. Blend thoroughly. Stir in artichoke pieces and water chestnuts. Season with onion powder, salt and pepper. Top with Parmesan cheese. Coat large casserole dish with cooking spray. Spoon mixture into casserole and bake 40 to 45 minutes.

MUSHROOM AND ARTICHOKE FLORENTINE

You might be surprised at just how good this recipe tastes. Since most of the ingredients are off-the-shelf items, you can whip this up in no time.

1 can (4-ounce) button mushrooms, drained	2 (15-ounce) cans spinach, well-drained
6 tablespoons butter	1 can (14-ounce) artichoke hearts, drained
2 tablespoons all-purpose flour	
½ cup milk	Salt and white pepper

Topping

½   cup sour cream   2   tablespoons fresh lemon juice
½   cup mayonnaise

Preheat oven to 350°F. Sauté mushrooms in butter; remove mushrooms from saucepan, leaving liquid in pan. Add flour to saucepan; stir and cook until bubbly. Add milk, spinach, mushrooms, artichoke, salt and pepper. Spoon mixture into a large casserole dish. To prepare topping, mix sour cream, mayonnaise and lemon juice in a small saucepan over low heat, stirring to blend. Pour over casserole and bake 30 minutes.

Marinated Artichoke Casserole

Friends won't believe how uncomplicated this recipe really is.
One taste and they'll be asking for your secret recipe!

	Butter-flavored cooking spray	8	ounces cream cheese, softened
2	(6-ounce) jars marinated artichoke hearts, drained	2	tablespoons butter, softened
2	(10-ounce) packages frozen chopped spinach, cooked and squeezed dry	½	cup freshly grated Parmesan cheese

Preheat oven to 350°F. Spray bottom of casserole dish with cooking spray. Spread artichoke hearts in bottom. Top with spinach. Mix together cream cheese, butter and Parmesan cheese, stirring until creamy. Spread cream cheese mixture over spinach layer. Cover and bake 30 minutes. Uncover and bake another 10 minutes.

ARTICHOKES STUFFED WITH SPINACH AND BREAD CRUMBS

There's an old South African saying, "When you have a lot to do, start with a meal." Prepare this recipe the night before a busy day, and simply steam it when you're ready to eat.

Artichokes

4	large artichokes
¼	cup fresh lemon juice

Boiling water, lightly salted
¼ cup extra virgin olive oil (more, if needed)

Stuffing

2 cups spinach leaves, thoroughly washed and finely chopped
1 cup Italian bread crumbs
1 cup freshly grated Parmesan cheese

1 garlic clove, mashed
1 teaspoon salt
¼ teaspoon white pepper
1 teaspoon dried basil
1 tablespoon dried parsley

Using a sharp knife, remove the top third of the artichokes; discard top portions. Use scissors to snip the thorns from the tips of the outer leaves. Cut stem so that artichoke sits up without falling over; soak in lightly salted water to rinse and clean. Parboil artichokes in a Dutch oven in boiling water and half the lemon juice, 15 to 20 minutes. Remove from water and drain upside down until cool. Use a large spoon to open the artichokes; remove the chokes and the lighter tender leaves on the inside that are underdeveloped. (The chokes are the fuzzy matter on the rim of the interior of the heart.) Return the artichokes to the water in the Dutch oven and cook 30 minutes. Remove artichokes; drain. To prepare stuffing, wilt spinach in small saucepan 2 minutes, using only the water that clings to the leaves. Combine spinach, bread crumbs, Parmesan cheese, garlic, salt, pepper, basil and parsley in a mixing bowl. Place about 2 tablespoons of stuffing over each heart, and spoon remaining stuffing between the leaves. Combine olive oil and remaining lemon juice. Place the stuffed artichokes, stem down, in a colander and drizzle oil mixture slowly over top, catching drippings in bowl underneath. Place the colander over a pot of boiling water, being certain that the water does not touch the colander. Steam the artichokes, covered with foil, 15 minutes. Drizzle reserved olive oil over stuffing between leaves and steam another 10 minutes, or until the stuffing is moist. Serve immediately, or prepare in advance and steam just before serving.

RED POTATOES AND SPINACH CASSEROLE

When preparing this recipe, you may want to bake it in more than one casserole dish, that way you can share with neighbors, care-givers or homeless shelters. One recipe is quite generous.

Vegetable cooking spray
1 ½ quarts chicken stock
    (preferably homemade)
1 ½ quarts beef broth
1 cup dry white wine
2 teaspoons dried tarragon
2 bay leaves
½ cup minced fresh parsley
4 garlic cloves, minced
3 pounds red potatoes, washed
    and thinly sliced
¼ pound butter (1 stick)

Salt and freshly ground pepper
4 (10-ounce) packages frozen
    chopped spinach, thawed
    and squeezed dry
¾ cup sour cream
1 cup freshly grated Parmesan
    cheese
6 scallions, minced
½ cup minced fresh dill
2 eggs
Freshly grated nutmeg

Preheat oven to 350°F. Coat a large casserole dish with cooking spray and set aside. Combine the chicken stock, beef broth and wine in a large saucepan. Add tarragon, bay leaves, parsley and garlic; bring to a boil. Put potatoes in boiling broth mixture and simmer up to 10 minutes, or until almost tender, yet still slightly crunchy. Carefully remove potato slices with a slotted spoon and set aside in a bowl; reserve cooking liquid. Add 4 tablespoons of the butter to the hot potato slices, turning to coat. Season with salt and pepper. Place a generous layer of potatoes in bottom of casserole dish. Combine spinach, sour cream, one-third of the Parmesan cheese, scallions, dill and eggs in a food processor. Season with salt, pepper and nutmeg; pulse until blended. Place spinach mixture on top of potatoes; top with remaining potatoes. Ladle 2 cups broth mixture over the potatoes. Sprinkle remaining Parmesan cheese on top and dot with remaining butter. Bake 1 hour and 15 minutes. Allow to stand 10 minutes before serving.

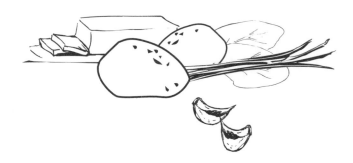

HAM AND HASH BROWNS AU GRATIN

With ham, hash browns, spinach, milk, cheese and eggs, this is a guaranteed winner. It's excellent served for breakfast, brunch or a late-night snack.

3	tablespoons butter
3	tablespoons all-purpose flour
1¾	cups milk
2	eggs, lightly beaten
6	ounces cheddar cheese, shredded (1½ cups)
¼	cup dry sherry
1	tablespoon Dijon mustard
¼	teaspoon freshly ground nutmeg
	Freshly ground pepper
2	small onions, thinly sliced

2	tablespoons extra virgin olive oil
1	package (10-ounce) frozen chopped spinach, thawed and squeezed dry
12	ounces fully cooked ham, julienned
1	package (24-ounce) frozen shredded hash browns (8 patties), thawed
¼	cup freshly grated Parmesan cheese

Preheat oven to 350°F. Melt butter in a large heavy saucepan; blend in flour. Add milk and cook until bubbly, stirring often. Cook 1 minute and remove from heat. Stir just 1 cup of hot milk mixture into beaten eggs; return egg mixture to saucepan. Stir in cheddar cheese, sherry, mustard, nutmeg and pepper; set aside. In a large skillet, cook onion in olive oil until tender. Stir in spinach; set aside. Place half of the ham strips in an ungreased baking dish. Break up hash brown patties and place half of them on top of ham. Spoon half of the cheese sauce over the potatoes. Spoon the spinach mixture on top of the cheese. Repeat layers with remaining ham, potatoes and cheese sauce. Sprinkle with Parmesan cheese. Bake, uncovered, 30 minutes. Allow to stand 10 minutes before serving.

GERMAN SCALLOPED POTATOES

Not far from my home is a little German community called Roberts Cove. I think of their annual Germanfest, held the first full weekend in October, whenever I prepare this recipe. They feature a folk dance troupe, folk singers and German folklore.

6	slices lean bacon		Milk and water (according to potato mix instructions)
1	small onion, thinly sliced		
1	package (10-ounce) frozen chopped spinach, thawed and squeezed dry	2	teaspoons caraway seed
		4	ounces provolone cheese, shredded (1 cup)
1	package (5-ounce) scalloped potato mix		

Preheat oven to 400°F. Cook bacon until crisp in a large skillet. Drain and reserve 2 tablespoons of drippings. Crumble bacon and set aside. In the same skillet, sauté onion until tender. Add spinach and heat through. In a casserole dish, combine potatoes and dry sauce mix from package. Stir in milk and boiling water called for in recipe on package, omitting the butter. Add bacon, spinach-onion mixture, and caraway seed. Bake, uncovered, 30 to 35 minutes, or until potatoes are tender. Sprinkle with provolone cheese and return to oven until cheese starts to bubble. Allow to stand 5 minutes before serving.

LEMONY STEAMED SPINACH

A perfect side dish for any meal.

2	pounds fresh spinach leaves	2	tablespoons fresh lemon juice
¼	pound butter, melted (1 stick)		Salt
2	teaspoons grated lemon zest		White pepper

Thoroughly wash spinach several times in cool water; shake off excess water. Remove and discard thick stems. Tear spinach leaves into bite-size pieces and place in large microwave-safe casserole dish. Cover casserole with thick plastic wrap and cook in microwave on HIGH 2 minutes. Stir and cook another minute or two. Drain well, squeezing out liquid. Combine butter, lemon zest, lemon juice, salt and white pepper in a small glass bowl and heat in microwave. Pour over spinach and toss.

HOBO PIE

"Hobo Pie" got its name from my fond memories of those Red Skelton television skits, back when television was only in black and white. He would laugh just as much as his audience, and he never forgot to say, "...and may God bless" at the end of every show. His light-hearted "anything goes attitude" entertained millions of viewers. This fun recipe has an "anything goes attitude" too, allowing you to be creative by swapping out veggies and sauces.

Filling

1	onion, chopped	¼	pound green beans, cut into 1-inch pieces
3	carrots, thinly sliced		
1	bell pepper, diced	1	bunch fresh spinach, stems removed, torn into bite-size pieces
1	broccoli head, coarsely chopped		Hungarian paprika

Sauce

2   cups brown gravy OR mushroom gravy OR tomato-based sauce

Topping

3   cups cooked potatoes, mashed with ¼ cup water

Preheat oven to 350°F. Steam onion, carrot, bell pepper, broccoli and green beans until crisp-tender. Remove from heat. Stir in spinach and gravy. Spoon this filling into a large casserole dish. Spread mashed potatoes over top. Sprinkle with a small amount of paprika. Bake 30 minutes.

STUFFED ONIONS

Vidalia onions are grown in Georgia and are only available one time during the year, usually around May and June. Mark your calendar now to prepare this recipe during their peak season.

3	large sweet Vidalia onions	¼	cup freshly grated Parmesan cheese
1	package (10-ounce) frozen chopped spinach, thawed and squeezed dry		Seasoned salt
			Dash of ground nutmeg
3	tablespoons mayonnaise		Freshly ground pepper
1	tablespoon fresh lemon juice		Pimiento strips (for garnish)

Peel the Vidalia onions and cut in half crosswise. Par-boil in lightly salted water until barely tender, 10 to 12 minutes; drain. Meanwhile, preheat oven to 350°F. Remove onion centers to form a cup for the filling. Chop centers of onions, reserving ¾ cup. Leftover chopped onion may be saved for another use. Combine chopped onion, spinach, mayonnaise, lemon juice, Parmesan cheese, salt, nutmeg, and pepper. Arrange onion cups in a shallow baking dish and fill with spinach filling. Bake, uncovered, 20 minutes. Garnish with pimiento slices.

FRIED CANNED SPINACH

A friend on the Internet sent this simple recipe to me all the way from Illinois. It's quick, easy and a real treat for spinach-lovers.

2	tablespoons butter	Balsamic vinegar (or fresh lemon juice)
1	small onion, chopped (½ cup)	
2	(14-ounce) cans spinach, drained	

Melt butter in a large skillet or saucepan. Sauté onion until soft. Add spinach and continue cooking until heated through, about 5 minutes. Serve with balsamic vinegar.

GARLICKY MUSHROOMS AND SPINACH

Mushrooms and garlic are the featured ingredients in this glorious recipe. Add fresh spinach, a touch of red wine, and you've got a real show-stopper.

2 teaspoons extra virgin olive oil
3 garlic cloves, minced
1 large fresh portobello mushroom, diced
1 cup fresh shiitake mushrooms, quartered
2 cups fresh button mushrooms, quartered
½ cup Burgundy wine

2 cups fresh spinach leaves, washed and torn into bite-size pieces
1 tablespoon low-sodium soy sauce
⅓ cup freshly grated Asiago or Parmesan cheese
   Freshly ground pepper

Heat olive oil in a large, non-reactive skillet over medium heat. Sauté garlic in oil 3 minutes. Stir in the mushrooms and sauté until lightly browned. Add the wine and stir. Use a wooden spoon to scrape any browned bits on the bottom of the pan. Cook until all liquid in the pan evaporates. Add the spinach and sauté 2 minutes. Add the soy sauce, Asiago cheese and pepper. Stir and cook until heated through.

NUTTY SPINACH

*Pine nuts and slivered almonds add crunch and
flavor to this spinach and prosciutto dish.*

¼	cup extra virgin olive oil	1	pound fresh spinach, cooked, drained and chopped
1	garlic clove, cut in half		
¼	cup pine nuts	¼	cup chopped prosciutto
¼	cup blanched slivered almonds		Salt and white pepper

Heat olive oil in medium saucepan. Add garlic and cook 2 minutes, stirring constantly. Remove garlic and discard. Add pine nuts and almonds; cook 3 minutes or until lightly browned. Stir in spinach, prosciutto, salt and pepper. Toss well and cook gently until heated through.

CREAMED LEMON SPINACH

*One of my husband's aunts has a lemon tree growing in her yard in New Orleans.
This dear, sweet lady had just sent a bag of lemons to us when I came upon this
recipe, making it a "must try."*

1	tablespoon butter	1	tablespoon fresh lemon juice
1	medium onion, chopped (¾ cup)	½	teaspoon fresh lemon zest
		3	tablespoons bottled real bacon pieces
1	garlic clove, minced		Salt and freshly ground pepper
2	tablespoons all-purpose flour		
1	cup milk	1	tablespoon freshly grated Parmesan cheese
1	package (10-ounce) frozen chopped spinach, thawed and squeezed dry		

Melt butter in heavy nonstick skillet. Sauté onion until tender. Add garlic and cook another 3 minutes. Stir in flour and cook 2 minutes, stirring frequently. Gradually whisk in milk. Increase heat to high setting and whisk 3 minutes, or until mixture begins to boil and thicken. Reduce heat to low and stir in spinach, lemon juice, lemon zest, and bacon pieces. Season with salt and pepper. Cook until heated through. Sprinkle with Parmesan cheese and serve hot.

Spinach with Raisins and Pine Nuts

Your broiler will finish off this wonderful dish,
forming a golden brown Parmesan veil on top.

2   pounds fresh spinach, washed, drained and cut into coarse shreds
3   tablespoons extra virgin olive oil
4   tablespoons butter, divided

2   garlic cloves, minced
    Pinch of cayenne
¼   cup seedless raisins
¼   cup pine nuts
2   tablespoons freshly grated Parmesan cheese

Preheat broiler. Place an empty, shallow baking dish in oven. Plunge spinach into pot of boiling water. Remove after 2 minutes; drain well, squeezing out all liquid. Heat olive oil and 2 tablespoons of the butter in a saucepan. Add garlic and cayenne. Cook over medium heat 3 minutes. Add raisins and pine nuts. Cook 2 minutes. Combine with spinach and transfer to hot baking dish. Sprinkle Parmesan cheese on top. Melt remaining 2 tablespoons butter and drizzle over cheese. Brown quickly under broiler.

Black-eyed Peas with Spinach

Are black-eyed peas a staple in your house? Dress them up with spinach and onion next time you need a new taste sensation. I like adding hot cooked rice to this recipe for a hearty lunch.

Vegetable broth (for cooking onion)
1   medium onion, chopped (¾ cup)
1   package (10-ounce) frozen chopped spinach, cooked and squeezed dry

2   (16-ounce) cans black-eyed peas, drained
    Freshly ground pepper
    Pinch of cayenne

In a large skillet, heat ¼ cup broth to boiling. Sauté onion, adding more broth as needed, until onion is tender. Add spinach to skillet, stir and cook two minutes, or until heated through. Add the black-eyed peas, pepper and cayenne. Bring to a simmer over medium heat. Serve hot.

ORZO WITH SPINACH AND PINE NUTS

Orzo, a rice-shaped pasta, is such a delightful food.

1 teaspoon butter	1 cup tightly packed chopped
1 garlic clove, minced	fresh spinach leaves
1¾ cups water	2 tablespoons freshly grated
¾ cup uncooked orzo	Parmesan cheese
Pinch of salt	2 tablespoons pine nuts, toasted

Melt butter in medium saucepan and sauté garlic about 2 minutes. Add water, orzo and salt; bring to a boil. Reduce heat to medium-low and cook 12 to 15 minutes, or until liquid is absorbed. Stir in spinach, Parmesan cheese and pine nuts; heat through, stirring frequently.

RICE AND SPINACH TIMBALES

Timbales are high-sided, drum-shaped molds, slightly tapered at the bottom, used for baked custards and various dishes. They are baked in an oven, and then unmolded onto a serving plate. Timbales are often served with a sauce, such as Béchamel.

⅔ cup low-fat cottage cheese	Salt and freshly ground pepper
½ cup plain nonfat yogurt	1 package (10-ounce) frozen
1 ounce feta cheese, crumbled	chopped spinach, thawed
2 eggs	and squeezed dry
2 egg whites	¾ cup cooked long-grain rice
¼ teaspoon dried basil	Vegetable cooking spray

Preheat oven to 350°F. In a large mixing bowl, combine cottage cheese, yogurt and feta cheese; blend well. Add eggs and egg whites and beat at medium speed of mixer until blended. Season with basil, salt and pepper. Stir in spinach and rice. Coat each of six 6-ounce custard cups with cooking spray. Spoon spinach mixture into cups, dividing equally. Place cups in a large baking pan and add hot water to pan to a depth of 1 inch. Bake 40 minutes, or until knife inserted near center comes out clean. Remove cups from water. Loosen edges of timbales with a small rubber spatula or knife. To serve, place a small plate upside down on top of each cup; invert timbale onto plate.

GREEN AND YELLOW RICE WITH HERBS

The International Rice Festival has been held in historic downtown Crowley, LA on the third weekend in October since 1937. It features a rice-cooking contest, a rice-threshing contest, and even the crowning of a Rice Queen. This spinach and cheddar cheese creation filled with wonderful herbs would surely win a prize!

1	cup milk	1	tablespoon Worcestershire sauce
4	eggs, beaten		
1	pound sharp cheddar cheese, shredded (4 cups)	½	teaspoon dried thyme
		½	teaspoon dried marjoram
1	package (10-ounce) frozen chopped spinach, cooked and squeezed dry	½	teaspoon dried rosemary
		½	teaspoon salt
		3	cups cooked rice
2	tablespoons minced onion	4	tablespoons butter, melted (½ stick)

Preheat oven to 350°F. In a large bowl, combine milk and eggs. Add cheese, spinach, onion and Worcestershire sauce; blend well. Season with thyme, marjoram, rosemary and salt. In a separate bowl, mix rice and butter. Add rice mixture to spinach mixture and stir until evenly blended. Pour mixture into a casserole dish. Set casserole dish in a larger pan, filled with 1 inch of hot water. Bake 40 to 45 minutes.

SPANAHORIZO

First cousin to spanikopita, this side dish uses rice instead of phyllo.

½	cup extra virgin olive oil	2	tablespoons tomato paste
1	large onion, finely chopped (1 cup)	1	large tomato chopped (1 cup)
			Salt and freshly ground pepper
1	garlic clove, minced	2	bunches fresh spinach, stems removed, chopped
1	bunch parsley, minced (discard stems)		
		1	cup white rice, uncooked
3	cups water		

Heat oil in a heavy saucepan and sauté onion until tender. Add garlic and cook another 3 minutes. Add parsley and continue cooking until soft; add water. Increase heat and bring water to a boil. Add the tomato paste, chopped tomato, salt and pepper. Stir to blend thoroughly. Add the spinach and rice. Simmer 30 minutes on low heat, or until rice is done.

TOMATOES ROCKEFELLER

Whether you're serving meat or poultry, potatoes or rice,
this recipe makes the perfect side dish.

1 package (10-ounce) frozen chopped spinach, cooked and squeezed dry	¼ teaspoon Worcestershire sauce
1 cup seasoned dry bread crumbs	¼ teaspoon granulated garlic
3 scallions, minced	½ teaspoon salt
3 eggs, lightly beaten	Freshly ground pepper
¼ pound butter, melted (1 stick)	½ teaspoon dried thyme
¼ cup freshly grated Parmesan cheese (extra, if desired)	4 large tomatoes, cut into 1-inch thick slices

In a large mixing bowl, combine spinach, bread crumbs, scallions and eggs; stir until thoroughly blended. Add butter, Parmesan cheese, Worcestershire sauce, garlic, salt, pepper and thyme, stirring until well mixed. Lay tomato slices on large baking sheet. Sprinkle salt and pepper on top-side of each slice. Spoon spinach mixture on each slice and broil until spinach mixture just starts to turn brown on the edges. Sprinkle with additional Parmesan cheese, if desired.

HERBED CANNELLINI AND OLIVES OVER WILTED SPINACH

Cannellini beans are large white Italian kidney beans. Prepared with spinach, bacon, Roma tomatoes and black olives, they're a bonus to good cooking and good eating.

8 cups spinach leaves, thoroughly washed	2 (15-ounce) cans cannellini beans, drained
6 slices lean bacon, chopped (uncooked)	1 pound firm, ripe Roma tomatoes, chopped
2 medium onions, cut into very thin slivers	¾ cup sliced black olives
½ teaspoon grated lemon zest	1 tablespoon balsamic vinegar
2 tablespoons water	1 ½ teaspoons chopped fresh oregano
Salt and freshly ground pepper	

Shred spinach leaves into thin strips. Cook bacon in saucepan over medium-high heat until crisp. Remove bacon with slotted spoon and set aside. Drain off most of drippings. Add onion and lemon zest to pan and cook until soft. Add half of spinach and 1 tablespoon water to pan; stir until spinach just starts to wilt. Add remaining spinach and another tablespoon of water, cooking and stirring until all spinach is wilted. Season to taste with salt and pepper. Transfer spinach mixture to serving platter and keep warm. Pour beans into pan. Add tomatoes, olives, vinegar and oregano. Cook just until beans are hot and tomatoes are soft, about 3 minutes. Spoon bean mixture over spinach. Sprinkle bacon on top and serve.

GRILLED SPINACH AND PESTO FILLED TOMATOES

When tomatoes and basil are plentiful, pull out this great recipe. Come to think of it, it's hard to imagine two foods more suited to each other than fresh basil straight from your herb garden and sun-ripened tomatoes.

3	large tomatoes, halved crosswise	3	ounces Monterey Jack cheese, shredded (¾ cup)
1	package (10-ounce) frozen chopped spinach, thawed and squeezed dry	6	scallions, sliced ¼-inch long
		3	tablespoons pesto sauce (recipe follows)

Preheat grill or oven to 350°F. Hollow out tomato halves, leaving a ¼-inch thick shell. Discard centers or use in a soup recipe. In a mixing bowl, combine spinach, ½ cup of the cheese, scallions and pesto sauce; mix well. Spoon mixture into tomato halves. Grill stuffed tomatoes until heated through. During the last 2 minutes of cooking, sprinkle remaining cheese over top. To prepare in oven, arrange filled tomatoes in a shallow baking dish and bake 20 to 30 minutes or until heated through. Sprinkle cheese on top and return to oven until cheese is melted.

PESTO SAUCE

I truly believe that there is no finer way to savor this magnificent herb than to prepare a batch of basil pesto.

2	cups firmly packed fresh basil leaves, washed and patted dry	3	garlic cloves, peeled
		4	tablespoons butter, softened (½ stick)
¼	cup pine nuts (walnuts, pecans, or pistachios may be substituted)	¾	cup freshly grated Parmesan cheese
		½	cup extra virgin olive oil

Combine basil leaves, pine nuts, garlic, butter and Parmesan cheese in electric blender container. Pulse with on-off process, scraping down sides of container with rubber spatula to push down ingredients. On lowest speed of blender, continue to process while slowly pouring oil through opening in cover. Blend until thoroughly incorporated. To store in refrigerator, transfer pesto to a small container and float a thin layer of olive oil on top. (The oil keeps the sauce from darkening.)

SPINACH AND ARTICHOKE
STUFFED TOMATOES

I recently invited some lady friends over for lunch, and asked what they would like me to prepare. One of them started laughing and said if I really wanted to make her happy, I should fix "those tomatoes thingies with that spinach and artichoke stuff you put in them." I did. They came. And we feasted.

3	large, firm tomatoes Salt and freshly ground pepper	2	ounces cream cheese, softened
1	jar (6-ounce) marinated artichoke hearts, drained and chopped	1	tablespoon butter
		2	tablespoons sour cream
1	package (10-ounce) frozen chopped spinach, thawed and squeezed dry	1	teaspoon dried oregano
		½	teaspoon salt
		½	cup freshly grated Parmesan cheese
4	scallions, chopped	2	tablespoons butter, melted
		½	cup dry bread crumbs

Preheat oven to 350°F. Cut tomatoes in half crosswise. Scoop out pulp and seeds, being careful not to puncture shells. Sprinkle inside of tomato shell with salt and pepper; set aside. In a medium bowl, combine artichoke, spinach and scallions. In a food processor, combine cream cheese, butter, sour cream, oregano, ½ teaspoon of salt and Parmesan cheese; process until puréed. Fold cream cheese mixture into spinach mixture until blended. In a small bowl, combine 2 tablespoons melted butter and bread crumbs with a fork. Stuff tomato halves with spinach-artichoke filling; top each with buttered crumbs. Place in a large baking dish and bake until heated through, about 10 minutes. Serve hot.

CURRIED SPINACH POTATO BOATS WITH CARAMELIZED ONION TOPPING

Want some serious baked potatoes? Try this hearty recipe,
crowned with caramelized onions.

¾ cup plain, fat-free yogurt, drained overnight or several hours
Vegetable cooking spray
1 small onion, minced (½ cup)
2 teaspoons curry powder
6 cups coarsely chopped fresh spinach leaves

1 teaspoon kosher salt
Freshly ground black pepper
1 large onion, peeled and halved lengthwise
4 large baked potatoes, halved lengthwise and scooped out

Put yogurt in a paper towel-lined strainer and allow liquid to drip out. Spray a nonstick skillet with cooking spray and place over medium heat. Add the minced onion and cook until tender. Lower heat, stir in curry powder and cook 3 minutes. Add spinach and sauté 3 to 5 minutes. Place mixture in a blender; add salt, pepper and yogurt; blend until smooth. Transfer mixture to a small saucepan and set aside. Coat a nonstick skillet with cooking spray and place over medium heat. Thinly slice large onion and put in skillet. Cook and stir until caramelized, 20 to 30 minutes. Warm the spinach mixture and use it to fill the potatoes. Pile the caramelized onions on top and serve.

BAKED EGGPLANT WITH TWO SAUCES

Having the "spinach reputation" that I do, it's kind of hard to get out of bringing a spinach dish when you're invited to a potluck dinner. I prepared this recipe for such an occasion, not realizing there would be over forty people there! What a fiasco. This went so quickly that I almost had to rush home and prepare another batch. However, my friends all joked about accepting a rain check from me.

Roasted Tomato and Red Wine Sauce

Olive Oil cooking spray
4 plum tomatoes
1 small onion, diced (½ cup)
¼ cup Burgundy wine
½ teaspoon chopped fresh oregano
Salt and freshly ground pepper

Garlic and Onion Sauce

1 small onion, thinly sliced
¼ cup dry white wine
8 garlic cloves, peeled
½ cup vegetable broth
Salt

Eggplant and Spinach

12 slices eggplant, ½-inch thick (remove peeling)
½ small onion, minced (¼ cup)
1 package (10-ounce) frozen chopped spinach, thawed and squeezed dry
2 ounces feta cheese, crumbled

To prepare tomato sauce, preheat oven to 425°F. Coat baking dish with cooking spray. Place tomatoes in baking dish and bake 30 minutes; set aside. Heat a saucepan coated with cooking spray. Sauté onion. Add tomatoes, Burgundy wine, oregano, salt and pepper; bring to a boil. Reduce heat and simmer 20 minutes. Place tomato mixture in blender and process until smooth; set aside and keep warm. To prepare garlic sauce, coat saucepan with cooking spray and set over high heat. Cook onion in wine 10 minutes. Add garlic and cook 3 minutes. Stir in broth and heat to boiling. Reduce heat and simmer 20 minutes. Place garlic mixture in a blender and process until smooth; set aside and keep warm. Preheat broiler. To prepare eggplant, lightly sprinkle salt over slices. Spray large baking sheet with cooking spray; arrange eggplant slices in a single layer and broil 5 to 7 minutes on each side. Spray a large nonstick skillet with cooking spray. Sauté onion 3 minutes or until soft. Add spinach and cook 10 minutes, stirring frequently. Remove from heat and add feta cheese. Preheat oven to 425°F. Arrange 4 eggplant slices 2 inches apart on a baking sheet.

Baked Eggplant with Two Sauces *(continued)*

Spread about 2 tablespoons spinach mixture on each slice. Place another eggplant slice on top of spinach. Spread spinach on top of eggplant slice and top with third eggplant slice. Bake 15 minutes. Place one eggplant stack on each serving plate, and spoon one-fourth of each sauce onto the plate. Serve hot.

Scalloped Florentine Potatoes

Here's a great side dish that's a snap to prepare in your microwave.

8	medium red potatoes	3	ounces cheddar cheese, shredded (¾ cup)
¼	cup water		
	Salt	½	(10-ounce) package frozen chopped spinach, thawed and squeezed dry
1	small onion, finely chopped (½ cup)		
4	tablespoons butter (½ stick)	1	tablespoon diced pimiento
¼	cup all-purpose flour		Hungarian paprika
2	cups milk		

Peel potatoes and slice ¼-inch thick. Place potato slices in a large microwave-safe casserole dish with water and salt. Cover with heavy plastic wrap and cook on high, stirring occasionally, until potatoes are just tender, about 8 minutes. Remove potato slices with slotted spoon and set aside. Drain water from casserole. Put onion and butter in casserole and cook in microwave on HIGH about 3 minutes or until onion is tender, stirring often. Stir in flour. Add milk all at once, stirring to blend. Cook, uncovered, 5 to 7 minutes or until bubbly and thick, stirring every 30 seconds. Add cheese and stir until cheese melts. Add the potato slices, spinach and pimiento. Cover and cook on HIGH 1 minute or until heated through; do not allow mixture to come to a boil. Sprinkle with paprika and serve.

BAKED POTATOES TOPPED WITH SPINACH SOUFFLÉ AND HAM

Stuffed potatoes make the perfect meal after a football game.
Prepare these ahead of time so the hungry crowd can jump right in.

1	package (12-ounce) frozen spinach soufflé		Salt
			Freshly ground black pepper
6	ounces cooked ham, diced into ⅛-inch pieces	¼	pound butter (1 stick)
		¼	cup freshly grated Parmesan cheese
4	baked potatoes, cut in half lengthwise		Sour cream (optional)

Transfer soufflé from packaging to a shallow microwave-safe baking dish. Cook on medium setting 4 to 5 minutes, rotating dish halfway through, or until soufflé can be broken up with a fork. Stir ham into soufflé. Cover loosely with plastic wrap and cook 4 minutes, or until heated through, stirring once while cooking. Meanwhile, scoop out centers of potato halves and place in a bowl; break up with fork. Add butter and season with salt and pepper. Return mashed potato to hollowed out potato shells and top with spinach mixture. Sprinkle Parmesan cheese on top. Broil for a few minutes just before serving, being careful not to burn tops. Serve each with a dollop of sour cream, if desired.

ELEGANT CREAMED SPINACH

Simple yet possessing a genteel taste all its own.

1	package (10-ounce) frozen chopped spinach, thawed	¼	teaspoon salt
			Freshly ground pepper
2	tablespoons butter		Dash of nutmeg
1½	tablespoons all-purpose flour		Dash of cayenne
½	cup heavy cream		

Cook spinach according to package instructions; drain, squeeze dry and set aside. Melt butter in saucepan. Add flour and stir to blend. Add cream and cook over medium heat 3 minutes, or until sauce thickens, stirring constantly. Add spinach, salt, pepper, nutmeg and cayenne. Cook 3 minutes and serve hot.

WHIPPED SPINACH POTATOES

When I first saw this recipe, I stopped what I was doing to prepare it.
It's even better on your plate than it is on this paper!

3 garlic cloves, minced	1 package (10-ounce) frozen
6 large baking potatoes, with	chopped spinach, cooked
skins	and squeezed dry
¾ cup skim milk, heated (more if	1 tablespoon crushed dried basil
needed)	Salt and freshly ground black
	pepper

Fill large saucepan three-fourths full with water; add garlic and bring to a boil. Scrub potatoes and cut into 1-inch cubes. Add potatoes to boiling water and cook until soft, about 12 minutes. Drain in colander. Mash potatoes until completely smooth. Gradually add heated milk and stir until potatoes are smooth. Add more milk a little at a time, if needed. Fold spinach and basil into potatoes. Season with salt and pepper.

SPINACH DUMPLINGS

Whenever I serve these, friends ask, "What are these? They're delicious!"

¼ pound butter (1 stick)	¾ cup freshly grated Parmesan
2 (10-ounce) packages frozen	cheese
chopped spinach, thawed	½ teaspoon salt
¾ cup ricotta cheese	Freshly ground pepper
½ cup all-purpose flour	Pinch of nutmeg
2 eggs, lightly beaten	Salted water for simmering

Melt half of the butter in a heavy skillet. Add spinach and cook 3 minutes, stirring frequently. Stir in ricotta cheese and cook another 5 minutes. In a large mixing bowl, combine spinach, flour, eggs, ¼ cup of the Parmesan cheese, salt, pepper and nutmeg. Refrigerate 1 hour, or until firm. Coat hands with flour and pinch off about 1 tablespoon of chilled mixture. Shape into a small ball to form a dumpling. Repeat, until all of the mixture is used. Meanwhile, bring a large pot of water to a simmer. Preheat oven to 350°F. Gently drop dumplings into simmering water and cook, uncovered, 6 to 8 minutes, or until they puff slightly. Remove dumplings onto paper towels to drain. Melt remaining butter and pour half in the bottom of a glass casserole dish. Arrange dumplings in a single layer, and pour the last of the butter on top. Sprinkle with remaining ½ cup Parmesan cheese and bake 5 minutes. Serve immediately.

95

BÉCHAMEL SPINACH

*Lots of alluring spinach needs only a hint of
Béchamel Sauce to complete this dish.*

Butter-flavored cooking spray
5 tablespoons butter
3 (10-ounce) packages frozen
   chopped spinach, thawed
   and squeezed dry
Salt and white pepper
2 tablespoons all-purpose flour

½ cup heavy cream
½ cup milk
Pinch of ground cloves
Pinch of ground nutmeg
⅔ cup freshly grated Parmesan
   cheese

Preheat oven to 375°F. Coat a glass pie plate with cooking spray. Melt 3 tablespoons of the butter in a heavy skillet over medium-high heat. Add spinach and sauté 3 minutes. Season with salt and pepper. Spread spinach in pie plate, smoothing with back of spoon. Melt the remaining 2 tablespoons butter in heavy saucepan and stir in flour. Whisk 2 minutes over medium heat; do not let mixture brown. Gradually add cream, then the milk, whisking until smooth. Continue to cook until sauce thickens, whisking frequently. Add cloves and nutmeg; season with salt and white pepper. Spoon sauce over spinach and sprinkle cheese on top. Bake until cheese browns just slightly on tips and sauce bubbles.

CHEESY SPINACH CASSEROLE

A great recipe for the beginner cook.

¼ pound butter (1 stick)	1 package (10-ounce) frozen
6 tablespoons flour	chopped spinach, thawed
8 ounces Velveeta cheese, cut	and squeezed dry
into ½-inch cubes	1 teaspoon seasoned salt
6 eggs, lightly beaten	Freshly ground pepper
24 ounces cottage cheese	Vegetable cooking spray

Preheat oven to 350°F. Melt butter in a large skillet. Add flour and stir to blend. Add Velveeta cheese, eggs, cottage cheese, spinach, salt and pepper. Cook and stir until thoroughly incorporated. Coat a large baking dish with cooking spray. Pour mixture into dish and bake 50 to 60 minutes.

BACONY CREAMED SPINACH

My first taste of creamed spinach with bacon was at a steak house in Baton Rouge, LA. To this day I can't remember anything about the steak, but I'll never forget that spinach!

2 (10-ounce) packages frozen	½ teaspoon salt
chopped spinach	Pinch of cayenne
6 slices lean bacon	2 tablespoons butter
1 small onion, chopped (½ cup)	2 tablespoons all-purpose flour
1 garlic clove, minced	1 cup half-and-half

Cook spinach according to package instructions; drain well and squeeze dry. Put spinach in a food processor and chop fine; set aside. Cook bacon in large skillet until crisp; remove from skillet and crumble. In about 2 tablespoons of the bacon drippings, sauté onion until tender. Add garlic and cook 3 minutes. Stir in spinach, lower heat, and season with salt and cayenne. In a separate skillet, melt butter over medium heat. Add flour, stirring constantly, until smooth. Gradually add the half-and-half and cook until bubbly and smooth. Stir in the spinach mixture and cook 3 minutes. Remove from heat, add crumbled bacon and serve.

SPINACH MADELINE

From the first time I was served Spinach Madeline, I knew it was a lovely dish with a lovely name. Even the most discriminating taste buds will savor every bite, because this is the way spinach was meant to be enjoyed.

2	(10-ounce) packages frozen chopped spinach	½	teaspoon freshly ground pepper
4	tablespoons butter (½ stick)	¾	teaspoon garlic salt
2	tablespoons chopped onion	¾	teaspoon celery salt
2	tablespoons flour	1	teaspoon Worcestershire sauce
½	cup heavy cream	1	roll (6-ounce) jalapeño cheese

Preheat oven to 325°F. Cook spinach according to package directions and drain, reserving ½ cup liquid; set aside. Melt butter in large saucepan; add onion and sauté until tender. Add flour, stirring until smooth. Do not allow to brown. Slowly add cream and spinach liquid, stirring constantly. Add pepper, garlic salt, celery salt, Worcestershire sauce and jalapeño cheese. Stir to blend. Add to spinach and mix well. Pour into round casserole dish and bake until heated through and bubbly. Serve with cocktail crackers or crusty bread.

SPINACH PANCAKES WITH ROMANO CHEESE SAUCE

Next time you sleep until noon on a cold and rainy Saturday, whip up a batch of these spinach pancakes. They are wonderful served alongside a slice of baked ham and a glass of warm apple juice. Enjoy while listening to the rain.

Pancakes

1 ½ cups all-purpose flour	2 cups tender spinach leaves,
Dash of salt	washed, patted dry and
1 ½ teaspoons baking powder	minced
2 eggs, lightly beaten	4 ounces Swiss cheese,
¾ cup milk	shredded (1 cup)
	Butter (for preparing skillet)

Sauce

¼ pound butter (1 stick)	1 tablespoon minced fresh
½ cup freshly grated Romano	Italian parsley (flat-leaf)
cheese (more, if needed)	1 teaspoon fresh lemon juice
	½ teaspoon fresh lemon thyme

In a mixing bowl, combine flour, salt and baking powder; sift. Add eggs and milk, stirring with a wire whisk. Add spinach and Swiss cheese, blending with a large spoon. Heat a nonstick griddle, melting a small amount of butter on griddle. Using a small ladle, spoon batter onto griddle, forming 4-inch pancakes. Cook until tiny bubble form on top of batter, and the outer edges start to form. Flip cakes using a spatula and continue cooking until done. Keep pancakes warm while preparing sauce. To prepare Romano sauce, melt butter in a separate skillet over medium heat. Add Romano cheese and stir gently to melt. Add parsley, lemon juice and lemon thyme, simmering to allow the flavors to marry. Pour warmed sauce over spinach pancakes and serve immediately.

CREAM CHEESE AND SPINACH ROULADE

This roulade offers one of the loveliest presentations in this cookbook.
It is impressive enough to serve on your finest china.

1 large bunch tender spinach, stems removed	¼ cup freshly grated Parmesan cheese
1 tablespoon butter	1 tablespoon milk
4 eggs, separated	8 ounces cream cheese, softened
Salt and freshly ground pepper	
Pinch of ground nutmeg	1 red bell pepper, roasted, peeled and julienned

Preheat oven to 400°F. Line a jelly-roll pan with wax paper. Thoroughly wash spinach; place in saucepan and cook with only the water that clings to the leaves, 3 to 5 minutes. Place spinach in a food processor, along with butter and egg yolks; blend until smooth. Season with salt, pepper and nutmeg. Beat the egg whites with a wire whisk until stiff. Fold spinach mixture into egg whites. Pour mixture into the jelly-roll pan and smooth the top with spatula or back of spoon. Sprinkle half of the Parmesan cheese on top. Bake 12 to 15 minutes or until just firm yet spongy in the center. Sprinkle the remaining Parmesan cheese onto a second sheet of wax paper, the same size as the jelly-roll pan. Unmold roulade onto paper; peel off lining paper. Beat the milk and cream cheese and spread in an even layer over the roulade. Arrange pepper strips on top. Roll roulade from one short end to the other, like a jelly-roll. Slice and serve.

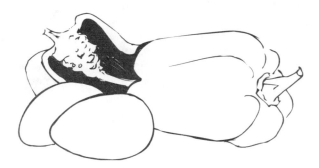

Meat
and
Poultry

i love spinach

MEAT & POULTRY

FLORENTINE BURGERS

Basking in a sauce of red wine, tomato sauce, sweet bell peppers and minced onion, these spinach-stuffed meat patties are bursting with flavor.

Filling

½ cup small curd cream-style cottage cheese

1 package (10-ounce) frozen chopped spinach, cooked and squeezed dry

1 tablespoon snipped fresh parsley

Salt

Patties

1 egg, lightly beaten

⅓ cup fine dry bread crumbs

½ teaspoon salt

¼ teaspoon cayenne

2 pounds extra-lean ground beef

Sauce

½ cup tomato sauce

¼ cup dry red wine

2 tablespoons minced bell pepper

2 tablespoons minced onion

In a mixing bowl, combine cottage cheese, spinach, parsley and a dash of salt. Mix well and set aside. Combine egg, bread crumbs, salt and cayenne; add ground beef and mix well with hands. On waxed paper, form meat mixture into 12 thin patties, 4 inches in diameter. Spoon about 3 tablespoons spinach filling on each of 6 patties. Top with remaining patties and seal edges. In a large skillet, brown half of the stuffed patties at a time. When patties are done, remove from skillet and set them aside. Discard excess fat in skillet. Add tomato sauce to skillet, along with wine, bell pepper and onion; cook until onions are tender. Return burgers to skillet, spooning some of the sauce over the burgers. Cover and simmer 20 minutes. Remove burgers to serving platter; cover with sauce.

GROUND BEEF WITH TOMATOES, RICE AND SPINACH

Why not cook a fabulous meal in one large skillet, making cleanup a breeze?

1	pound extra-lean ground beef	1	package (10-ounce) frozen chopped spinach, thawed and squeezed dry
1	medium onion, chopped (¾ cup)		
1	garlic clove, minced	¾	cup long-grain white rice, uncooked
4	cups canned crushed tomatoes	1	teaspoon crushed dried dill Freshly ground pepper

In a deep, nonstick skillet, sauté beef, onion and garlic until meat is browned and crumbly. Drain off excess fat and stir in tomatoes, spinach, rice, dill and pepper. Bring to a boil and reduce heat to low. Cover and simmer 30 to 35 minutes, or until rice is tender.

STUFFED TENDERLOIN

Spinach and mushrooms accented with herbs,
form the stuffing for this juicy beef tenderloin.

Stuffing

½   **pound fresh spinach leaves, heavy stems removed, thoroughly washed**
    Vegetable cooking spray
¼   **pound fresh mushrooms, diced**
¼   **cup freshly grated Parmesan cheese**

1   **egg, lightly beaten**
½   **teaspoon fennel seeds**
½   **teaspoon ground sage**
½   **teaspoon salt**
½   **teaspoon freshly ground pepper**

Tenderloin

1   **beef tenderloin, well trimmed (4 to 5 pounds)**
3   **garlic cloves, crushed**

¾   **teaspoon fennel seeds**
1   **teaspoon freshly ground pepper**

Preheat oven to 500°F. To prepare stuffing, place spinach in a nonstick skillet, cover and cook until just wilted, about 3 minutes. Remove from heat, uncover and allow to cool. Chop spinach and drain well by pressing between layers of paper towels; set aside. Coat a nonstick skillet with cooking spray; place over medium-high heat until hot. Add mushrooms and sauté until tender and liquid cooks out. Remove from heat and add spinach, Parmesan cheese, egg, fennel seeds, sage, salt and pepper. To prepare tenderloin, cut tenderloin lengthwise to within 1 inch of each side, leaving bottom of tenderloin connected. Combine garlic, fennel seeds and pepper; rub on tenderloin. Spoon spinach mixture into opening of tenderloin. Press gently to close; tie securely with heavy string at 1-inch intervals. Spray roasting rack with cooking spray and place tenderloin on it; place rack in a roasting pan. Insert meat thermometer into thickest part of tenderloin. Put roasting pan in oven and immediately reduce temperature to 350°F. Cook 50 to 60 minutes, or until meat thermometer registers 160°F for medium doneness. Remove from oven and allow to stand, loosely covered with foil, for 10 minutes before slicing.

VEAL RIB-EYE WITH SHRIMP AND ARTICHOKE CREAM SAUCE

Celebrating some good news or lifetime accomplishment? Prepare a meal befitting the occasion! This refined list of ingredients reads like a "Who's Who."

1 whole veal rib-eye	Salt and freshly ground pepper

Stuffing

6	ounces fresh spinach leaves, thoroughly washed	6	ounces prosciutto
4	ounces fresh mushrooms	½	teaspoon fennel seeds
4	ounces artichoke hearts		Salt

Sauce

½	pound headless shrimp, uncooked (peeled and deveined)	2	ounces extra virgin olive oil
		6	artichoke bottoms
	White pepper	¼	cup dry white wine
		24	ounces heavy cream

Preheat oven to 350°F. Prepare stuffing by combining spinach, mushrooms, artichoke hearts, prosciutto, fennel seeds and salt in a blender; purée until very fine. Stuff rib-eye and season with salt and pepper. Bake 40 to 50 minutes, or until desired doneness. Meanwhile, sauté shrimp in olive oil; add artichoke bottoms. Cook 3 minutes. Deglaze pan with wine and heavy cream. Cook and reduce to desired consistency. Serve sauce with sliced rib-eye.

SAVORY STUFFED STEAK

*One of the oldest spinach recipes in my collection,
this stuffed round steak still remains a favorite.*

1   (2-pound) round steak,
    trimmed of excess fat

Salt and cayenne

Vegetable Filling
2   cups water
½   cup long-grain white rice,
    uncooked
2   (10-ounce) packages frozen
    chopped spinach, thawed
    and squeezed dry

Salt and freshly ground pepper
1   teaspoon dried basil
1   egg, lightly beaten
3   large carrots, shredded

Gravy
1   medium onion, sliced
1   large carrot, sliced
1   stalk celery, sliced

1 ½ cups tomato juice
2   tablespoons cornstarch
¼   cup cold water

Place steak on large cutting board. Cover with plastic wrap and pound with side of meat mallet into large rectangle. Season well with salt and cayenne. To prepare vegetable filling, bring water to a boil in a medium saucepan; add rice. Reduce heat, cover and simmer until tender, 15 to 20 minutes. Drain well; transfer rice to a medium bowl. Season spinach with salt and pepper. Use a spatula to spread spinach in a flat layer 4 inches wide, crosswise along center of steak. Add salt, ½ teaspoon of the basil and egg to rice; mix well. Spoon rice mixture on top of spinach, spreading evenly with spatula. Add salt, pepper and remaining basil to shredded carrots; mix well. Spoon carrot mixture over rice; pat evenly into place. Bring both ends of the steak over the filling, overlapping slightly; secure with wooden picks. Scatter onion slices, carrot slices, and celery slices in bottom of large Dutch oven. Place rolled steak in pot, seam side down. Pour tomato juice around the bottom of the pan. Bring to a boil; cover and reduce heat. Simmer 1 ½ to 2 hours, or until meat is tender. Baste occasionally with pan drippings. Remove the meat onto a serving platter. Mix cornstarch and cold water; pour over pan drippings. Cook over medium heat until thickened, stirring frequently. Strain, discarding vegetables.

ORANGE-BEEF STIR-FRY

The flavors in this recipe all come together in a most intriguing fashion.

Sauce

1 tablespoon cornstarch	1 teaspoon freshly grated
1 teaspoon sugar	orange zest
1 teaspoon instant beef bouillon	½ cup orange juice
granules	1 tablespoon soy sauce

Beef

1 (12-ounce) beef top-round	1 tablespoon peanut oil
steak, partially frozen for	8 ounces fresh spinach, washed
easier slicing	and torn into bite-size pieces
Vegetable cooking spray	½ (8-ounce) can sliced water
1 garlic clove, minced	chestnuts, drained
4 scallions, bias cut into 1-inch	2 cups hot cooked rice
lengths	

To prepare sauce, combine cornstarch, sugar, granules, orange zest, orange juice and soy sauce; set aside. Slice steak into thin pieces across the grain. Spray a wok or large skillet with cooking spray. Stir-fry garlic 1 minute; remove from wok and discard. Stir-fry scallions 1 minute; remove from wok and reserve. Add oil to wok and stir-fry half of the beef strips. Remove meat from wok and stir-fry remaining strips. Return all meat to the wok and add sauce. Cook and stir until bubbly. Stir in spinach, water chestnuts and reserved onion. Cover and cook 1 minute. Serve hot over rice.

STUFFED PORK ROAST

This produces a juicy and succulent meal.

1 boneless pork roast, rolled and	½ (10-ounce) package frozen
tied (about 5 pounds)	chopped spinach, thawed
1 tablespoon vegetable oil	and squeezed dry
½ small onion, chopped (¼ cup)	1 cup soft bread crumbs
¼ cup chopped red bell pepper	Salt and freshly ground pepper
¼ cup chopped fresh	⅛ teaspoon ground sage
mushrooms	⅛ teaspoon garlic powder

Preheat oven to 325°F. Untie roast and set aside. To prepare stuffing, heat oil in skillet until hot. Sauté onion and bell pepper until tender; add mushrooms and cook until soft. Stir in spinach, bread crumbs, salt, pepper, sage and garlic powder. Spread stuffing over one loin to within 1-inch of edges. Top with remaining loin and tie securely with string. Place stuffed roast on rack in open roasting pan. Bake, uncovered, 1 to 1½ hours, or until meat thermometer registers 160°F. Remove from oven; allow to stand 10 minutes before carving.

PORK CHOPS STUFFED WITH SPINACH AND SHRIMP

Your butcher will be happy to slit a pocket in some thick pork chops for you when you tell him about this splendid recipe. He knows you'll be back for more when your family showers you with rave reviews.

Stuffing

1 tablespoon butter	½ cup chopped leeks (white part only)
1 cup chopped headless shrimp, uncooked (peeled and deveined)	1 garlic clove, minced
Creole seasoning	⅓ cup celery, minced
	1 cup cooked chopped spinach leaves

Pork Chops

4 pork chops (1 ½ inches thick)	¼ bell pepper, chopped
Creole seasoning	¼ cup fresh chopped parsley
Pinch of cumin	1 garlic clove, minced
Flour (for dusting chops)	½ cup dry white wine
Vegetable cooking oil for pan-frying	½ cup water
6 scallions, finely chopped	2 tablespoons soy sauce
1 small onion, chopped (½ cup)	Tabasco

To prepare stuffing, melt butter in a large nonstick skillet over medium heat. Add shrimp and seasoning; cook 2 minutes. Add leeks, garlic and celery; simmer 3 to 5 minutes. Add spinach and cook until wilted, about 5 minutes. Remove from heat and set aside. To prepare pork chops, split meat with a sharp knife to form pocket for stuffing. With the side of a meat mallet, pound each pork chop until flattened. Sprinkle Creole seasoning on meat and rub with a pinch of cumin. Stuff each chop with ½ cup of spinach stuffing. Tie the chops with heavy string so that the stuffing will not fall out. Dust each chop with flour. Heat just enough oil in heavy skillet to generously cover the bottom; add chops and sear on both sides until deep brown. Remove chops and add scallions, onion, bell pepper, parsley, and garlic. Cook for 4 minutes on medium heat. Add wine, water, soy sauce and Tabasco. Return chops to skillet and cook on each side 15 minutes.

STUFFED HAM

*You'll want to take a picture of your spinach-stuffed ham
before cutting into it...it's that impressive.*

Ham

1   fully cooked half ham (about
    10 pounds)
2   (10-ounce) packages frozen
    chopped spinach, thawed
    and squeezed dry

1   large onion, chopped (1 cup)
¾   cup packed watercress
½   cup packed celery leaves
½   teaspoon salt
    Freshly ground pepper

Glaze

½   cup honey
2   tablespoons cider vinegar

2   teaspoons prepared mustard
2   teaspoons ground ginger

Cut away rind from ham and trim all but ¼ inch of fat. Using a small knife, make "X-shaped" cuts about 2 inches deep and 1 inch apart all over the fat side of the ham. Preheat oven to 325°F. Put spinach, onion, watercress, celery leaves, salt and pepper in a food processor and pulse until vegetables are finely chopped. Press the vegetable mixture into the cavities of the ham, packing in as much as possible. Place ham, fat side up, in a shallow roasting pan. Bake about 2 hours. Meanwhile, stir together honey, vinegar, mustard and ginger and brush onto ham. Continue baking and basting 30 minutes, or until ham is richly glazed. Remove ham from oven and allow to stand 20 minutes before carving.

CREOLE SPINACH JAMBALAYA WITH SMOKED SAUSAGE

My husband has a favorite saying: "There are two things in this world I really enjoy...and eating is both of them."

¼ cup vegetable oil
1 large onion, chopped (1 cup)
½ bell pepper, chopped
1 stalk celery, minced
1 garlic clove, minced
1 pound smoked sausage, cut into ½-inch slices and then diced
½ (6-ounce) can tomato paste (4 to 5 tablespoons)

1 package (10-ounce) frozen chopped spinach, thawed and squeezed dry
2 teaspoons salt
Cayenne
2 cups uncooked long-grain rice
1 can (14 ½-ounce) beef broth
2 cups water
1 scallion, chopped
1 tablespoon chopped fresh parsley

Heat vegetable oil in a large Dutch oven. Chop onion, bell pepper, celery and garlic in food processor; sauté in oil until tender. Meanwhile, brown sausage pieces in a skillet; drain well on paper towels. Add tomato paste to cooked onion mixture; stir and cook 2 minutes. Chop spinach in food processor. Add sausage and spinach to onion mixture; season with salt and cayenne. Add rice, beef broth and water; stir. Bring to a boil; cover and reduce heat. Cook over medium-low heat until rice is tender, 25 to 30 minutes. Stir in scallion and parsley and heat through. Serve hot.

INDIAN LAMB WITH SPINACH

During a business trip to Houston several years ago, a few of us decided to try out a little East Indian restaurant. Although we didn't understand most of the items on the menu, we did manage to find one with spinach. When we got back home, one of the men in our group created his rendition of that meal, and added this recipe to my collection.

2	tablespoons vegetable oil	¼	cup plain yogurt
1	large onion, finely chopped (1 cup)	1	piece (1-inch) finely chopped ginger
1	pound lean lamb, cut into 1-inch cubes	2	garlic cloves, peeled and crushed
4	teaspoons ground coriander		Water
1	tablespoon brown mustard seeds	2	pounds fresh spinach, trimmed, washed and torn into bite-size pieces
2	teaspoons ground cumin		Salt
½	teaspoon chili powder		Hot cooked rice
1	teaspoon turmeric		

Heat oil in a heavy skillet and cook onion until soft. Stir in lamb, coriander, mustard seeds, cumin, chili powder and turmeric; stir well to blend. Add 1 tablespoon of the yogurt and cook over high heat until the yogurt is absorbed. Repeat with one tablespoon of yogurt at a time until all is incorporated. Stir in ginger and garlic and just enough water to cover meat and bring to a boil. Cover the skillet, lower heat and simmer 1 to 1 ½ hours, or until meat is cooked. Increase heat slightly and add spinach, one handful at a time, stirring each batch until it is wilted. Cook, uncovered, over high heat to allow any excess liquid to evaporate, about 5 minutes. Season with salt just before serving. Serve over hot rice.

CHICKEN AND SPINACH POTATO SALAD

Potato salad has always been a tradition at our back yard barbeques. This recipe takes it several steps higher, by adding chicken and lots of fresh, tender spinach leaves.

Dressing

1	egg, lightly beaten	1	tablespoon chopped fresh tarragon
3	tablespoons grainy mustard		
¼	cup heavy cream	3	tablespoons extra virgin olive oil

Salad

1 ½	pounds thin-skinned red potatoes, cut into 1-inch cubes	2	cups diced cooked chicken meat
¼	cup white wine vinegar	2	tablespoons vegetable oil
		4	cups fresh spinach leaves, washed and chopped

To prepare the dressing, combine the egg and mustard in a large mixing bowl, mix well and set aside. In a small saucepan, bring cream to a boil over medium heat. Remove pan from heat. Immediately pour hot cream into the bowl with the egg mixture and beat with a wire whisk to fully incorporate. Add tarragon. Slowly whisk in the olive oil; set dressing aside. To prepare the salad, cook potato in boiling salted water until soft but not mushy; drain. Place potatoes in a mixing bowl and add vinegar, cover and allow to stand 5 minutes. Heat cooking oil in a medium skillet; add the chicken, cover and cook 5 minutes. Spoon the chicken into the bowl with the dressing; add the potatoes and mix well. To serve, add spinach to the bowl, toss well to coat, and mound on plates.

ROASTED GARLIC AND CHICKEN WITH SPINACH AND TOMATOES

Tender chicken breasts are topped with a spinach, mushroom and tomato mixture, seasoned to perfection with garlic and fresh rosemary.

Roasted Garlic

1 large garlic head, cloves separated, unpeeled

1 tablespoon extra virgin olive oil

Chicken

4 boneless skinless chicken breast halves

All-purpose flour

2 tablespoons extra virgin olive oil

½ pound shiitake or button mushrooms, sliced

1 cup dry white wine

4 medium tomatoes, peeled, seeded and diced

2 cups packed fresh spinach leaves

2 teaspoons chopped fresh rosemary

3 tablespoons butter

Preheat oven to 350°F. Place garlic head in a small baking dish. Rub 1 tablespoon of the olive oil all over the garlic. Bake until soft, 15 to 20 minutes. Remove from oven and allow garlic to cool. Pinch garlic between fingers to release from peel. Transfer garlic to bowl. Using the flat side of a meat mallet, pound chicken between sheets of plastic wrap to thickness of ½ inch. Coat chicken with flour, shaking off excess. Heat olive oil in heavy skillet over medium-high heat. Add chicken and sauté until cooked through, about 5 minutes per side. Transfer chicken to serving plates. Tent with aluminum foil to keep warm. Add mushrooms to skillet and cook 4 minutes. Add wine to skillet and boil until liquid is reduced by half, about 5 minutes. Add tomato, spinach, rosemary and roasted garlic; sauté until spinach wilts, about 3 minutes. Add butter and mix just until melted. Spoon mixture over chicken and serve.

ROASTED CHICKEN STUFFED WITH SPINACH AND RICE

If you thought stuffed turkey was good at Thanksgiving, just wait until you try this smaller version of stuffed poultry. It's spectacular!

1 large roasting chicken (3 ½ to 4 pounds)	1 cup cooked rice
Salt and freshly ground pepper	1 bag (10-ounce) fresh spinach leaves, washed, stems removed, chopped
2 tablespoons butter, softened	½ teaspoon freshly grated nutmeg
1 scallion, minced	
2 tablespoons all-purpose flour	2 teaspoons fresh lemon juice
½ cup hot chicken broth	1 garlic clove, lightly roasted to soften
½ cup heavy cream	
2 ounces chopped cooked ham (½ cup)	1 tablespoon butter, softened

Preheat oven to 375°F. Rinse chicken and pat dry using paper towels. Rub salt and pepper inside and out of chicken. Melt 2 tablespoons butter in a medium saucepan. Add scallion and cook until tender. Add the flour; cook, stirring constantly, 3 minutes. With a wire whisk, beat in the broth and cream. Heat mixture to boiling, stirring constantly until very thick. Remove from heat and stir in ham, rice, spinach, nutmeg and lemon juice. Mix thoroughly. Stuff the chicken with the spinach mixture. Sew up cavity so the stuffing will not fall out. Truss. Rub the chicken with the garlic and 1 tablespoon softened butter. Place chicken in a shallow baking pan. Roast 20 minutes in oven. Reduce heat to 350°F and continue to roast about 1 hour, basting occasionally with pan juices. Check for doneness by pricking with fork. Chicken is done when juices run clear. Remove string before transferring chicken to a serving platter.

CHICKEN, SPINACH AND BACON CAKES

You'll be staring at the oven in eager anticipation
as these scrumptious little cakes bake to perfection.

¼ cup extra virgin olive oil
4 scallions, finely chopped
¼ pound lean bacon, uncooked, coarsely chopped (4 slices)
1 ½ pounds boneless skinless chicken breasts

1 package (10-ounce) frozen chopped spinach, thawed and squeezed dry
⅓ cup heavy cream
1 ⅓ cups fresh bread crumbs
Freshly ground pepper
Salt
¼ teaspoon cayenne

Heat 2 tablespoons of the olive oil in a large saucepan; add scallions and cook until light golden, about 7 minutes; set aside. Place bacon in food processor and pulse until finely chopped. Transfer bacon to a large mixing bowl. Process chicken in food processor until minced. Add chicken meat to bowl with bacon along with spinach, heavy cream, ⅓ cup of the bread crumbs, scallions, pepper, salt and cayenne. Mix thoroughly to blend. Shape ¼ cup of the mixture into little round cakes. At this point, preheat oven to 400°F. In a shallow bowl, mix the remaining 1 cup of bread crumbs and pepper to taste. Dredge each little cake in the bread crumbs. Heat remaining olive oil in a large skillet over moderately-high heat. Fry the cakes, several at a time, turning once, until lightly browned on each side. Use remaining olive oil, if needed for frying. Transfer cakes to a baking sheet. Repeat with remaining chicken cakes. When all cakes have been fried, bake 10 to 12 minutes until firm. Serve warm.

CREAMY CHICKEN WITH SPINACH AND MUSHROOMS

Smooth and creamy, yet not too rich or overpowering, this meal is a crowd pleaser.

1   teaspoon canola or vegetable oil
1   small onion, chopped (½ cup)
2   cups sliced fresh mushrooms
2   garlic cloves, minced
1   tablespoon all-purpose flour
1   cup skim milk
½   cup chicken broth
12 ounces boneless skinless chicken breasts, cut into ½-inch cubes

1   package (10-ounce) frozen chopped spinach, thawed and squeezed dry
    Freshly ground pepper
8   ounces pasta shells, cooked al dente (4 cups)
2   tablespoons freshly grated Parmesan cheese

Heat oil in a large nonstick skillet; add onion and sauté until soft. Add the mushrooms and garlic and cook another 5 minutes, stirring often. Add the flour and cook 1 minute, stirring constantly. Gradually stir in the milk and chicken broth. Cook, stirring constantly, until the mixture begins to boil and thicken. Stir in the chicken and spinach; season with pepper. Return to a boil, stirring as needed until chicken is cooked through, about 8 minutes. Place the hot pasta in a large serving bowl. Add the chicken mixture; toss to coat. Serve hot with Parmesan cheese sprinkled on top.

TARRAGON-ORANGE SAUCE OVER SPINACH-STUFFED CHICKEN BREASTS

The name tarragon comes from the French "estragon" and the Latin "dracunculus", meaning "a little dragon." This high-spirited tarragon with its fiery tang, (well-tamed when blended with fresh orange juice), gives this dish a character all its own.

Stuffed Chicken Breasts

6	large boneless skinless chicken breast halves	1	can (11-ounce) mandarin orange segments, drained, (reserve liquid)
¾	cup cooked orzo		
1	package (10-ounce) frozen chopped spinach, thawed and squeezed dry	½	small onion, minced (¼ cup)
		1	garlic clove, pressed
		½	teaspoon salt
			Freshly ground pepper

Tarragon-Orange Sauce

⅔	cup orange juice, preferably fresh-squeezed	1	tablespoon cornstarch
⅔	cup reserved mandarin orange liquid	2	teaspoons chopped fresh tarragon
		¼	teaspoon salt

Garnish

Mandarin orange sections   Fresh tarragon sprigs

Using the flat side of a meat mallet, pound chicken breast halves, one at a time, between sheets of plastic wrap to about ¼-inch thick. In a medium mixing bowl, combine orzo, spinach, orange segments, onion, garlic, salt and pepper; mix well. Divide stuffing equally among chicken breasts; placing about ½ cup spinach mixture in center of meat, bringing ends together and securing with wooden picks. Place stuffed chicken breasts, seam side down, in large ungreased baking dish. Preheat oven to 350°F. To prepare sauce, combine orange juice, mandarin orange liquid, corn starch, tarragon, and salt in a small saucepan. Bring to a boil over medium-high heat. Cook 5 minutes, or until sauce thickens, stirring constantly. Pour sauce over chicken. Bake 35 to 40 minutes, or until chicken is fork tender and the juices run clear. Garnish with additional mandarin oranges and fresh tarragon, if desired.

118

BLUE CHEESE AND SPINACH STUFFED CHICKEN BREASTS

You'll be tempted to nibble on the spinach and blue cheese-stuffing before it ever even gets into the chicken. Be patient because the end result is well worth the wait.

Stuffing

1	teaspoon vegetable oil	½	cup frozen chopped spinach, thawed and squeezed dry
½	small onion, minced (¼ cup)	1	ounce blue cheese, crumbled
2	garlic cloves, minced	1	teaspoon Dijon mustard

Chicken

4	boneless skinless chicken breast halves		Freshly ground pepper
		1	teaspoon vegetable oil

Sauce

1	large onion, chopped (1 cup)	1	cup low-salt chicken broth
⅓	cup dry white wine	2	tablespoons Dijon mustard
½	teaspoon dried thyme		

To prepare stuffing, heat the oil in a large nonstick skillet over medium heat. Add onion and sauté 6 to 8 minutes, or until soft. Add garlic and cook 1 minute. Add spinach and sauté 3 minutes. Combine spinach mixture, blue cheese and mustard in a small bowl; stir well and set aside. Wipe skillet dry with paper towel. To prepare chicken, cut a horizontal slit through thickest portion to form a pocket. Stuff about 2 tablespoons spinach mixture into each pocket. Season chicken with pepper. Heat oil in skillet over medium-heat. Sauté chicken 6 minutes on each side, or until chicken is cooked through. Remove chicken from skillet; set aside and keep warm. To prepare sauce, put onion in skillet and sauté 5 minutes. Add wine and thyme; cook 3 minutes or until reduced by half. Add broth and mustard, cooking and stirring until thick. Return chicken to skillet; cover and simmer until thoroughly heated. Serve sauce with chicken.

119

CHICKEN ROCKEFELLER IN PHYLLO

Working with phyllo sheets may take a bit of practice for the beginner cook. However, this is one of the best recipes for practicing. Because the ingredients are so alluring, no one will notice if the pastry sheets aren't perfect.

4	boneless skinless chicken breast halves	1	teaspoon dried dill
			Salt and freshly ground pepper
6	scallions, finely chopped	2	ounces feta cheese, crumbled
2	garlic cloves, minced	16	sheets frozen phyllo dough, thawed
1	teaspoon butter		
1	package (10-ounce) frozen chopped spinach, thawed and squeezed dry	½	pound butter, melted (2 sticks)

Preheat oven to 350°F. Using the flat side of a meat mallet, pound chicken breasts, one at a time, between sheets of plastic wrap to about ¼-inch thick. Set aside. Sauté scallions and garlic in 1 teaspoon of butter until onions are tender. Add spinach, dill, salt and pepper. Cook until mixture is heated through. Add feta cheese. Divide mixture among chicken breasts and roll up meat. Place on a greased baking sheet and bake 20 minutes. Using a pastry brush, coat each sheet of phyllo with a thin layer of melted butter. When four sheets have been buttered and stacked one on top of the other, place one breast in the middle of the short side, fold sides over and roll up, completely encasing chicken. Continue until all sheets and chicken breasts have been used. Place phyllo packets on greased pan and bake until golden brown.

CHICKEN AND SHRIMP
OVER SPINACH FETTUCCINE

"Creamy, rich and succulent" best describes this recipe.

4	tablespoons butter (½ stick)	2	cups diced cooked chicken
8	ounces sliced fresh mushrooms	8	ounces headless shrimp, uncooked (peeled and deveined)
4	scallions, thinly sliced		
1	can (10 ¾-ounce) condensed cream of chicken soup (full strength)	3	tablespoons sherry
		2	tablespoons snipped fresh parsley
2	tablespoons half-and-half cream	12	ounces spinach fettuccine, cooked al dente
3	ounces cream cheese, cubed and softened	2	ounces cheddar cheese, shredded (½ cup)

Melt butter in a large saucepan; add mushrooms and scallions; sauté 5 minutes. Remove from heat. Stir in soup and half-and-half until well combined. Add the cream cheese and cook over low heat, stirring occasionally, until cream cheese is melted. Stir in chicken, shrimp and sherry. Simmer 12 minutes, but do not allow mixture to come to a boil. Just before serving, stir in parsley. Mound spinach fettuccine on large pasta bowl. Spoon chicken mixture over fettuccine. Sprinkle with cheddar cheese. Serve hot.

BISCUIT AND SPINACH POT PIES

These little pot pies are another one of my favorite spinach recipes. Serve them for brunch, a light luncheon, or a late night treat. You will be amazed at just how delicious they are.

Vegetable cooking spray
4 tablespoons butter (½ stick)
½ small onion, minced (¼ cup)
⅓ cup all-purpose flour
½ teaspoon salt
    Dash of white pepper
1 can (10 ¾-ounce) condensed cream of chicken soup (full strength)
¾ cup milk or half-and-half

¼ cup chicken stock (white wine or milk may be substituted)
2 cups cubed, cooked chicken
1 can (4-ounce) mushroom pieces, drained
1 package (10-ounce) frozen chopped spinach, thawed, squeezed dry
1 can (19-ounce) refrigerator buttermilk biscuits (8 "grand-size" biscuits)

Preheat oven to 350°F. Spray 8 (10-ounce) custard cups or aluminum pot pie bowls with cooking spray. Melt butter in a large heavy skillet. Sauté onion until tender. Add flour and stir. Season with salt and pepper. Cook until smooth and bubbly, stirring constantly, about 1 minute. Gradually stir in soup, milk and chicken stock; cook until mixture boils and thickens, stirring constantly. Add chicken pieces, mushrooms, and spinach; stir well and cook until heated through. Divide mixture evenly among the eight custard cups. Remove biscuits from package and separate. Press each biscuit into a circle the same size as the top of the custard cups. Cut four slits in each biscuit. (This will allow steam to vent during cooking.) Place one biscuit on top of each custard cup. Bake 20 to 30 minutes, or until biscuits are golden brown. Serve warm.

TURKEY BREAST FLORENTINE

Whether you need a satisfying evening entrée, or something to bring to a new neighbor, this stuffed turkey breast is sure to please.

1	(3-pound) turkey breast portion, (debone, butterfly and pound ½-inch thick)	1½	cups milk
6	slices lean bacon	1	package (10-ounce) frozen chopped spinach, cooked and squeezed dry
1	small onion, chopped (½ cup)		
3	tablespoons all-purpose flour	1	jar (2 ½-ounce) sliced mushrooms, drained
½	teaspoon dried tarragon		
	White pepper	1	tablespoon butter, melted
		1	ounce Swiss cheese, shredded (¼ cup)

Preheat oven to 350°F. Chop 2 slices of the bacon. Cook just until done; drain; reserve drippings. Cook onion in bacon drippings until tender. Blend in flour, tarragon, and pepper. Add milk. Cook and stir until thick and bubbly; remove from heat. Combine ½ cup of milk sauce, cooked bacon, spinach and mushrooms. Cover remaining sauce and chill in refrigerator. Place turkey skin side down; top with spinach mixture. Roll up and secure with heavy string. Place rolled turkey breast on rack in baking pan. Brush turkey with butter and stick meat thermometer in center. Bake, loosely covered with foil, 1 ½ hours. Uncover and remove string. Lay remaining bacon slices over turkey. Bake 30 minutes or until meat thermometer reaches 180°F. Meanwhile, stir cheese into remaining sauce; heat through. Slice turkey roll and serve with warmed sauce.

TURKEY HAM, ARTICHOKE AND SPINACH CASSEROLE

Here's a light and pleasing dish, filled with tasty ingredients.

4	ounces cream cheese or Neufchâtel cheese, softened	1	package (10-ounce) frozen chopped spinach, cooked and squeezed dry
1	tablespoon mayonnaise		Salt and freshly ground pepper
¼	cup milk	1	pound turkey ham, cut into ½-inch cubes
	Vegetable cooking spray		
1	package (9-ounce) frozen artichoke hearts, thawed	¼	cup seasoned bread crumbs

Preheat oven to 375°F. In a mixing bowl, combine cream cheese, mayonnaise and milk. Beat with electric mixer until light and fluffy. Coat bottom of casserole dish with cooking spray; place artichoke hearts in the bottom. Evenly distribute spinach over artichoke hearts. Season with salt and pepper. Sprinkle turkey ham pieces over spinach. Spread cream cheese mixture over turkey ham. Sprinkle bread crumbs on top. Bake 35 to 40 minutes, or until golden.

GROUND TURKEY AND SPINACH LOAF

The first time I prepared this recipe, I also made old-fashioned cornbread in a cast iron skillet. It was so good, I wrote a note on my recipe to be sure to serve this loaf with hot buttered cornbread.

1	pound ground turkey	5	tablespoons Dijon mustard
1	package (10-ounce) frozen		Vegetable cooking spray
	chopped spinach, thawed	1	jar (2-ounce) chopped
	and squeezed dry		pimientos, drained
½	cup seasoned bread crumbs	2	ounces mozzarella cheese,
½	small onion, minced (¼ cup)		shredded (½ cup)

Preheat oven to 350°F. Combine turkey, spinach, bread crumbs, onion and 4 tablespoons of the mustard in a medium bowl. Spray a 9-inch pie plate with the cooking spray. Shape turkey mixture into a small loaf; place in pie plate. Bake 50 to 55 minutes or until meat thermometer inserted in center of loaf registers 160°F and juices run clear. Remove from oven; spread remaining 1 tablespoon of mustard over top of loaf and top with pimientos and mozzarella cheese. Return to oven and bake 5 minutes or until cheese is melted. Cut into wedges and serve.

TURKEY BREAST STUFFED WITH SPINACH, CHEESE AND HAM

Rather than putting the stuffing inside the turkey, this mixture of mushrooms, spinach, cheese and ham is carefully stuffed under the skin that covers the turkey breast.

8 ounces fresh mushrooms, coarsely chopped (3 cups)	½ cup diced fully cooked ham
1 small onion, minced (½ cup)	Freshly ground pepper
4 tablespoons butter (½ stick)	Dash of ground nutmeg
2 (10-ounce) packages frozen chopped spinach, thawed and squeezed dry	1 whole turkey breast (5 to 5½ pounds)
3 ounces Swiss cheese, shredded (¾ cup)	2 tablespoons butter, melted
	2 tablespoons fresh lemon juice
	Salt

Preheat oven to 325°F. In a large sauce pan, sauté mushrooms and onion in 4 tablespoons of butter. Remove from heat; cool slightly. Stir in spinach, Swiss cheese, ham, pepper and nutmeg; set aside. Loosen skin from turkey breast, lifting carefully and pulling it back. Leave skin attached near neck area. Do not cut or tear the skin. Spoon spinach mixture on breast meat, under skin. Replace skin over spinach mixture; secure with small skewers or wooden picks. Place turkey breast on rack in roasting pan. Combine the remaining butter, lemon juice, salt and pepper; brush onto breast. Roast 2 hours or until meat thermometer inserted in thickest portion of breast registers 170°F. Brush occasionally with pan drippings to keep skin moistened. Cover with foil and allow to stand 10 minutes. Cut across the grain into slices and serve.

SAUTÉED WILD DUCK BREASTS WITH CREAMED SPINACH AND CRANBERRY-BOURBON RELISH

One of my neighbors shared this recipe with me, claiming he was first introduced to it one weekend during duck hunting season. Well, he wasn't kidding when he said it gets better every time it's prepared. The Cranberry-Bourbon Relish completes this meal in a manner befitting a king.

8	wild duck breasts	1	cup all-purpose flour
1	tablespoon salt	3	tablespoons extra virgin olive
1	teaspoon cayenne		oil
1	teaspoon freshly ground	3	(9-ounce) packages frozen
	pepper		creamed spinach
1	teaspoon crushed dried sage		Cranberry-Bourbon Relish
1	teaspoon crushed fresh		(recipe follows)
	rosemary		

Remove any bones and skin from duck breasts. In a small bowl, combine salt, cayenne, pepper, sage and rosemary. Rub seasoning into breasts and allow to stand in refrigerator at least one hour. To prepare duck, dip breasts in flour and pan-fry in olive oil; turn to cook on both sides. Remove to a heated platter. Slice each breast thinly; keep warm. Prepare creamed spinach according to package instructions; divide among serving plates. To serve, fan slices over spinach and spoon Cranberry-Bourbon Sauce on the side.

CRANBERRY-BOURBON RELISH

1	cup bourbon	1	bag (12-ounce) fresh
4	scallions, minced		cranberries
½	teaspoon freshly grated ginger	1	cup sugar
	Zest of 1 small orange	1	teaspoon freshly ground
			pepper

In a stainless steel saucepan, combine bourbon, scallions, ginger and orange zest. Bring to a boil; lower heat and simmer until a syrupy glaze forms, about 10 minutes. Add cranberries and sugar; raise heat and bring to a boil, stirring constantly. Lower heat and cook until cranberries start to burst. Remove from heat and add pepper. Cool; refrigerate until needed.

ROASTED DUCK BREASTS IN
CRANBERRY AND WINE SAUCE

I stumbled across this recipe in my files when I was looking for something to cook, using some of the Burgundy wine my husband and I bought on our honeymoon. Since I didn't have juniper berries, I used gin.

3	scallions, finely chopped	2	tablespoons cranberry sauce
2	tablespoons canola oil	4	duck breasts
5	ounces Burgundy wine		Salt
¼	cup beef stock		Freshly ground pepper
1	tablespoon fresh lemon juice		Fresh rosemary, minced
	Pinch of ground nutmeg	2	packages (9-ounce) frozen
4	dried juniper berries, crushed		creamed spinach, cooked
	slightly to release flavor (or 1		
	tablespoon gin)		

Preheat oven to 350°F. In a heavy nonstick skillet, sauté scallions gently in oil; do not allow to brown. Mix in the Burgundy wine, beef stock, lemon juice, nutmeg and juniper berries. Bring to a boil and stir in the cranberry sauce. Stir until dissolved. If desired, remove juniper berries from sauce. Meanwhile, season the duck with salt, pepper and rosemary; roast in a baking pan 20 to 30 minutes, or until cooked through. Remove from oven; discard skin and slice. Divide cooked spinach among four plates, place the sliced breasts on top, and spoon the sauce on the side of the plate.

Seafood
and
Fish

i love spinach

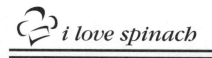

SEAFOOD & FISH

NEW ORLEANS STYLE
OYSTERS ROCKEFELLER

Many of the famous New Orleans restaurants offer Oysters Rockefeller on their menus. Their recipes are top secret and have been handed down from one family generation to another. One taste of this dish, and you'll soon realize that pearls are not the only precious gift that oysters can provide.

4	stalks celery	1	tablespoon fresh lemon juice
3	bunches scallions	2	teaspoons anchovy paste
3	garlic cloves	3	tablespoons ketchup
½	pound plus 4 tablespoons butter, melted (2 ½ sticks)		Dash of Tabasco
2	(10-ounce) packages frozen chopped spinach, thawed and squeezed dry	¼	cup chopped fresh parsley Fine dry bread crumbs Freshly grated Parmesan cheese
2	teaspoons salt Pinch of cayenne		Rock salt
½	teaspoon ground anise seed	4	dozen fresh oysters on the half shell, drained
3	tablespoons Worcestershire sauce		

Preheat oven to 400°F. Combine celery, scallions and garlic in a food processor or blender and purée; using a large heavy saucepan, sauté puréed vegetables in butter until tender; stir in spinach and cook on low until heated through. Remove from heat. Add salt, cayenne, anise seed, Worcestershire sauce, lemon juice, anchovy paste, ketchup, Tabasco and parsley; stir well. Purée a small amount of the mixture at a time in the food processor or blender. Transfer mixture to a large bowl. Spread rock salt generously over bottom of baking pans with shallow sides. Arrange the oysters on the half shell in a single layer on top of rock salt. Spoon a dollop of spinach on top of each oyster, sprinkle bread crumbs on top and flatten with back of spoon. Cover with Parmesan cheese. Place baking pans in oven and bake until lightly browned on top. Serve hot.

OYSTER BISQUE WITH SPINACH

*Close your eyes and just imagine how delicious this bisque tastes.
It's amazing how so few ingredients can yield such an aristocratic elegance.*

2   tablespoons butter
1   bag (10-ounce) fresh ready-to-
      use spinach leaves, chopped
1   container (10-ounce) shucked
      fresh oysters, undrained

1   cup chicken stock (preferably
      homemade)
½   cup heavy cream
¼   cup heavy cream, whipped
      (for garnish)

Preheat broiler. Melt butter in a nonstick saucepan. Add spinach and cook until tender, 3 to 5 minutes. Pour spinach and moisture in saucepan into a food processor or blender and purée. Add the oysters and their juices and purée until smooth. Return the spinach mixture to the saucepan, add the chicken stock and heat 2 minutes. Gradually add the ½ cup heavy cream and simmer 1 minute. Ladle into heatproof bowls and float whipped cream on top of each portion. Run under broiler for a minute or two to brown lightly. Serve immediately.

OYSTERS WRAPPED IN SPINACH AND BACON

*Excellent for serving at a cocktail party, these oysters will
have your guests asking, "What's in these? They're terrific!"*

18   thin slices lean bacon
2   (10-ounce) containers shucked
       oysters, drained

18   large fresh spinach leaves,
       thoroughly washed and
       patted dry
2   ounces Pernod (or other
       licorice-flavored liqueur)

Partially cook bacon in the microwave, using paper towels to absorb fat. Bacon should still be pliable with as much fat cooked out as possible. Preheat broiler. Wrap a spinach leaf around each oyster. Wrap a slice of bacon around the spinach. Drizzle Pernod on top of each oyster. Arrange the wrapped oysters seam side down on a broiler pan and broil about 3 minutes. Remove pan from broiler when bacon is crisp and oysters are hot. Serve immediately.

SMOKED OYSTER, SPINACH AND RICE STUFFING

Looking for a unique and exciting stuffing recipe?
This is probably the one for you.

3¾ cups reduced-sodium, fat-free chicken broth
¼ cup bourbon whiskey
2 teaspoons dried basil
2 teaspoons dried thyme
2¼ cups long-grain white rice, uncooked
1 tablespoon canola oil
1 large onion, chopped (1 cup)
1 large stalk celery, minced

3 leeks, white and light green parts, washed and chopped
2 garlic cloves, minced
3 cups fresh spinach, washed and chopped
2 (3.75-ounce) tins smoked oysters, drained and sliced
Salt
Freshly ground pepper

Preheat oven to 450°F. In a heavy saucepan, combine chicken broth, whiskey, basil and thyme. Bring to a boil. Spread rice into a large casserole dish. Pour chicken broth mixture over rice and cover tightly with heavy foil. Bake in oven 30 minutes, or until rice is tender. Meanwhile, heat oil in a large saucepan over medium heat. Add onion, celery and leeks. Cook until tender, stirring occasionally, about 10 minutes. Add garlic and cook 1 minute more. Add spinach and oysters, stirring until spinach is just wilted. Pour spinach mixture into rice and stir gently until blended evenly. Season with salt and pepper; stir again. Casserole may be kept warm in a slow oven, or refrigerated for up to 2 days, and reheated before serving.

ROCKEFELLER CREOLE TOMATOES

Don't tell your friends just how easy this dish is to throw together, and they'll think you spent hours preparing it. These thick, broiled tomato slices topped with an oyster and spinach mixture make the perfect side dish.

4   Creole tomatoes, tops and bottoms removed, cut into eight 1-inch thick slices
Salt
1   package (10-ounce) frozen chopped spinach, cooked and squeezed dry
3   scallions, finely chopped
3   eggs, lightly beaten
¼   pound butter, melted (1 stick)
¼   cup freshly grated Parmesan cheese

½   teaspoon Worcestershire sauce
¼   teaspoon garlic powder
Freshly ground pepper
1   teaspoon fresh thyme
Dash of Tabasco
Seasoned bread crumbs (about 1 cup)
1   container (10-ounce) shucked oysters, drained and patted dry
Freshly grated Parmesan cheese for topping (optional)

Preheat broiler. Arrange tomato slices in a large shallow baking pan. Lightly sprinkle salt on top. In a mixing bowl, combine spinach, scallions, eggs, butter, Parmesan cheese, Worcestershire sauce, garlic powder, pepper, thyme and Tabasco. Stir in just enough bread crumbs to form a medium consistency. Place 1 oyster on top of each tomato slice and mound spinach mixture on top. If desired, sprinkle a little Parmesan cheese over spinach. Place baking pan under broiler, 4 to 6 inches from the heat, and cook 10 to 15 minutes, or until heated through and spinach just begins to show signs of browning on the edges.

CREAMY ROCKEFELLER CASSEROLE

Need to prepare Oysters Rockefeller for a large group? Consider this casserole. Its allure is just as captivating as those that are served on the half shell.

2 (10-ounces) packages frozen chopped spinach	1 package (8-ounce) cream cheese, softened
2 chicken bouillon cubes	1 quart shucked oysters, drained (about 24 large)
1 tablespoon instant minced onion, soaked in 2 tablespoons milk Tabasco	½ cup buttered bread crumbs (see Note)

Preheat oven to 375°F. Cook spinach according to package instructions, omitting salt and adding bouillon instead. Squeeze spinach dry and return to pot. Add onion, Tabasco and cream cheese, mixing well. Heat over low heat but do not allow to boil. Arrange oysters in a lightly greased shallow casserole dish. Top with spinach mixture and sprinkle with buttered bread crumbs. Bake 25 to 30 minutes or until heated through.

Note: To make buttered bread crumbs, melt 2½ tablespoons butter. Add ½ cup dry bread crumbs and dash of salt. Mix well.

Oysters on the Half Shell with Puff Pastry Tops

If prizes were awarded for the best recipes in this cookbook, my vote for the "blue ribbon winner" would have to go to this recipe. Its presentation is every bit as impressive as is its exceptionally fine flavor.

1	package (10-ounce) frozen chopped spinach	1	ounce hazelnut liqueur White pepper
½	cup dry white wine	4	ounces Swiss cheese, shredded (1 cup)
2	slices lean bacon, chopped		
½	small onion, chopped (¼ cup)	2	ounces freshly grated Asiago cheese, divided
1	small garlic clove, minced		
12	oysters in their shells (tops and bottoms)	1	egg, lightly beaten
		1	tablespoon water
½	teaspoon dried thyme	1	frozen puff pastry sheet, thawed
½	cup heavy cream		

Preheat oven to 400°F. Combine frozen spinach and wine in saucepan. Cover and cook over low heat until done. Cool and drain by squeezing spinach; reserve liquid. In a medium sauté pan, cook bacon until almost done; add onion and cook until golden. Add garlic and cook another 2 minutes. Remove bacon mixture from pan, place in a bowl and set aside. Add cooking liquid from spinach to sauté pan. Open oysters; make sure to keep the top half of each shell right next to the bottom half containing the oyster. Drain liquid from each oyster into saucepan containing spinach liquid. Add thyme and boil over medium heat until reduced to about ¼ cup. Add cream and liqueur; continue cooking until mixture is thickened and reduced; season with white pepper. In a medium bowl, combine spinach with bacon mixture and cream sauce, blending thoroughly. Top each oyster with about 2 tablespoons of spinach mixture. Sprinkle with Swiss cheese and half the Asiago cheese. Roll out puff pastry. Use the top half of each oyster shell as a template for cutting out the puff pastry sheet. Lift each cut-out and place on top of corresponding bottom half. Continue until all oysters are topped with pastry. Beat egg with water to form egg wash. Using a pastry brush, brush tops of pastry with egg wash. Place oysters on a baking sheet and bake 30 to 40 minutes, or until pastry is a rich golden brown. Serve immediately.

SHRIMP AND POTATOES

*Layers of spinach, shrimp, potatoes and a smooth,
creamy cheese sauce create a harmony of delectable flavors.*

4   small potatoes, peeled
     (½ pound total)
2   tablespoons butter
1   garlic clove, pressed or
     minced
1   bag (10-ounce) fresh spinach
     leaves, heavy stems
     removed, chopped

Pinch of nutmeg
Salt and freshly ground pepper
8   ounces fresh or defrosted
     headless shrimp (peeled and
     deveined)

Sauce
1   tablespoon butter
2   tablespoons all-purpose flour,
     more if needed
6   ounces milk (¾ cup)

2   ounces cheese of your choice,
     shredded (½ cup)
     Salt and white pepper

Bring a pan of salted water to a boil. Put potatoes in water and cook for only 10 minutes; drain, slice ¼-inch thick; set aside. Melt the butter in a large pan and gently sauté garlic; add spinach and cook until wilted. Season with nutmeg, salt and pepper. Cook another 2 minutes then spoon into a casserole dish. Arrange single layer of shrimp on top of spinach mixture. Preheat oven to 375°F as you prepare the sauce. Melt butter in a saucepan; stir in flour and cook 1 minute. Add milk and bring to a boil, whisking briskly. Continue cooking another 3 minutes, being careful not to scorch mixture in bottom of pot. Remove from heat, add half the cheese, and season to taste with salt and pepper. Pour the sauce over the shrimp. Top with the sliced potatoes and the remaining cheese. Bake 20 minutes, or until golden brown and bubbly.

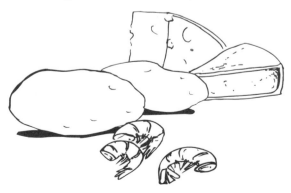

PASTA PRIMAVERA WITH SHRIMP

Lots of fresh vegetables make this pasta dish heart-healthy, as well as appetizing.

2 pounds headless shrimp, uncooked (peeled and deveined)
1 pound long fusilli or linguine
½ cup extra virgin olive oil
2 medium yellow squash, julienned
2 large carrots, julienned
2 medium zucchini, julienned (optional)
1 garlic clove, minced
½ cup chopped fresh parsley
   Salt and freshly ground pepper
1 package (10-ounce) frozen chopped spinach, cooked and squeezed dry

Bring a large pot of water to a rolling boil. Drop shrimp into water and cook for 2 minutes. Remove immediately with a slotted spoon and set aside. Cook pasta in shrimp water until al dente; drain and set aside. Reserve 1 cup of the cooking water in case the pasta seems too dry in the final step. In a large heavy skillet, heat the olive oil and sauté squash, carrots and zucchini. Add the garlic, parsley, salt and pepper. Add the spinach and sauté 3 minutes. Add the shrimp and stir until heated through. Combine the vegetable mixture with the pasta. If needed, add a little of the reserved cooking water. Serve immediately.

SHRIMP WITH ORZO AND FETA

Light enough to be a side dish, yet bountiful enough to satisfy as a meal.

1	pint cherry tomatoes, washed and quartered	1	package (10-ounce) frozen chopped spinach, thawed and squeezed dry
2	tablespoons chopped fresh dill		
1	tablespoon extra virgin olive oil	12	ounces headless shrimp, cooked (peeled and deveined)
1	garlic clove, pressed		
½	teaspoon salt	2	ounces feta cheese, crumbled
	Freshly ground pepper	1	tablespoon freshly grated Parmesan cheese
1	package (8-ounce) orzo		

In a large bowl, combine tomatoes, dill, olive oil, garlic, salt and pepper. Allow to stand 15 minutes. Meanwhile, cook orzo according to package instructions; drain. Combine tomato mixture, orzo, spinach, shrimp, feta cheese and Parmesan cheese. Pour mixture into a microwave-safe casserole dish. Cover and cook on HIGH 5 minutes, or until heated through.

SHRIMP ALFREDO IN A HEARTBEAT

A package of spinach pasta, a jar of Alfredo sauce and
some fresh shrimp make this meal as easy as 1-2-3.

1	jar (16-ounce) light Alfredo Sauce	1	teaspoon chopped fresh basil
½	pound headless shrimp, cooked (peeled and deveined)	12	ounces spinach fettucine, cooked al dente
		2	tablespoons freshly grated Parmesan cheese

Pour Alfredo Sauce into medium saucepan and warm over low heat. Add shrimp and basil. Simmer 15 to 20 minutes to allow flavors to marry. Pour over hot pasta and sprinkle with Parmesan cheese.

Shrimp Florentine

Individual servings make for a lovely presentation.

2	tablespoons butter
3	tablespoons flour
2	cups milk
4	egg yolks
½	teaspoon dried thyme
¼	teaspoon granulated garlic
	Salt and freshly ground pepper
1	tablespoon minced onion
1	can (4-ounce) mushroom pieces, drained
2	teaspoons chopped fresh parsley

1	package (10-ounce) frozen chopped spinach, cooked and squeezed dry
½	pound headless shrimp, cooked (peeled and deveined)
¼	cup freshly grated Parmesan cheese
3	tablespoons dry bread crumbs

Preheat oven to 400°F. In a heavy skillet, melt butter. Stir in flour; add milk and egg yolks. Cook over medium heat; remove before boiling. Add thyme, garlic, salt, pepper, onion, mushrooms and parsley. Gently press spinach into individual casserole dishes. Place shrimp on top of spinach and pour sauce on top. Cover with Parmesan cheese and bread crumbs. Bake 20 to 25 minutes, or until tops are golden brown.

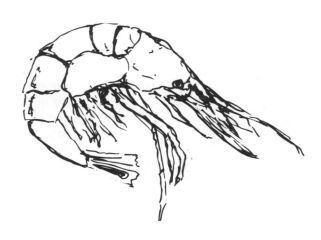

SAFFRON CREAM SAUCE WITH SHRIMP

Saffron is the most expensive seasoning in the world due to the labor required for harvesting the individual stamens. Over a quarter of a million crocus flowers must be harvested to obtain one pound of saffron. Fortunately, it takes just a pinch of saffron to flatter this rich cream sauce.

¼ teaspoon saffron threads	3 scallions, finely chopped (¼ cup)
¼ cup dry white wine	
1 bag (16-ounce) fresh spinach leaves, rinsed but not dried	2 small garlic cloves, pressed
	⅔ cup whipping cream
1 tablespoon butter	2 tablespoons shrimp stock (see note below)
1 pound headless shrimp, uncooked (see note below)	
Salt and white pepper	1 medium tomato, seeded
	Fresh lemon wedges
1 tablespoon extra virgin olive oil	Hot cooked rice

Crush the saffron threads using a mortar and pestle. Place saffron and wine in a small bowl; set aside. Meanwhile, heat a large stainless steel (nonreactive) skillet over medium-high heat. Add spinach a handful at a time and cook with only the water that clings to the leaves. When spinach is evenly wilted, transfer to a colander and allow to drain. Squeeze out moisture and coarsely chop. Wipe the skillet with a paper towel and melt the butter over medium heat. Add the shrimp; season with salt and pepper. Cook until shrimp start to curl and turn pink, about 3 minutes. Transfer shrimp and liquids from skillet to a warm plate. Heat the olive oil in the skillet. Add the scallions and cook until softened. Add the garlic and cook another minute. Increase heat and add the saffron mixture; boil until wine is reduced by half. Lower heat. Add cream and 2 tablespoons of the shrimp stock; simmer. Cut tomato into ½-inch cubes and add to skillet, along with spinach. Simmer 1 minute. Add shrimp with liquid and cook until heated through. Adjust seasoning. Serve with freshly squeezed lemon over hot steamed rice.

Note: To prepare shrimp stock, peel and devein shrimp reserving heads and shells. Rinse heads and shells in clear water; drain. Place heads and shells in a saucepan with enough water to cover. Simmer over medium heat 15 minutes. Strain liquid and discard heads and shells; set aside to cool. Unused shrimp stock may be frozen for future use.

SHRIMP AND SPINACH LOAF

Reaching the heights of culinary bliss, this recipe will undoubtedly be the first dish eaten on any buffet table. It would be a nice selection to serve after a music recital or after an evening at the opera.

½	pound headless shrimp, uncooked (peeled and deveined)	1	large onion, minced (1 cup)
		6	eggs, separated, at room temperature
1	large bunch fresh spinach, stems removed, washed and patted dry	¼	pound butter, melted (1 stick)
		1	teaspoon salt
			Freshly ground pepper
2	cups Italian bread crumbs		Tabasco

Preheat oven to 350°F. Coarsely chop shrimp. Combine shrimp, spinach, bread crumbs and onion; set aside. Beat egg yolks in a large mixing bowl. Add butter, salt, pepper and Tabasco. Blend in spinach mixture. In a separate bowl, beat egg whites until stiff but not dry. Gradually fold egg whites into spinach mixture. Spoon mixture into a lightly greased loaf pan. Place loaf pan into a larger baking dish. Pour boiling water into the baking dish 1-inch deep. Bake 45 to 55 minutes, or until wooden pick inserted in center comes out clean. Invert loaf onto serving platter and serve.

EASY SHRIMP APPETIZERS

Looking for "something a little different"
to bring to a holiday gathering? Try these.

1	package (10-ounce) frozen chopped spinach, thawed and squeezed dry	2	tablespoons chopped fresh parsley
4	ounces chive-flavored cream cheese, at room temperature	1	egg, lightly beaten
½	pound cooked headless tiny shrimp (canned shrimp may be used)	¼	cup freshly grated Parmesan cheese
		6	tablespoons cracker crumbs
		¼	teaspoon poultry seasoning
			Salt and freshly ground pepper

Topping

½	cup freshly grated Parmesan cheese	½	cup Ritz cracker crumbs
		3	tablespoons butter, melted

Preheat oven to 350°F. In a large mixing bowl, combine spinach and cream cheese until well blended. Add shrimp, parsley, egg, Parmesan cheese and cracker crumbs; stir well. Season with poultry seasoning, salt and pepper. Divide mixture into scallop shells or suitable baking dish. To prepare the topping, toss together the Parmesan cheese, cracker crumbs and butter. Sprinkle topping over spinach mixture. Place scallop shells on a baking sheet and heat in oven until piping hot. Serve immediately.

ALL-IN-ONE-POT FETTUCCINE WITH SHRIMP AND SPINACH

If you're one of those people who doesn't like to wash a lot of pots and pans, yet you enjoy great-tasting food, you've come to the right recipe. For a great meal with minimal cleanup, this recipe can't be beat. The pasta, shrimp and spinach are all cooked in the same pot!

12	ounces fettuccine, uncooked	1	cup plain nonfat yogurt
1	pound headless shrimp, uncooked (peeled and deveined)	4	ounces feta cheese, crumbled
		2	garlic clove, minced
1	package (10-ounce) frozen chopped spinach, thawed	1	teaspoon dried dill
			Freshly ground pepper
			Salt

Bring large pot of salted water to a boil; add pasta and set timer according to package instructions, less four minutes. When timer goes off, add shrimp and reset timer for two minutes. When timer goes off again, add spinach and cook two minutes. Meanwhile, mix together yogurt, feta cheese, garlic, dill and pepper in a large mixing bowl. Drain pasta, shrimp and spinach thoroughly. Add pasta mixture to yogurt mixture in bowl, and toss to coat. Sprinkle lightly with salt, if desired. Serve immediately.

CRAWFISH AND SPINACH STUFFED CHICKEN BREASTS WITH ANDOUILLE CREAM SAUCE

Andouille is a spicy, heavily smoked sausage. A specialty of Cajun cooking, it is the traditional sausage used in jambalaya and gumbo. Teamed with chicken, crawfish, spinach and a list of mouth-watering ingredients, this unique sausage will have your guests asking for refills.

Stuffed Breasts

6	large deboned chicken breasts	6	ounces ricotta cheese (¾ cup)
½	pound crawfish tail meat, veins removed	2	small garlic cloves, minced
1	package (10-ounce) frozen chopped spinach, thawed and squeezed dry	¼	cup freshly grated Parmesan cheese
		1	tablespoon dried oregano

Andouille Cream Sauce

1	cup heavy cream	6	ounces fresh mushrooms, coarsely chopped
½	cup chicken stock (preferably homemade)		Freshly ground pepper
4	ounces andouille sausage, chopped and browned	4	scallions, finely chopped

Preheat oven to 350°F. Using a sharp knife, carefully cut a slit into each chicken breast, forming a pocket for the stuffing. Do not cut all the way through or stuffing will fall out. Set aside. In a large mixing bowl, combine crawfish meat, spinach, ricotta cheese, garlic, Parmesan cheese and oregano. Stuff chicken breasts with spinach mixture. Arrange chicken in a large baking dish and bake 45 to 50 minutes, or until juices run clear when meat is poked with a fork. While chicken bakes, prepare sauce. Pour heavy cream and chicken stock in a heavy saucepan. Add cooked andouille and mushrooms; season with pepper. Allow to simmer, stirring occasionally, until sauce thickens; add scallions and stir. Pour sauce over stuffed chicken breasts and serve.

CAJUN FETTUCCINE WITH CRAWFISH, SHRIMP AND CRAB

Deep in the heart of south Louisiana live the luckiest people in the world. They are surrounded by rich resources and fresh seafood...including crawfish, shrimp and crabs.

¼ pound butter (1 stick)	4 ounces crawfish tail meat, veins removed
2 garlic cloves, minced	1 ounce dry white wine
4 scallions, finely chopped (¼ cup)	1 tablespoon fresh lemon juice
4 ounces andouille, diced	1 cup heavy cream
1 small tomato, seeded and diced	½ red bell pepper, diced (¼ cup)
½ red bell pepper, diced (¼ cup)	¼ pound cold butter (1 stick), chip by cutting into tiny pieces
1 can (4-ounce) mushroom pieces, drained	2 tablespoons chopped fresh parsley
8 ounces small headless shrimp, uncooked (peeled and deveined)	Salt
	Freshly ground pepper
4 ounces lump crabmeat	8 ounces spinach fettuccine, cooked al dente

In a heavy saucepan, melt 1 stick of butter over medium-high heat. Add garlic, scallions, andouille, tomatoes, bell pepper and mushrooms. Cook until all vegetables are wilted, about 5 minutes. Add shrimp, crabmeat and crawfish; stir occasionally and cook 10 minutes. Pour seafood mixture in a bowl. Deglaze pan with wine and lemon juice, cooking to reduce volume. Return seafood mixture to pan; add heavy cream. Cook until sauce has thickened, about 5 minutes. Add chipped butter a little at a time; swirl pot to blend but do not stir with a spoon. Continue adding butter until all is incorporated. Remove from heat. Add parsley and season with salt and pepper. Fold mixture into hot spinach fettuccine and serve.

CORN AND CRAWFISH SALAD

*On your next day at the park, pack a container
of this great salad in your picnic cooler.*

¼ cup minced celery
¼ cup minced scallions
1 tablespoon minced fresh parsley
½ teaspoon Hungarian paprika
Dash of cayenne
1 tablespoon Dijon mustard
2 tablespoons white wine vinegar
¼ cup extra virgin olive oil

2 cups canned corn kernels, drained
1 cup chopped cucumbers (peeled and seeded)
1 tablespoon minced pimientos
1 pound cooked crawfish tail meat, veins removed
1 bag (10-ounce) fresh spinach leaves, washed and patted dry

In a large mixing bowl, combine celery, scallions, parsley, paprika, cayenne, mustard and white wine vinegar. In a slow, steady stream, pour olive oil into mixture while beating with a wire whisk. Add corn, cucumbers, pimientos and crawfish. Toss to coat. Cover and refrigerate for 1 hour. Serve over a bed of spinach leaves.

BÉCHAMEL CREAM CHICKEN BREASTS WITH CRAWFISH AND SPINACH

A royal dish fit for a king, this recipe is rich, bountiful and exquisite.

6	large deboned chicken breasts	1	tablespoon fresh oregano, minced
½	pound crawfish tail meat, veins removed and coarsely chopped	½	cup white wine
1	pound fresh spinach leaves, stems removed, thoroughly washed and patted dry	1	cup Béchamel Cream (recipe follows)
6	ounces ricotta cheese (¾ cup)	½	cup fresh basil leaves, chopped
1	garlic clove, pressed	¼	cup pine nuts, toasted
¼	cup freshly grated Parmesan cheese	¼	cup heavy cream

Preheat oven to 350°F. Using a sharp knife, carefully cut a slit into each chicken breast, forming a pocket for the stuffing. Do not cut all the way through or stuffing will fall out. Set aside. In a large mixing bowl, combine crawfish tail meat, spinach, ricotta cheese, garlic, Parmesan cheese and oregano. Stuff chicken breasts with spinach mixture. Arrange chicken in a large baking dish and bake 25 to 35 minutes, or until juices run clear when meat is poked with a fork. While chicken bakes, prepare sauce. Combine wine, Béchamel Cream, basil, pine nuts and heavy cream in a saucepan. Cook over medium heat until mixture thickens. When chicken is done, cover with sauce and serve.

BÉCHAMEL CREAM

6	ounces chicken stock (¾ cup) (preferably homemade)	3	peppercorns
2	teaspoons minced onion	2	tablespoons butter
½	small carrot, sliced	2	tablespoons all-purpose flour
½	bay leaf	½	cup half-and-half or whole milk
1	sprig parsley		Salt
			White pepper

In a small saucepan, combine chicken stock, onion, carrot, bay leaf, parsley and peppercorns. Simmer 30 minutes. Strain and discard vegetables. Melt butter in saucepan. Add flour and stir until blended. Gradually add strained chicken stock, stirring constantly. Slowly add half-and-half and cook until thick. Season with salt and white pepper.

SUCCULENT SCALLOPS
OVER SPINACH FETTUCCINE

Don't let the ease and simplicity of this meal fool you. It's a sumptuous feast for both the eyes to behold and the taste buds to enjoy.

¼ cup pine nuts	1 pound bay scallops, rinsed and drained
1 tablespoon extra virgin olive oil	½ cup minced fresh parsley
2 garlic cloves, minced	Juice of one lemon
2 large tomatoes, coarsely chopped	1 pound spinach fettuccine, cooked al dente
½ cup dry white wine	¼ cup freshly grated Parmesan cheese

Put pine nuts in a nonstick skillet over medium heat and stir until lightly toasted. Remove pine nuts and set aside. Heat olive oil in skillet and sauté garlic. Add tomatoes and wine to skillet, and simmer 3 minutes. Stir in scallops and parsley. Squeeze lemon juice over scallops and stir to blend. Cook until scallops are opaque. Pour scallop mixture over hot spinach pasta and sprinkle pine nuts on top. Shake Parmesan cheese on top and serve immediately.

SEA SCALLOPS WITH
FRESH ORANGE DRESSING

*A perfect luncheon dish, this light entrée will set the mood
for relaxed conversation among old and new friends alike.*

2	(10-ounce) bags fresh spinach leaves, tough stems removed	2	tablespoons chopped fresh chives
			Salt
3	tablespoons fresh orange juice	1 ½	pounds sea scallops, rinsed and drained
1	teaspoon Dijon mustard		
	Freshly ground pepper	2	teaspoons fresh orange zest, for garnish
4	tablespoons extra virgin olive oil		Orange slices, for garnish

Wash spinach thoroughly. Put spinach in a small saucepan with a lid and set aside. In a small bowl, combine fresh orange juice, mustard and pepper. Blend well using a wire whisk. Slowly drizzle 2 tablespoons of the olive oil, whisking well. Stir in 1 tablespoon of the chives; season with salt and set aside. Pour the remaining olive oil in a large nonstick skillet over medium heat. Add half the scallops and cook 5 minutes, or until they are opaque and lightly golden, shaking the pan and turning the scallops over once. Remove scallops from skillet and keep warm. Repeat procedure with remaining scallops. Keep warm. Wilt the spinach by heating over medium heat about 3 minutes. Drain all moisture from the spinach and place spinach on serving plates. Using a fork, push spinach to form a ring; place scallops in center of ring. Pour orange dressing over scallops and spinach; garnish with remaining chives, orange zest and orange slices. Serve immediately.

SCALLOPS AND VEGGIES WITH SPINACH LINGUINE

Hot spinach linguine is tossed with scallops, mushrooms, and carrots.
To tie it all together, a light wine-based sauce is added.

4 ounces spinach linguine	½ teaspoon instant chicken bouillon granules
1 ½ cups sliced fresh mushrooms	
1 large carrot, thinly sliced	1 pound bay scallops, rinsed and drained
4 scallions, chopped	
2 tablespoons butter	1 tablespoon minced fresh parsley
1 garlic clove, minced	
¼ cup dry white wine	¼ teaspoon lemon-pepper
1 tablespoon cornstarch	Fresh lemon wedges

In a large pasta pot, bring 2 quarts water to a rolling boil. Add spinach linguine; return to boil. Cook 5 minutes; add mushrooms, carrots and scallions. Return to boiling; cook, uncovered, 5 minutes or until pasta and vegetables are tender. Drain pasta and vegetables; keep warm. Meanwhile, melt the butter in a large skillet. Add garlic and cook about 1 minute. In a small cup combine wine, cornstarch and bouillon granules. Add wine mixture to skillet, along with scallops, parsley and lemon-pepper. Cook and stir until thick and bubbly. Continue cooking another minute or two until scallops are opaque. Serve scallop mixture over hot linguine mixture.

SCALLOPS AND SPINACH IN CURRIED CREAM SAUCE

Next time you visit a specialty gourmet shop or an international grocery market, ask the clerk which brand is their best-selling curry powder. Quality ingredients are the key to this simple yet stunning recipe.

2 tablespoons butter	1 cup half-and-half
1 small onion, minced (½ cup)	2 cups fresh spinach leaves, cut chiffonade style
½ teaspoon salt	
2 teaspoons curry powder	2 pounds sea scallops, rinsed and drained
2 teaspoons tomato paste	
½ cup chicken stock (preferably home made)	

In a large heavy skillet, melt butter over medium-low heat. Add onion and sauté until tender; season with salt. Stir in curry powder and cook 2 minutes. Transfer onion mixture to a blender and add the tomato paste, chicken stock and half-and-half. Purée until smooth. Return sauce to skillet and bring to a simmer. Add spinach and scallops; cover and simmer 5 to 7 minutes.

CRAB AND ARTICHOKE CASSEROLE

Has it been awhile since you received a standing ovation?
Try preparing this magnificent casserole and it just might do the trick!

2   (10-ounce) packages frozen
    chopped spinach, thawed
2   teaspoons instant chicken
    bouillon granules
8   ounces sour cream
    Dash of cayenne

1   can (14-ounce) artichoke
    hearts, drained and
    quartered
1   can (6-ounce) crabmeat, rinsed
    in cold water and drained
1   tablespoon butter

Place spinach in a large microwave-safe casserole dish. Sprinkle chicken granules on top. Cover with wax paper and heat on DEFROST setting, rotating dish and stirring every 2 minutes, until heated through. Squeeze moisture from spinach. Return spinach to casserole dish. Stir in sour cream and season with cayenne. Press down lightly with back of spoon, and arrange artichoke hearts and crabmeat on top. Dot with butter and cover with wax paper. Microwave on HIGH 5 minutes, or until heated through. Serve immediately.

SEAFOOD AND SPINACH

A delectable meal that gets better with every bite.

6 tablespoons butter	1 can (14-ounce) artichoke
1 large onion, chopped (1 cup)	hearts, drained and coarsely
4 scallions, finely chopped	chopped
(¼ cup)	½ teaspoon salt
2 (10-ounce) packages frozen	Freshly ground pepper
chopped spinach, thawed	1 teaspoon Worcestershire
and squeezed dry	sauce
16 ounces sour cream	Tabasco
½ cup freshly grated Parmesan	½ pound headless shrimp,
cheese	uncooked (peeled and
	deveined)
	1 pound crabmeat

Preheat oven to 350°F. In a heavy skillet, melt butter and sauté onion until tender. Add scallions and cook until soft but not brown. Add spinach, sour cream and Parmesan cheese. Stir well to blend. Reduce heat and simmer until heated through. Add artichoke, salt, pepper, Worcestershire sauce, Tabasco, and shrimp; simmer 3 to 5 minutes. Gently fold in crabmeat. Transfer mixture into a large casserole dish and bake 20 to 30 minutes, or until piping hot.

CRABMEAT FETTUCCINE

Packed with richness and captivating taste sensations, this fettuccine is perfect.

2 tablespoons butter	¼ cup freshly grated Romano
2 tablespoons all-purpose flour	cheese
¼ teaspoon granulated garlic	¼ cup freshly grated Parmesan
Freshly ground pepper	cheese
1 cup heavy cream	8 ounces spinach fettuccine,
8 ounces lump crabmeat	cooked al dente

Melt butter in a saucepan; add flour and blend. Season with garlic and pepper. Stir in heavy cream, cooking over low heat until thickened. Simmer 5 minutes, stirring frequently. Add crabmeat. Cook until heated through. Add Romano cheese and Parmesan cheese; stir until melted. Pour over spinach fettuccine in large pasta bowl; toss to coat.

LOBSTER AND SPINACH BISQUE

*Worth every moment it takes to prepare, this Lobster and
Spinach Bisque is grand enough as a first course at a formal meal.*

Bisque

2	tablespoons butter	3	cups half-and-half
2	scallions, minced	1	package (10-ounce) frozen chopped spinach, cooked and puréed
½	cup dry white wine		
1 ½	cups chicken stock (preferably home made)		Salt
⅓	cup all-purpose flour		Freshly ground pepper
3	cups lobster stock or clam juice		Chunks of cooked lobster meat
¼	teaspoon dry mustard		Parmesan cheese

Lobster Stock

	Lobster shells and unusable lobster legs	1	stalk celery, sliced
		1	small onion, quartered
	Water	1	bay leaf

Prepare lobster stock by placing lobster shells in large saucepan and cover with water. Add celery, onion and bay leaf. Simmer 30 to 40 minutes. Remove from heat, skim and strain. Meanwhile, melt butter in a large saucepan; sauté scallions until tender. Add wine and chicken stock and simmer until reduced by half. Whisk in flour. Add lobster broth and dry mustard. Stir until the mixture returns to simmering and thickens. Add the half-and-half, spinach, salt and pepper. Do not allow to come to boil at this point. Pour into serving bowls and garnish with lobster meat and Parmesan cheese.

SALMON AND SPINACH PUFF WITH GOLDEN MUSHROOM SAUCE

Salmon and spinach were meant for each other in this tasty pie.

Pie

1   frozen pie crust (9-inch)
1   can (14¾-ounce) salmon, drained

½   can (4-ounce) mushroom pieces, drained
2   (12-ounce) packages frozen spinach soufflé, thawed

Golden Mushroom Sauce

1   can (10¾-ounce) condensed golden mushroom soup (full strength)

⅓   cup milk

Preheat oven to 350°F. Thaw pie crust 20 minutes at room temperature. Prepare the salmon by removing the fat, skin, bones, etc. and flake. Spread salmon in bottom of pie crust. Sprinkle mushrooms on top. Spoon soufflé over mushrooms. Bake 35 to 40 minutes or until puffed and firm. Allow to stand 5 to 10 minutes before cutting into wedges. Serve with Golden Mushroom Sauce spooned over each serving. To prepare sauce, heat soup and milk in a small saucepan.

NORTH PACIFIC PASTA PRIMAVERA

Vegetables, herbs, salmon and spinach...a winning combination.

2 tablespoons butter	1 small tomato, cored and diced (½ cup)
2 tablespoons minced onion	
1 ½ cups sliced fresh mushrooms	2 tablespoons minced fresh parsley
1 tablespoon unbleached all-purpose flour	
¼ teaspoon dried basil	2 tablespoons dry white wine
¼ teaspoon dried oregano	8 ounces spinach fettuccine, cooked al dente
¼ teaspoon dried thyme	
½ cup milk	Salt and freshly ground pepper
12 ounces smoked salmon, flaked	Lemon or lime wedges for garnish
1 small zucchini, thinly sliced	
1 carrot, shredded	Fresh parsley sprigs for garnish
½ cup frozen peas, thawed	

Melt butter in a large saucepan and sauté onion until tender. Add mushrooms and simmer 3 minutes, stirring frequently. Stir in flour, basil, oregano and thyme. Cook 1 minute. Gradually add milk, cooking and stirring until mixture thickens. Add salmon, zucchini, carrot, peas, tomato, parsley and wine; simmer until heated through. Pour over hot spinach pasta and toss to coat. Season with salt and pepper; garnish with citrus wedges and parsley, if desired.

SALMON WITH CURRIED CREAM SAUCE ON DILLED FETTUCCINE

*Remember this recipe when fresh dill is plentiful
because you will want to enjoy it over and over again.*

Salmon and Sauce

½ cup dry white wine
1 tablespoon butter
Salt and freshly ground pepper
1 salmon fillet (1 ½-pound),
skinned and quartered

1 large onion, minced (1 cup)
1 cup sliced fresh mushrooms
1 teaspoon curry powder
1 teaspoon all-purpose flour
2 cups half-and-half

Dilled Fettuccine

1 pound fresh spinach fettuccine
4 tablespoons butter (½ stick)

2 tablespoons chopped fresh dill
(not dried)
1 tablespoon fresh lemon juice

Combine wine, butter, salt and pepper in a skillet and bring to a boil. Add salmon, cover and poach 3 minutes. Turn salmon over, cover and cook another 3 minutes. Remove salmon from skillet and keep warm by covering with foil on a plate. Add onions and mushrooms to poaching liquid and cook over medium-high heat 6 minutes. Sprinkle curry powder and flour over mushroom mixture and cook, stirring 2 minutes. Gradually add cream in a steady stream, and gently bring to a low boil and let thicken 3 minutes. Cover and reserve. Put salmon and any juices on the plate back into the curried cream sauce to reheat. Pour salmon and sauce over hot dilled fettuccine. To prepare pasta, bring a large pot of salted water to a boil. Cook pasta until al dente. Meanwhile, heat the butter in a small skillet over high heat until butter starts to turn brown. Remove skillet from heat and add dill and lemon juice. Drain pasta and toss with dill butter. Serve on heated plates.

EMERALD SAUCE

The luck of the Irish may be headed your way with this beautiful emerald-green sauce. Excellent when served with poached salmon and boiled potatoes.

2	tablespoons butter	1	egg yolk
2	tablespoons all-purpose flour	¼	cup half-and-half
1	cup milk		Salt
4	ounces fresh spinach, puréed in food processor		White pepper

Melt butter in saucepan over low heat. Add flour and stir until well blended; cook 1 minute longer. Increase heat slightly and slowly add milk, stirring constantly. When mixture thickens, add spinach and cook 1 minute. Pour mixture into blender container and process; return mixture to saucepan. Combine egg yolk and light cream. Gradually add hot mixture to egg yolk mixture, a small amount at a time, stirring constantly. Cook over medium-low heat 1 minute, stirring constantly. Season with salt and pepper.

SALMON AND SPINACH LOAF

Prepare in a loaf pan and slice for presentation.

	Shortening for preparing loaf pan	24	unsalted saltines, broken up
		4	scallions, chopped
	Dry bread crumbs for preparing loaf pan	½	cup chopped fresh parsley
2	(14¾-ounce) cans salmon	2	eggs, lightly beaten
1	package (10-ounce) frozen chopped spinach, thawed and squeezed dry	¼	cup evaporated milk
		1	lemon (zest and juice only)
		1½	teaspoons crushed dried dill
			Freshly ground pepper

Preheat oven to 350°F. Prepare a loaf pan by rubbing with shortening. Sprinkle bread crumbs inside the pan and shake the pan until evenly coated. Drain salmon, debone and discard dark skin. Put salmon in a large bowl and set aside. Combine spinach, saltines, scallions, parsley, eggs, evaporated milk, lemon zest, lemon juice, dill and pepper in a food processor. Whirl until vegetables are chopped fine. Add to salmon, mixing well with clean hands to blend. Spoon mixture into the prepared loaf pan. Bake 50 minutes, or until lightly browned. Allow to stand 10 minutes before inverting onto a serving platter.

ATHENIAN FLOUNDER STUFFED WITH SPINACH AND FETA CHEESE

The best that Athens has to offer is proudly displayed in this enticing dish.

1	package (10-ounce) frozen chopped spinach, cooked and squeezed dry		Freshly ground pepper
4	ounces feta cheese, crumbled	4	flounder fillets
2	tablespoons fresh lemon juice	½	cup water
½	teaspoon fresh dill	¼	cup dry white wine
		2	tablespoons chopped parsley
		¼	teaspoon Hungarian paprika

Preheat oven to 375°F. In a medium mixing bowl, combine spinach, feta cheese, 2 teaspoons of the lemon juice, dill and pepper. Mix well. Spoon one-fourth of the spinach-cheese mixture onto the center of each fillet and roll fish lengthwise to enclose; transfer seam side down to a baking dish. In a small bowl, combine water, wine, parsley, paprika and remaining lemon juice; pour over fillets and bake 15 to 20 minutes, or until fish flakes easily when tested with a fork.

FENNEL AND SPINACH RICE WITH TARRAGON FISH

If there was ever a reason to plant your own little herb garden, this is it. Fresh fennel bulbs and tarragon make a fitting combination.

½	fennel bulb, chopped (1 cup)	1	cup shredded fresh spinach leaves
½	small onion, minced (¼ cup)		
2	tablespoons water	4	(4-ounce) lean fish fillets
2	cups chicken stock (preferably homemade)		Hungarian paprika
1	cup long-grain rice, uncooked	1	tablespoon chopped fresh tarragon
			Lemon wedges

Cook fennel and onion in water in large nonstick skillet over medium heat until crisp-tender, stirring occasionally. Stir in chicken stock, rice and spinach. Heat to boiling; reduce heat and cover. Simmer 10 minutes. Lay fish fillets on rice mixture. Sprinkle fish with paprika and tarragon. Replace cover and simmer 15 to 20 minutes longer, or until fish flakes easily with fork and liquid is absorbed. Serve with lemon wedges.

FLOUNDER PINWHEELS

Delectable flounder fillets are rolled around a spinach mixture, then baked to perfection and topped with a light vegetable sauce.

3   cups fresh spinach leaves, thoroughly washed and chopped
1   egg, lightly beaten
¼   cup soft bread crumbs
1   teaspoon fresh thyme (or ¼ teaspoon dried)
2   tablespoons freshly grated Parmesan cheese

White pepper
4   flounder fillets, rinse in cold water and pat dry
1 ½   teaspoons cornstarch
2   tablespoons cold water
1   can (6-ounce) vegetable cocktail juice
Fresh parsley sprigs
Lemon wedges

Preheat oven to 375°F. Place spinach in a saucepan with only the water that clings to the leaves. Cook and stir until just wilted; remove from pan; squeeze dry, and place in a mixing bowl. Add egg, bread crumbs, thyme, Parmesan cheese and white pepper; set aside. Spoon one-fourth of spinach mixture in center of each fillet and roll up jelly-roll fashion. Place seam side down in a square baking dish. Cover and bake 15 to 20 minutes, or until fish is fork tender. Meanwhile, combine cornstarch and water in a small saucepan, stirring until smooth. Stir in cocktail juice. Cook over medium heat until thickened and bubbly. Transfer flounder pinwheels to a serving platter and pour sauce over top. Garnish with parsley and lemon wedges. Serve immediately.

ROASTED SNAPPER WITH LEMON-DILL SPINACH

Just the name of this recipe makes one's mouth water in anticipation.

	Vegetable cooking spray	1	teaspoon extra virgin olive oil
4	(6-ounce) skinless snapper fillets	2	(10-ounce) bags fresh spinach leaves, stems removed, washed and drained
1	tablespoon fresh lemon juice		
4	teaspoons Dijon mustard	1	garlic clove, minced
½	cup finely chopped fresh dill	1	lemon, quartered lengthwise

Preheat oven to 400°F. Spray glass baking dish with cooking spray. Arrange snapper fillets in dish and sprinkle with lemon juice. Spread Dijon mustard over each fillet. Sprinkle all but 1 tablespoon of the fresh dill over the fish. Bake 15 to 20 minutes, or until just cooked through. Meanwhile, heat olive oil in large nonstick skillet over medium heat. Add spinach and minced garlic; stir until spinach is wilted, 3 to 5 minutes. Transfer spinach to serving platter with tongs, leaving pan juices behind. Place hot fish fillets over spinach and sprinkle remaining dill on top, along with lemon wedges. Serve immediately.

FISH FLORENTINE WITH HERBED TOMATOES

Invite your dearest friends over for a light meal before an evening at the symphony, and serve this wonderful dish.

1	cup cooked spinach, drained and chopped	8	ounces firm-fleshed fish (such as Cod, Halibut or Red Snapper)
1	tablespoon instant onion flakes		
	Pinch of garlic powder	2	medium tomatoes, sliced
¼	teaspoon ground nutmeg	3	tablespoons freshly grated Parmesan cheese
	Salt and freshly ground pepper	2	tablespoons chopped fresh parsley
¼	cup sour cream		
		½	teaspoon Italian mixed herbs

Preheat oven to 400°F. Combine spinach, onion, garlic powder, nutmeg, salt and pepper. Stir in sour cream. Spread mixture over bottom of small shallow baking dish. Place fish fillets over spinach mixture. Cover with tomato slices. In a small bowl, combine Parmesan cheese, parsley and Italian herbs; sprinkle over tomatoes and fish. Bake 15 minutes, or until fish flakes when tested with fork.

RED SNAPPER WITH SPINACH-HERB PESTO AND CREAMY THYME SAUCE

Fresh herbs make this dish extraordinary! The Spinach-Herb Pesto and Creamy Thyme Sauce are both prepared the night before and kept in the refrigerator. The sauces are reheated, separately, in a double boiler before being poured over the fish fillets.

Spinach-Herb Pesto

1	cup chopped fresh spinach leaves	1 ½	tablespoons extra virgin olive oil
½	cup chopped fresh basil leaves	2	tablespoons premium chicken broth
1	garlic clove, roasted and minced	2	tablespoons chopped fresh cilantro
3	tablespoons freshly grated Parmesan cheese		

Creamy Thyme Sauce

½	cup part-skim ricotta cheese	1	tablespoon chopped fresh thyme leaves
2	tablespoons milk	1	tablespoon sherry
2	tablespoons plain yogurt		White pepper
	Pinch of salt		

Red Snapper

6	fresh carrots	3	scallions, finely chopped
16	ounces bottled clam juice	¼	cup chopped fresh parsley
1	cup dry white wine	6	(4-ounce) red snapper fillets
⅓	cup white wine vinegar		

To prepare pesto, combine spinach, basil, garlic, Parmesan cheese, olive oil, chicken broth and cilantro in a blender; purée until smooth, scraping sides with spatula as needed. Refrigerate several hours. To prepare cream sauce, combine ricotta cheese, milk, yogurt, salt, thyme, sherry and white pepper in a blender; purée until smooth. Refrigerate several hours. To prepare meal, steam carrots until fork tender; set aside. Bring clam juice, wine, vinegar, scallions and parsley to a boil in a large skillet; add the fish fillets. Reduce heat and simmer 10 minutes, or until fish is opaque throughout. Gently reheat the Pesto Sauce and the Creamy Thyme Sauce, separately, in top of a double boiler or on low setting of microwave. Avoid high heat as the sauces may curdle. Evenly divide the Creamy Thyme Sauce among the six serving plates and place a fish fillet on top. Spoon Pesto on top of fish; place carrot alongside each serving of fish. Serve immediately.

Baked Trout, Spinach and Toasted Pine Nuts in Foil Packets

Neat little foil packets hold the juiciest and most aromatic spinach and fish you've ever tasted.

¼	cup pine nuts		Salt
3	large garlic cloves, peeled		White pepper
1	tablespoon butter	4	trout fillets
1	bag (10-ounce) fresh spinach leaves		Extra virgin olive oil
			Lemon wedges

Heat small nonstick skillet over medium-high heat. Put pine nuts in, stir and shake until nuts are toasted. Remove from heat and set aside. Preheat oven to 350°F. Bring a small saucepan of water to a boil and blanch the garlic 3 minutes. Rinse in cold water and cut into chunks. Melt the butter in a medium saucepan over medium-high heat. Cook the spinach with a pinch of salt, stirring frequently until wilted. Remove spinach from skillet, cool enough to handle, and squeeze out excess moisture. Place spinach in a bowl; add garlic and pine nuts; set aside. Season inside of each fish with salt and white pepper. Spread spinach mixture evenly in each fish, covering with the other side. Brush the outside with olive oil and sprinkle with salt and pepper. Place each fish in the center of a piece of foil. Use a pharmacy fold to secure each packet, pressing out excess air before sealing. Place packets on baking sheet and bake 20 minutes. The foil packets will puff when done. To serve, cut packets open with a knife, being careful to avoid getting burned by rising steam. Transfer fish with a spatula onto serving plates. Pour packet juice over fish. Garnish with lemon wedges and serve immediately.

CATFISH BUNDLES

A popular saying around "watering holes" here in the Deep South is, "Are the catfish jumping?" That's a way of asking if the fishing is good. Dinner forks will be jumping as your guests try to scoop up every last morsel of this delicious creation.

1	pound fresh catfish fillets	1	jar (2 ½-ounce) sliced
½	teaspoon lemon-pepper		mushrooms, drained
	seasoning	¼	cup freshly grated Parmesan
1	package (10-ounce) frozen		cheese
	chopped spinach, thawed	1	scallion, finely chopped
	and squeezed dry	1	egg yolk
1	cup corn bread stuffing mix	2	tablespoons water
1	small carrot, shredded		

Preheat oven to 350°F. Line sides of four lightly greased 10-ounce custard cups with fish, piecing as necessary. Sprinkle with lemon-pepper seasoning. In a mixing bowl, combine spinach, stuffing mix, carrot, mushrooms, Parmesan cheese and scallion. Beat egg yolk and water; add to spinach mixture. Spoon one-fourth of spinach mixture into center of each cup. Cover loosely with foil. Bake 25 to 35 minutes, or until fish flakes easily when tested with a fork.

CATFISH STUFFED WITH SPINACH SOUFFLÉ

*Using already prepared spinach soufflé helps
you make this meal in a hurry. Great for busy days.*

4	tablespoons butter, melted (½	1	package (12-ounce) frozen
	stick)		spinach soufflé
2	tablespoons fresh lemon juice	½	cup creamy buttermilk salad
6	catfish fillets		dressing
¾	cup cheese-flavored cracker		
	crumbs		

Preheat oven to 375°F. Combine butter and lemon juice; using a pastry brush, coat both sides of fish fillets. Roll fillets in cracker crumbs. Cut frozen spinach soufflé into 6 equal squares. Place one soufflé piece in the center of each fillet; fold ends over. Pour salad dressing over bottom of baking dish. Place fillets seam side down in dish. Bake 30 to 40 minutes, or until fish flakes easily when tested with fork. Serve hot with pan drippings poured over each serving.

CREOLE PLANTATION CATFISH FILLETS

Cooking in a big cast iron skillet always takes me back in time to memories of my grandmothers. They would hoist those big heavy pots without blinking an eye. What strong yet tender-hearted women they were.

Seasoned Flour

½   cup all-purpose flour
½   teaspoon salt
¼   teaspoon freshly ground
    pepper

½   teaspoon Hungarian paprika
    Pinch of granulated garlic

Catfish

8   catfish fillets

⅓   cup vegetable shortening

Creole Sauce

2   small garlic cloves, minced
1   can (28-ounce) whole
    tomatoes, undrained
4   cups fresh spinach leaves,
    thoroughly washed

¼   cup freshly grated Parmesan
    cheese
8   ounces sour cream
    Salt

Preheat broiler. Make seasoned flour by combining the flour, salt, pepper, paprika and granulated garlic; dredge catfish fillets through flour until evenly coated. In a large cast iron skillet, heat shortening and sauté fillets until crisp and golden; remove fish and transfer to warm platter. Add garlic to skillet and sauté 1 minute; add tomatoes and cook until heated through. With slotted spoon, lift out tomatoes and set them aside. Heat liquid in skillet and add spinach; cook just until tender. Arrange spinach and tomatoes in center of each serving plate; place fish fillets on top. Blend 1 tablespoon of the Parmesan cheese with the sour cream and a little salt; spoon over fillets. Sprinkle remaining cheese on top and brown under broiler.

Pastas
and
Lasagne

i love spinach

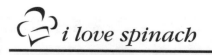 *i love spinach*

PASTAS & LASAGNE

ANGEL HAIR PASTA WITH LEMON AND GARLIC

Spinach produces superb-tasting pasta, as well as being a beautiful speckled-green color.

1 teaspoon extra virgin olive oil
4 garlic cloves, minced or pressed
½ cup dry white wine
¼ cup fresh lemon juice
1 medium tomato, chopped (1 cup)
4 ounces dried spinach angel hair pasta

4 ounces dried semolina angel hair pasta
¼ cup finely chopped fresh basil
2 tablespoons freshly grated Parmesan cheese
Freshly ground pepper

Fill a large pot with water and bring to a boil over high heat; maintain boil. Heat the olive oil in a small sauté pan; add garlic and cook 3 minutes. Remove the pan from heat and add wine. Return it to the heat and cook another 2 minutes, or until the wine has reduced by half. Stir in lemon juice and tomato. Remove pan from heat. Carefully add pasta to boiling water and cook 3 to 5 minutes; test for doneness. Drain and transfer pasta to a warm serving platter. Add the basil, Parmesan cheese and pepper; toss with tomato mixture. Serve immediately.

Vodka and Red Pepper Flakes with Tomatoes and Fresh Basil

You'll be shouting "Bravo!" as you experience the symphony of taste in this magnificent recipe. One taste and you will instantly be reminded that this dish is custom-suited for the adventuresome spirit!

⅓ cup vodka
1 teaspoon hot red pepper flakes (more, if desired)
1 pound dried spinach fettuccine

1 can (28-ounce) crushed tomatoes, undrained
1 cup fresh basil leaves, chopped
Pinch of salt

Pour the vodka over the red pepper flakes in a small bowl; allow to stand 10 minutes. Strain and discard the pepper flakes. Cook pasta in boiling water 5 to 7 minutes, or until tender but still firm. Combine tomatoes and basil; pour into a microwave-safe bowl. Stir in the vodka and microwave on HIGH 2 to 3 minutes. Transfer hot pasta to a large serving bowl and top with tomato mixture. Toss well and serve.

Tortellini with Creamy Mushroom Sauce

Spinach tortellini is topped with a creamy mushroom sauce, creating a shining example of simplicity with a flattering taste.

8 ounces spinach tortellini
3 tablespoons butter
½ small onion, minced (¼ cup)
1 cup sliced fresh mushrooms
1 teaspoon fresh lemon juice
3 tablespoons all-purpose flour
1 cup fat-free chicken stock

2 ounces heavy cream (¼ cup)
1 teaspoon salt
Freshly ground pepper
¼ cup dry white wine
1 cup frozen sweet peas, cooked
Chopped parsley (garnish)
Scallion rings (garnish)

Cook spinach tortellini according to package instructions. Meanwhile, heat butter in a medium saucepan; add onion and cook until tender. Stir in mushrooms and lemon juice and cook another 2 minutes. Sprinkle flour into saucepan and stir well. Add chicken stock and cream, stirring until mixture is thick and comes to a boil. Add salt, pepper and wine; cook 1 minute. Divide tortellini among individual serving plates and cover with sauce. Sprinkle with cooked peas and garnish, if desired. Serve immediately.

ROASTED RED BELL PEPPER SAUCE WITH SPINACH PASTA

Homemade roasted bell peppers are the secret to this dish's genteel taste.

6 red bell peppers	1 ½ cups chicken stock (preferably homemade)
2 tablespoons extra virgin olive oil	Salt and freshly ground pepper
2 tablespoons butter	2 tablespoons chopped fresh basil
1 medium onion, chopped (¾ cup)	½ cup heavy cream
1 garlic clove, minced	8 ounces spinach fettuccini, cooked al dente

Broil peppers until charred on all sides. Place in paper bag, close and allow to stand 10 minutes. Remove from bag and discard skin, seeds and membranes; chop. Heat olive oil and butter in saucepan; add onion and cook until transparent. Stir in garlic and cook until tender. Add bell peppers and stock; simmer, uncovered, 15 minutes. Transfer to blender and purée. Season with salt and pepper. Add basil and cream. Heat gently but do not allow to boil. Pour sauce over spinach pasta and toss. Serve immediately.

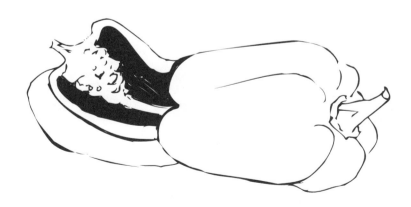

SPINACH LINGUINE WITH GOAT CHEESE

Light the candles, dim the lights and surround yourself with relaxing music...now you're all set for a memorable evening. What could be better than this fitting combination of flavors?

3	tablespoons extra virgin olive oil	½	teaspoon chopped fresh oregano
1	bunch scallions, finely chopped	1	tablespoon chopped fresh parsley
4	plum tomatoes, chopped	1	tablespoon chopped fresh basil
1	red bell pepper, seeded and chopped		Salt
			White pepper
6	sun-dried (oil-packed) tomatoes, drained and chopped	8	ounces spinach linguine, cooked al dente
1	garlic clove, roasted and minced	4	ounces soft Montrachet goat cheese, sliced

Heat olive oil in heavy skillet; add scallions and sauté. Stir in tomatoes, bell pepper, sun-dried tomatoes, garlic and oregano; cook about 15 minutes. Add parsley, basil, salt and white pepper. Stir in pasta and toss thoroughly. Divide pasta onto serving dishes and top each with goat cheese.

Fresh Tomato Fettuccine with Prosciutto

When I was a child, I would sneak out of my grandmother's back screen door with her salt shaker. On the side of the barn was her garden filled with beautiful tomato plants. They reminded me of Christmas trees with round red ornaments, even though it was the middle of July with temperatures well into the 90's. When no one was looking, I would snatch a tomato off a plant, bite into it, and then sprinkle a little salt for the next bite. Looking back now, I suspect that my grandmother was watching me the whole time from her kitchen window...and smiling.

1	tablespoon extra virgin olive oil	1	pound fresh tomatoes, peeled, seeded and chopped (2 cups)
3	tablespoons butter		Dash of ground nutmeg
1	small onion, chopped (½ cup)	9	ounces refrigerated spinach fettuccine, cooked al dente
1	garlic clove, minced		
8	ounces fresh mushrooms, sliced	¾	cup shredded Parmesan cheese
⅓	cup dry white wine		
¼	cup finely chopped prosciutto		

Heat olive oil and 2 tablespoons butter in a large skillet; add onion and cook until tender. Stir in garlic and cook 2 minutes more. Add mushrooms and cook, uncovered, 10 minutes or until tender. Combine wine and prosciutto and add to skillet; simmer until liquid evaporates. Add tomatoes and nutmeg; simmer 15 minutes, stirring occasionally. Toss hot cooked pasta with remaining butter and half of the Parmesan cheese. Transfer to a platter and cover with tomato sauce. Sprinkle remaining cheese on top. Serve hot.

GRILLED RED BELL PEPPERS AND VIDALIA ONIONS WITH SPINACH FETTUCCINE

Vidalia Onions were first grown in Georgia in the 1940's. They are extremely mild, as well as sweet, and have none of the bitter taste often found with yellow onions. Although the reason why they are so good is not known, many think it is because of the soil conditions. Whatever the reason, these onions are a delicious part of this dish.

2	medium Sweet Vidalia Onions		½	cup chicken broth
2	red bell peppers		¾	cup heavy cream
2	tablespoons extra virgin olive oil		⅓	cup fresh flat-leaf parsley, minced
2	garlic cloves, minced or pressed		8	ounces dried spinach fettuccine, cooked al dente
	Pinch of crushed red pepper			
½	cup dry white wine			

Cut onions and bell peppers into quarters. Roast or grill until charred and place in a paper bag until cooled. Remove from bag and discard seeds, core, and skins. Slice onions and bell peppers into strips; set aside. Heat olive oil in a large skillet and sauté garlic; add crushed red pepper, and cook until fragrant. Add wine, chicken broth and heavy cream; stir to blend. Bring to a boil; reduce heat and simmer gently 3 minutes. Add parsley, onions and bell peppers to sauce; toss with spinach fettuccine and serve.

CHICKEN TEQUILA

Deep in the heart of Texas near the San Antonio River Walk, my husband and I stumbled upon a little restaurant that prepared this beguiling sensation. Although we've never been able to find that little place on return visits, its memory lives on in this recipe.

½	cup chopped fresh cilantro	1 ¼	pounds chicken breast meat, diced ¾-inch thick
2	garlic cloves, minced		
1	tablespoon minced jalapeño pepper (seeds removed)	½	small red onion, thinly sliced
		½	red bell pepper, thinly sliced
3	tablespoons unsalted butter	½	yellow bell pepper, thinly sliced
½	cup chicken broth		
2	tablespoons gold tequila	½	green bell pepper, thinly sliced
2	tablespoons fresh lime juice	1 ½	cups heavy cream
3	tablespoons soy sauce	1	pound spinach fettuccine, cooked al dente

Cook ⅓ cup of the cilantro, garlic and jalapeño in 2 tablespoons of the butter 5 minutes over medium heat. Add chicken broth, tequila and lime juice. Bring to a boil and cook until reduced to paste-like thickness; set aside. Pour soy sauce over diced chicken and set aside 5 minutes. Meanwhile, cook onion and bell peppers with remaining butter until limp. Add the chicken mixture; stir in tequila paste and cream. Bring sauce to a boil, cooking gently until chicken is cooked and the sauce is thick. When sauce is done, pour it over the hot pasta and toss with reserved cilantro.

BLACK OLIVES, TOMATOES AND CAPERS OVER SPINACH PASTA

Prepare this sauce ahead of time for a quick meal on a busy day.

1 tablespoon extra virgin olive oil	1 tablespoon balsamic vinegar
1 small onion, chopped (½ cup)	2 tablespoons tomato paste
3 garlic cloves, minced	2 teaspoons sugar
1 can (16-ounce) salt-free whole tomatoes	½ tablespoon crushed dried oregano
1 cup chopped black olives	8 ounces spinach pasta, cooked al dente
3 tablespoons capers, drained and rinsed	

Heat olive oil in a large skillet; sauté onion until tender. Add garlic, stir and cook 3 minutes. Add tomatoes, breaking them with a fork. Stir in olives, capers, vinegar, tomato paste, sugar, and oregano. Simmer sauce until slightly thickened, 5 to 7 minutes. Serve over hot spinach pasta.

SPINACH-RICOTTA STUFFED JUMBO SHELLS

A favorite among young and old alike, these spinach and ricotta stuffed pasta shells are crowned with a magnificent Italian Tomato Sauce.

Italian Tomato Sauce

1 small onion, chopped (½ cup)	¾ cup water
2 tablespoons extra virgin olive oil	2 ounces dry white wine
	½ teaspoon dried basil
2 garlic cloves, roasted and mashed	½ teaspoon dried oregano
	2 teaspoons chopped fresh parsley
1 can (28-ounce) crushed tomatoes, undrained	Salt and freshly ground pepper
3 ounces tomato paste	

Stuffing

1 tablespoon extra virgin olive oil	1 egg, beaten
	⅔ cup ricotta cheese
2 tablespoons chopped onion	½ cup freshly grated Parmesan cheese
1 package (10-ounce) frozen chopped spinach, cooked and squeezed dry	Pinch of ground nutmeg

Shells

20 jumbo pasta shells, cooked al dente (pour 1 teaspoon olive oil in water)

Preheat oven to 350°F. To prepare tomato sauce, sauté onion in olive oil until tender. Add garlic, tomatoes, tomato paste, water, wine, basil, oregano, parsley, salt and pepper; simmer 30 minutes. To prepare stuffing, pour olive oil into skillet, add onion and cook until onion is tender but not brown. Add spinach and heat through. Remove from heat. In a large mixing bowl, combine spinach mixture, egg, ricotta cheese, Parmesan cheese, and nutmeg. Pour half the tomato sauce in a large baking dish. Stuff the cooked shells with the spinach mixture. Arrange shells in baking dish and top with remaining tomato sauce. Bake 20 to 30 minutes; serve hot.

GIANT SPINACH SHELLS

Mozzarella and cottage cheese, along with spinach and tomato sauce, accent these jumbo shells, creating a dish your whole family will enjoy.

24 giant pasta shells, cooked al dente	16 ounces cottage cheese (2 cups)
1 tablespoon vegetable oil	1 egg, beaten
1 small onion, minced (½ cup)	½ teaspoon salt
2 tablespoons butter	Freshly ground pepper
1 package (10-ounce) frozen chopped spinach, thawed and squeezed dry	30 ounces tomato sauce
	4 ounces mozzarella cheese, shredded (1 cup)

Gently toss shells in vegetable oil; set aside. Preheat oven to 350°F. Sauté onion in butter until tender. Stir in spinach and cook 2 minutes. Pour contents of skillet into a mixing bowl. Add cottage cheese, egg, salt and pepper; blend thoroughly. Stuff pasta shells with spinach mixture. Pour half of the tomato sauce into a large baking dish. Arrange stuffed shells in dish and cover with remaining tomato sauce. Bake 20 to 30 minutes. Remove from oven and sprinkle with mozzarella cheese. Return to oven and cook 5 minutes, or until cheese is melted and bubbly.

GREEK PENNE

Simple and unimposing, Greek Penne can be prepared in minutes.

2 teaspoons extra virgin olive oil	6 cups fresh spinach leaves, thoroughly washed and chopped
1 large red onion, chopped (1 cup)	
2 garlic cloves, minced	3 scallions, finely chopped
3 tablespoons pine nuts, roasted	2 ounces feta cheese, crumbled
1 ½ pounds ripe plum tomatoes, coarsely chopped	1 cup plain nonfat yogurt
	Pinch of salt
1 tablespoon tomato paste	Freshly ground pepper
	8 ounces penne pasta, cooked al dente

Heat olive oil in skillet over medium-high heat; sauté onion until tender; add garlic. Reduce heat to medium-low and add pine nuts. Stir in tomatoes and tomato paste; cover. Add spinach and scallions to skillet. Blend feta cheese and yogurt in a food processor. Remove the tomato mixture from the heat and stir in yogurt mixture. Season with salt and pepper. Pour penne in a large pasta bowl and top with sauce. Serve immediately.

BASIC RAVIOLI

The only thing better than homemade ravioli with a fantastic filling, is homemade ravioli with two fantastic fillings. You'll have a hard time choosing between the "cheese and spinach," and the "meat and spinach."

Dough

1 ½	cups all-purpose unbleached flour
½	teaspoon salt
1	egg yolk
	Warm water
	Freshly grated Parmesan cheese

Choice of Filling (see recipes below)
Italian Tomato Sauce
(see recipe on page 177)

Cheese and Spinach Filling

¼	cup cracker crumbs
½	cup freshly grated Parmesan cheese
⅓	cup cooked chopped spinach

1   egg, beaten
Chicken stock
Salt and freshly ground pepper

Meat and Spinach Filling

½	cup cooked beef or chicken, drained
½	cup cooked chopped spinach
1	egg, beaten

2   tablespoons freshly grated Romano cheese
Salt and cayenne

In a large mixing bowl, sift flour and salt. Make a well in the center and add egg yolk. Mix thoroughly using a knife, moistening with just enough warm water to make a stiff dough. Knead on a breadboard until smooth. Cover bowl and keep in a warm place 30 minutes. Meanwhile, prepare one or both fillings. To make cheese and spinach filling, mix cracker crumbs, Parmesan cheese, spinach and egg. Moisten with a little chicken stock; season. To prepare meat and spinach filling, mix meat, spinach, egg and Romano cheese; season with salt and cayenne. Roll dough paper-thin and cut into strips 2-inches wide. Put 1 teaspoon of filling on half of the strips, about 2 inches apart. Cover with the remaining strips, lining up all sides. Seal the edges by pressing with your thumbs; seal between the fillings in the same manner, creating little square "pillows." Cut apart, forming individual squares, each filled with a spinach mixture. Allow to dry 2 hours. Drop ravioli into rapidly boiling water and cook about 20 minutes. Remove with slotted spoon and arrange in layers on a heated plate or platter. Sprinkle between layers with a generous layer of Parmesan cheese. Top with Italian Tomato Sauce (see recipe on page 177) and serve.

CHICKEN AND SPINACH RAVIOLI

A bold yet unimposing taste all tucked inside a little
pillow of dough awaits you and your guests.

Pasta

3	cups all-purpose unbleached flour	2	tablespoons butter
2	eggs		Warm water
			Pinch of salt

Filling

1	cup minced cooked chicken	1	tablespoon chopped parsley
1	cup chopped cooked spinach leaves	1	small garlic clove, minced
½	cup Italian bread crumbs		Salt and freshly ground pepper
⅓	cup freshly grated Parmesan cheese (extra for sprinkling on top, if desired)	2	eggs, lightly beaten

To prepare the pasta, sift flour and salt into a large mixing bowl. Transfer to a work surface. Drop eggs in center of flour; mix well. Add butter. Gradually add just enough water to make a stiff dough; knead until smooth. Cover with a warm bowl and allow to stand 15 minutes. Roll into two thin sheets and cut each sheet into 2-inch wide strips. To prepare filling, combine chicken, spinach, bread crumbs, Parmesan cheese, parsley, garlic, salt and pepper. Blend in enough beaten egg to hold together firmly. Spoon 1 teaspoonful of spinach mixture along half the dough strips, spacing 2 inches apart. Place remaining strips on top, matching all sides. Pinch down to seal the edges. Pinch in between each mound to form individual squares; cut squares apart using a sharp knife or pastry cutter. Reseal cut edges. Allow to stand 2 hours before cooking. Bring 2 gallons of water to a hard boil and carefully drop in ravioli. Cook 10 to 20 minutes, or until dough is tender, depending on size and thickness of each ravioli. Remove cooked ravioli with a slotted spoon and place on heated plates. Top with Parmesan cheese, if desired. Serve immediately.

MINTED TOMATO SAUCE FOR SPINACH-FETA FILLED SHELLS

For a refreshing change of pace, this recipe incorporates mint leaves in its tantalizing list of fine ingredients.

12 jumbo pasta shells, cooked al dente

1 ounce mozzarella cheese, shredded (¼ cup)

Filling
1 package (10-ounce) frozen chopped spinach, thawed and squeezed dry
2 ounces feta cheese, crumbled
½ cup ricotta cheese

¼ cup chopped walnuts, toasted
1 egg white, lightly beaten
Pinch of salt
½ teaspoon ground cinnamon
Freshly ground pepper

Sauce
1 can (14 ½-ounce) cut-up tomatoes, undrained
⅓ cup tomato paste (half of a 6-ounce can)

2 tablespoons water
2 teaspoons dried mint leaves
1 teaspoon sugar
Dash of garlic powder

Preheat oven to 350°F. Set aside cooked pasta shells. Prepare filling in a medium mixing bowl by combining spinach, feta cheese, ricotta cheese, 3 tablespoons of the walnuts, egg white, salt, cinnamon and pepper. Blend well; Set aside. Make the sauce in a medium saucepan by combining the undrained tomatoes, tomato paste, water, mint, sugar and garlic powder. Bring to a boil; reduce heat and simmer, uncovered, 5 to 8 minutes until thickened. Stuff each shell using 2 tablespoons of the spinach filling. Arrange shells in an ungreased baking dish. Top with sauce and remaining walnuts. Bake, covered, 25 minutes. Remove from oven and sprinkle with mozzarella cheese. Return baking dish to oven and continue baking, uncovered, 3 minutes. Serve immediately.

FETTUCCINE WITH SPINACH, SAUSAGE AND ROQUEFORT CREAM

Here's a rich and creamy fettuccine, bursting with flavor.

¼ cup extra virgin olive oil	1 garlic clove, minced
6 ounces Italian sausage, casings removed	2 cups heavy cream
8 ounces fresh mushrooms, sliced	4 ounces Roquefort cheese, crumbled
2 bunches fresh spinach, stems removed, thoroughly washed	2 teaspoons Dijon mustard
¼ cup chopped walnuts	Salt and freshly ground pepper
	1 pound fettuccine

Heat olive oil in heavy skillet; add sausage and lightly brown, about 5 minutes. Crumble sausage with fork and transfer with a slotted spoon to a bowl. Add mushrooms to the skillet and gently sauté 2 minutes. Add spinach to skillet and cook until wilted. Stir in walnuts and garlic, stirring to blend. Add heavy cream and Roquefort cheese and bring to a boil; reduce heat and simmer until thick. Add sausage, mustard, salt and pepper. Cook pasta according to package instructions until just tender but firm to the bite. Drain and transfer to a large serving bowl. Pour spinach sauce over pasta and toss gently to coat. Serve immediately.

LINGUINE WITH CHICKEN, ORANGES AND SPINACH

*Delightful and delicious, here's one linguine dish
sure to captivate your taste buds.*

½   cup extra virgin olive oil
1   small onion, sliced
1   small garlic clove, minced
1   pound boneless skinless
    chicken breasts
1   teaspoon dried basil
2   (10-ounce) packages frozen
    chopped spinach, thawed
    and squeezed dry

Freshly ground pepper
8   ounces linguine, cooked al
    dente
1   cup orange chunks, peeled
    and seeds removed
1   cup freshly grated Parmesan
    cheese

Heat olive oil in heavy skillet and sauté onion until tender but not browned. Add garlic and cook another 3 minutes. Cut chicken into 1-inch strips. Stir in basil and chicken and cook 10 minutes. Add spinach and pepper; stirring and cooking another 5 minutes. Pour hot linguine in a large serving bowl and cover with chicken mixture. Top with orange chunks and Parmesan cheese. Serve immediately.

SPINACH PESTO

Many years ago, pesto was made by hand, using a mortar and pestle. Modern electric blenders have cut the preparation time down to just minutes, rather than hours.

3   cups fresh spinach leaves,
    thoroughly washed, stems
    removed, patted dry
2   tablespoons pine nuts, toasted
1   garlic clove, chopped
½   teaspoon salt
½   cup extra virgin olive oil

½   cup freshly grated Parmesan
    cheese
2   tablespoons freshly grated
    Romano cheese
    Angel hair pasta, cooked al
    dente

Combine spinach, pine nuts, garlic and salt in a food processor or blender. Pulse several times using a start-and-stop technique. You will need to scrap the sides of the blender several times with a rubber spatula. While blades are running, slowly add olive oil. Continue to blend until a smooth pasta forms. When the ingredients are puréed, transfer them to a small mixing bowl and stir in the Parmesan and Romano cheeses. Blend thoroughly and toss with hot angel hair pasta.

TOMATO AND SAUSAGE LINGUINE WITH SHREDDED SPINACH

Fresh shredded spinach is added at the end of this recipe. The heat from the steaming pasta gently wilts the spinach for a succulent flavor.

8   ounces linguine
1   tablespoon extra virgin olive oil
½   small red onion, chopped (¼ cup)
3   scallions, chopped
3   medium tomatoes, seeds removed, chopped

8   ounces Italian sausage links, casings removed
1   cup water
8   ounces fresh spinach leaves, julienned
¼   cup freshly grated Parmesan cheese

Cook linguine according to package instructions while preparing sauce. Heat oil in a skillet; add onion and scallions, cooking until softened. Add tomatoes and cook 8 to 10 minutes. Cut sausage into small pieces and boil in water, cooking over medium heat until water evaporates and sausage is lightly browned. Add sausage to tomato mixture. When linguine is cooked al dente, drain it in a colander. Place shredded spinach in a shallow pasta bowl. Combine linguine and tomato mixture; pour over spinach and toss well. Sprinkle Parmesan cheese on top and serve.

PASTA WITH SPINACH, SUN-DRIED TOMATOES AND PINE NUTS

Sun-dried tomatoes explode with rich flavor as they blend with tender, fresh spinach. On a trip from San Francisco to Louisiana, I stopped at specialty markets on the side of the road to purchase pine nuts and sun-dried tomatoes. When I got home, I prepared this recipe and knew immediately that it would be included in my first cookbook.

1 pound spaghetti, broken in half	¼ cup pine nuts, toasted
½ cup sun-dried tomatoes, rinsed (not oil packed)	2 garlic cloves, minced
1 pound fresh spinach, thoroughly washed, stems removed, coarsely chopped	1 teaspoon dried basil
	Freshly ground pepper
	Freshly grated Parmesan cheese
2 tablespoons extra virgin olive oil	

Put pasta cooking in boiling salted water according to package instructions. Place sun-dried tomatoes in a bowl and cover with very hot water. When tomatoes are softened, drain and chop. When pasta is almost ready, add spinach to pasta pot and continue cooking 2 minutes. Drain. Heat olive oil in empty pasta pot. Add pine nuts and stir until toasted. Add garlic and cook 2 minutes. Add tomatoes and remove from heat. Return pasta to pot and toss to coat. Season with basil and pepper. Sprinkle generously with Parmesan cheese. Serve warm.

LEMON TURKEY STIR-FRY

*Lighter and less imposing than other meats, these turkey cutlets
blend well with spinach and a touch of lemon.*

1 ½	pounds turkey cutlets, cut into ½-inch strips	6	scallions, thinly sliced
1	tablespoon soy sauce	1	lemon, sliced very thin and slivered
1	tablespoon white wine vinegar	1	garlic clove, minced
2	teaspoons cornstarch	1	bag (10-ounce) fresh spinach leaves, washed, patted dry and chopped
1	teaspoon lemon pepper		
1	pound spaghetti, uncooked		
2	tablespoons extra virgin olive oil		Fresh parsley and lemon slices (optional)

Combine turkey, soy sauce, vinegar, cornstarch and lemon pepper in a plastic zip-top bag; shake well. Place bag in refrigerator 30 minutes to allow flavors to blend. Meanwhile, boil pasta according to package instructions; drain well. Heat olive oil in skillet and sauté contents of plastic bag 3 to 5 minutes. Add scallions and lemon slivers, cooking until scallions are tender. Stir in garlic and cook 3 minutes longer. Add spinach and cook until just wilted. Spoon over hot pasta and garnish with fresh parsley and lemon slices, if desired.

EASY OVERNIGHT SPINACH MANICOTTI

Got relatives arriving on Friday evening, just about the time you knock off work? No problem. Prepare this dish the night before and place it in the refrigerator. When you get home from work the next day, simply remove it from the refrigerator and pop it in the oven. Your guests will think you spent all day preparing this heart-warming meal.

1   package (10-ounce) frozen
      chopped spinach, thawed
      and squeezed dry
15 ounces ricotta cheese
6   ounces mozzarella cheese,
      shredded (1 ½ cups)
¾   cup freshly grated Parmesan
      cheese
1   egg, lightly beaten
1   tablespoon minced fresh
      parsley

½   teaspoon onion powder
     Freshly ground pepper
     Pinch of garlic powder
2   (28-ounce) jars spaghetti
      sauce (meat flavored)
1   cup water
8   ounces manicotti shells,
      uncooked

In a large bowl, combine spinach, ricotta cheese, 1 cup of the mozzarella cheese, ¼ cup of the Parmesan cheese, egg, parsley, onion powder, pepper and garlic powder. In a separate bowl, combine spaghetti sauce and water. Spread 1 cup sauce in bottom of an ungreased baking dish. Stuff manicotti with spinach mixture and arrange in baking dish over sauce. Pour remaining sauce over manicotti; sprinkle with remaining mozzarella and Parmesan cheeses. Cover and refrigerate overnight. Remove from refrigerator 30 minutes before baking. Meanwhile, preheat oven to 350°F. Bake, uncovered, 40 to 50 minutes. Serve hot.

FLORENTINE CHICKEN LASAGNE WITH PECAN TOPPING

"Stylish elegance" best describes this lasagne recipe. The pecan topping adds an enchanting hint of charm. Serve with white or red wine and a fresh garden salad.

Lasagne

1	package (10-ounce) frozen chopped spinach, thawed and squeezed dry
2	cups chopped cooked chicken
8	ounces cheddar cheese, shredded (2 cups)
½	small onion, chopped (¼ cup)
¼	teaspoon ground nutmeg
1	tablespoon cornstarch
½	teaspoon salt
	Freshly ground pepper
1	tablespoon soy sauce

1	can (10 ¾-ounce) condensed cream of mushroom soup (full strength)
8	ounces sour cream
1	can (4-ounce) sliced mushrooms, drained
⅓	cup mayonnaise
6	lasagne noodles, cooked al dente
1	cup freshly grated Parmesan cheese

Pecan Topping

2	tablespoons butter	1	cup chopped pecans

Preheat oven to 350°F. In a large bowl, combine spinach, chicken, cheddar cheese, onion, nutmeg, cornstarch, salt, pepper, soy sauce, soup, sour cream, mushrooms, and mayonnaise. To prepare topping, melt butter in a heavy skillet over medium heat. Stir in pecans and cook about 3 minutes; set aside to cool. Arrange 3 lasagne noodles in bottom of a lightly greased baking dish. Spread half of chicken mixture on top. Proceed with second layer of lasagne noodles, topped with remaining chicken mixture. Sprinkle Parmesan cheese and Pecan Topping over lasagne. Bake, covered, 50 to 60 minutes or until bubbly. Allow to stand 10 minutes before cutting.

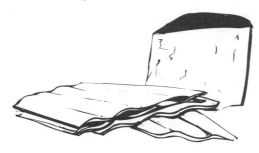

CHICKEN LASAGNE

Certainly worth the effort, this recipe is truly a sumptuous feast.
It is filled with lots of creamy cheeses, moist chicken and of course, spinach.

¼ pound butter (1 stick)
½ cup all-purpose flour
½ teaspoon salt
½ teaspoon dried basil
3 cups chicken broth from
   Simmered Chicken
   (see below)
2 ½ cups cubed chicken from
   Simmered Chicken
1 egg, lightly beaten
2 cups creamed cottage cheese

½ pound lasagne noodles,
   cooked al dente (about
   10 noodles)
1 package (10-ounce) frozen
   chopped spinach, thawed
   and squeezed dry
4 ounces mozzarella cheese,
   thinly sliced
¼ cup freshly grated Parmesan
   cheese

Simmered Chicken
1 whole chicken
   (3 to 3 ½ pounds)
3 cups water (approximately)
1 small onion, sliced

2 celery tops
1 whole bay leaf
1 teaspoon salt
Freshly ground pepper

Preheat oven to 375°F. In a large heavy skillet, melt butter over medium heat. Stir in flour, salt and basil. Pour in chicken broth, stirring until mixture thickens and comes to a boil. Remove from heat and add chicken. Stir egg into cottage cheese in a small mixing bowl. Lightly grease a large baking dish and place ⅓ of the chicken mixture on the bottom. Top with half the noodles, half the cottage cheese mixture, half the spinach and half the mozzarella cheese. Repeat the layers, ending with chicken mixture on top. Bake 40 minutes; remove from oven and top with Parmesan cheese. Return lasagne to oven and continue baking 7 to 10 minutes. Allow to stand 10 minutes before cutting. To prepare Simmered Chicken, put chicken in a heavy pot; cover with water. Add onion, celery tops, bay leaf, salt and pepper. Bring to boil; cover and reduce heat. Simmer 1 hour or until chicken is tender. Remove from heat; strain broth and reserve. When chicken is cool to the touch, remove meat from bones and coarsely chop.

MICROWAVE LASAGNE

For years I used my microwave oven just for heating food.
However, when I found this recipe, that all changed.

1	pound lean ground beef, browned and drained	½	teaspoon salt Freshly ground pepper
1	package (10-ounce) frozen chopped spinach, thawed and squeezed dry	9	Dash of cayenne pepper lasagne noodles (uncooked)
1	jar (32-ounce) spaghetti sauce	8	ounces mozzarella cheese, shredded (2 cups)
¼	cup water	½	cup freshly grated Parmesan cheese
12	ounces cottage cheese		
2	eggs, lightly beaten		

In a large casserole dish, combine beef, spinach, spaghetti sauce and water. Microwave on HIGH 5 minutes. In a small bowl, mix cottage cheese, eggs, salt, pepper and cayenne. In an oblong casserole, layer 1½ cups meat mixture, 3 lasagne noodles, ⅓ cottage cheese mixture, and ¾ cup mozzarella cheese. Repeat with two more layers. If desired, reserve ½ cup tomato mixture to spread on top layer of noodles. Top with Parmesan cheese. Cover with double layer of plastic wrap. Microwave on HIGH 8 minutes; reduce to 50% power and cook another 30 minutes, or until noodles are tender. Allow to stand 10 to 15 minutes before cutting.

SPANIKOPITA LASAGNE

Just when I thought spanikopita couldn't be improved upon, this lasagne recipe came in the mail from the mother of a dear friend. It takes the best of both worlds, spanikopita and lasagne, with the end result being exceptional.

	Vegetable cooking spray	¾	cup milk
1	tablespoon vegetable oil	4	ounces feta cheese, crumbled
2	medium onions, chopped	2	eggs, lightly beaten
	(1 ½ cups)	2	garlic cloves, minced or
2	cups sliced fresh mushrooms		pressed
1	package (10-ounce) frozen		Salt and freshly ground pepper
	chopped spinach, thawed	½	teaspoon dried dill
	and squeezed dry	9	lasagne noodles, uncooked
2	medium tomatoes, chopped	4	plum tomatoes, sliced
	(1 ½ cups)	8	ounces mozzarella cheese,
15	ounces ricotta cheese		shredded (2 cups)

Preheat oven to 350°F. Spray a large baking dish with cooking spray. Heat oil in a large nonstick skillet; add onions and cook until tender. Add mushrooms and cook until limp. Stir in spinach and chopped tomatoes, cooking another 10 minutes. In a large mixing bowl, combine ricotta cheese, milk, feta cheese, eggs, garlic, salt, pepper and dill. Add cooked vegetables from skillet. Spread 1 ½ cups vegetable mixture in bottom of baking dish. Cover with a single layer of noodles. Repeat layers, ending with mixture on top. Arrange tomato slices on top and sprinkle with mozzarella cheese. Cover with heavy-duty foil and bake 30 minutes. Remove foil and continue baking 15 minutes. Allow to stand 15 minutes before cutting.

FOUR-CHEESE VEGETABLE LASAGNE

"Cheeseheads," this one's for you! Combine cottage cheese, mozzarella cheese, Swiss cheese and Parmesan cheese for a spinach lasagne that is out of this world.

Vegetable cooking spray
1 tablespoon vegetable oil
2 cups chopped fresh broccoli
1 ½ cups thinly sliced carrots
1 bunch scallions, sliced
½ cup chopped red bell pepper
3 garlic cloves, minced
½ cup unbleached all-purpose flour
3 cups low-fat milk
½ cup freshly grated Parmesan cheese

Salt and freshly ground pepper
1 package (10-ounce) frozen chopped spinach, thawed and squeezed dry
12 ounces low-fat cottage cheese
4 ounces mozzarella cheese, shredded (1 cup)
2 ounces Swiss cheese, shredded (½ cup)
12 lasagne noodles, cooked al dente

Preheat oven to 375°F. Coat a Dutch oven with cooking spray. Heat oil in pot over medium heat. Add broccoli, carrots, scallions, bell pepper, and garlic; sauté 8 minutes; set aside. Put flour in a medium saucepan; slowly add milk, blending well with a wire whisk. Bring to a boil, stirring constantly, until thickened. Add ¼ cup of the Parmesan cheese, salt and pepper; stir. Remove from heat and add spinach. Remove ½ cup spinach mixture from pot and set aside. In a mixing bowl, combine cottage cheese, mozzarella cheese and Swiss cheese. Spread ½ cup spinach mixture, (not the reserved spinach), in a large baking dish coated with vegetable cooking spray. Arrange 4 lasagne noodles over spinach mixture; top with half the cheese mixture, half the broccoli mixture and half the remaining spinach. Repeat layers, ending with noodles on top. Spread reserved ½ cup spinach mixture over noodles, and sprinkle with remaining ¼ cup Parmesan cheese. Cover with heavy foil and bake 35 to 40 minutes. Allow to stand 10 minutes before cutting.

CANNED SPINACH LASAGNE

Quick, easy and delicious! Laura Ingalls Wilder once said, "I am beginning to learn that it is the sweet, simple things of life which are the real ones after all."

1 pound extra-lean ground beef	2 (14-ounce) cans spinach, drained
1 can (28-ounce) diced tomatoes, drained	15 ounces ricotta cheese
½ teaspoon dried basil	12 ounces mozzarella cheese, shredded (3 cups)
½ teaspoon dried oregano	9 lasagne noodles, cooked al dente
1 small garlic clove, minced	

Preheat oven to 350°F. Brown meat in a heavy skillet; drain. Stir in tomatoes, basil, oregano and garlic and cook 5 minutes; set aside. Blend spinach with ricotta cheese. In a large baking dish, layer 3 noodles, ⅓ spinach mixture, ⅓ tomato mixture, and ⅓ mozzarella cheese. Repeat layers, ending with cheese on top. Bake 30 to 40 minutes. Allow to stand 10 minutes before cutting.

LASAGNE WITH THREE CHEESES AND SPINACH

Herbs, cheeses, mushrooms and spinach all come together in this splendid lasagne. Serve with a nice Chianti and some authentic Italian music.

3 tablespoons extra virgin olive oil	2 tablespoons chopped fresh parsley
1 medium onion, chopped (¾ cup)	1 pound fresh spinach leaves, thoroughly wash, patted dry and chopped
2 small garlic cloves, minced	
2 large tomatoes, chopped	8 ounces mozzarella cheese, shredded, divided (2 cups)
4 ounces fresh mushrooms, sliced	1 cup cottage cheese
½ teaspoon dried oregano	½ cup freshly grated Parmesan cheese
½ teaspoon dried basil	
½ teaspoon dried rosemary	8 ounces lasagne noodles, cooked al dente

Preheat oven to 350°F. Heat oil in a large skillet and sauté onion until tender. Add garlic, tomatoes and mushrooms and cook another 5 minutes stirring often. Add oregano, basil, rosemary, parsley and spinach; cook until wilted. Simmer over low heat. Reserve ½ cup mozzarella cheese and set aside. Combine remaining mozzarella cheese, cottage cheese and Parmesan cheese in a large bowl; stir in vegetable mixture. Layer noodles alternately with vegetable mixture in a baking dish. Top with reserved mozzarella cheese. Bake 30 to 40 minutes. Allow to stand 10 minutes before cutting.

POTATO, SPINACH AND BEEF LASAGNE

Potato slices replace the traditional lasagne noodles in this recipe. The thinly sliced potatoes cook quickly and add an interesting texture to this dish.

3	medium potatoes, sliced ¼-inch thick	1	pound extra-lean ground beef, browned and drained
1	tablespoon butter	1	package (10-ounce) frozen chopped spinach, cooked and squeezed dry
1	small onion, finely chopped (½ cup)		
½	cup celery, diced	1	can (8-ounce) tomato sauce
1	garlic clove, minced		Salt and freshly ground pepper
1	can (4-ounce) mushroom stems and pieces, drained	½	teaspoon dried oregano
		2	ounces cheddar cheese, shredded (½ cup)

Preheat oven to 400°F. Line a large baking dish on sides and bottom with potato slices; set aside. Heat butter in large skillet and sauté onion, celery, garlic and mushrooms. Add cooked beef, spinach, tomato sauce, salt, pepper, and oregano. Pour mixture into baking dish and sprinkle cheddar cheese on top. Bake 35 to 40 minutes. Allow to stand 5 minutes before cutting.

AMATEUR SPINACH LASAGNE

Undoubtedly one of the easiest recipes in this cookbook, this one will impress your friends and family. Just don't tell them how easy it really was to prepare, and they will think you spent all day in the kitchen!

15 ounces ricotta cheese	2 (30-ounce) jars spaghetti sauce
6 ounces mozzarella cheese, shredded (1 ½ cups)	8 ounces lasagne noodles, uncooked (about 10 noodles)
1 egg, lightly beaten	½ cup water
Freshly ground pepper	½ cup vegetable juice cocktail or tomato juice
½ teaspoon dried oregano	¼ cup freshly grated Parmesan cheese
½ teaspoon dried basil	
1 package (10-ounce) frozen chopped spinach, thawed and squeezed dry	

Preheat oven to 350°F. In a large mixing bowl, combine the ricotta cheese, mozzarella cheese, egg, pepper, oregano and basil. Add the spinach and blend well. Put a small amount of sauce in bottom of large baking pan; spread with back of spoon to evenly coat. Place ⅓ of the uncooked noodles on the bottom; top with ⅓ of the spinach mixture, and then ⅓ of the spaghetti sauce. Make 3 layers, ending with spaghetti sauce on top. Combine water and vegetable juice cocktail. Carefully pour juice mixture around the inside edges of the baking dish, gently moving the noodles with a spatula to get the liquid evenly distributed. Sprinkle Parmesan cheese on top. Cover baking dish tightly with heavy foil and bake 1 hour. Remove foil and continue baking until lightly browned. Allow to stand 15 minutes before cutting.

GREEK VEGETARIAN LASAGNE

Looking for a vegetarian lasagne recipe that uses top-quality ingredients? If so, you've come to the right place.

- ¼ cup vegetable stock
- 1 large leek, chopped (white part only)
- 1 large onion, chopped (1 cup)
- 5 scallions, finely chopped (¼ cup)
- ½ cup chopped fresh parsley
- ¼ cup chopped fresh dill
- 1½ pounds fresh spinach, stems removed, cooked, squeezed dry and chopped
- 1 cup low-fat cottage cheese
- 4 ounces feta cheese, crumbled
- 4 eggs, beaten
- 3 tablespoons butter
- 3 tablespoons whole wheat flour
- 2½ cups skim milk
- ¼ cup freshly grated Parmesan cheese
- 12 ounces lasagne noodles, cooked al dente (about 15 noodles)

Preheat oven to 350°F. Heat vegetable stock in large skillet; add leeks, onions, and scallions. Cook over low heat until soft, but not brown. Add parsley and dill, stirring until parsley is wilted. Add spinach to onion mixture and cook on low heat until all moisture is evaporated. Pour skillet contents into a large mixing bowl. Add cottage cheese, feta cheese and eggs. Melt butter in skillet, stir in flour, and continue cooking over low heat for 3 minutes. Gradually add milk and stir until sauce thickens. Remove from heat and add Parmesan cheese; blend thoroughly. Place half of white sauce in bottom of large baking dish. Add a layer of noodles and a layer of spinach mixture. Repeat layers until all ingredients are used, ending with white sauce on top. Bake 25 to 30 minutes. Allow to stand 15 minutes before cutting into serving pieces.

CREAMY LASAGNE FLORENTINE WITH BÉCHAMEL SAUCE

This elegant and tempting lasagne is assembled several hours before being baked and served. Prepare ingredients and keep in refrigerator the night before a special luncheon, or prepare in the morning for a hassle-free dinner party that evening.

1 pound bulk pork sausage	3 ounces Swiss cheese, shredded (¾ cup)
1 small onion, chopped (½ cup)	½ cup freshly grated Parmesan cheese
1 large boneless, skinless chicken breast, cooked and cubed (2 cups)	Pinch of garlic powder
2 (10-ounce) packages frozen chopped spinach, thawed and squeezed dry	9 lasagne noodles, cooked al dente
Béchamel Sauce (recipe follows)	¼ cup soft bread crumbs

Brown sausage and onion in a large skillet, stirring to crumble. Drain well. Add chicken, spinach, half of the Béchamel Sauce and half of the Swiss cheese. Stir in Parmesan cheese and garlic powder. Spread about ¼ cup of the remaining Béchamel Sauce in the bottom of a lightly greased baking dish. Place 3 lasagne noodles over sauce and top with one-third of meat mixture. Repeat layering until ending with Béchamel Sauce on top; sprinkle with breadcrumbs. Cover with plastic wrap and refrigerate lasagne for 8 hours. An hour and a half before mealtime, remove lasagne from refrigerator and set on counter top. Allow lasagne to stand at room temperature 30 minutes. In the meantime, preheat oven to 350°F. Bake, uncovered, 35 minutes. Cover and continue baking another 10 minutes. Uncover and sprinkle with remaining Swiss cheese. Return lasagne to oven until cheese melts.

BÉCHAMEL SAUCE

3	cups milk
½	cup half-and-half
1	small onion, minced (½ cup)
2	bay leaves
¼	teaspoon dried thyme
3	tablespoons unsalted butter

⅓	cup unbleached all-purpose flour
½	teaspoon salt
	Freshly ground pepper
	Pinch of ground nutmeg

Combine milk, half-and-half, onion, bay leaves and thyme. Bring to boil over medium heat. Remove from heat and allow to cool. Melt butter in a heavy saucepan over low heat. Stir in flour, blending until smooth. Cook 1 minute, stirring constantly. Gradually pour milk mixture into flour mixture, stirring until thick and bubbly. Add salt, pepper and nutmeg; remove bay leaves.

LASAGNE ROLLS WITH WILTED SPINACH

During a potluck gathering, a group of ladies were busy talking in the kitchen about how one of the recipes was beautifully presented. It was these spinach-stuffed lasagne rolls, swimming in a lavish marinara sauce.

1	tablespoon extra virgin olive oil	15	ounces ricotta cheese
			Salt and freshly ground pepper
1	garlic clove, minced	9	lasagne noodles, cooked al dente
2	fresh carrots, shredded		
2	bunches fresh spinach, stems removed, washed, patted dry and chopped	2	cups Marinara Sauce (recipe follows—spaghetti sauce may also be used)
½	cup currants (optional)	¼	cup freshly grated Parmesan cheese
½	cup pine nuts		

Preheat oven to 350°F. Heat olive oil over medium-low heat in a large skillet; add garlic and sauté until soft. Add carrots and cook 5 minutes, stirring often. Add spinach and cook until spinach wilts. Stir in currants and pine nuts. Pour contents of skillet into a large bowl. Add ricotta cheese and stir well. Season with salt and pepper. Lay lasagne noodles flat on a clean work surface. Evenly spread the spinach mixture over entire length of noodles. Carefully roll up each noodle jelly-roll style. Pour half of the Marinara Sauce into a shallow baking dish. Place rolled up noodles on top of sauce so that the spiral pattern is on top. Pour remaining sauce over rolls and sprinkle with Parmesan cheese. Bake until sauce bubbles and cheese just starts to darken. Serve warm.

MARINARA SAUCE FOR LASAGNE ROLLS

2 tablespoons extra virgin olive oil	4 cups canned Italian plum tomatoes, undrained
2 tablespoons unsalted butter	1 tablespoon tomato paste
1 large onion, finely chopped (1 cup)	Freshly ground pepper
1 cup finely chopped carrot	3 flat anchovy fillets, drained, rinsed in ice water and finely chopped
1 tablespoon dried basil	
2 tablespoons finely chopped Italian parsley	Dash of red pepper flakes
1 bay leaf	Salt

Place olive oil and butter in a large, heavy skillet on low heat. Add the onion and cook until tender. Stir in the carrot and cook another 5 minutes. Add the basil, parsley and bay leaf. Simmer 2 more minutes, stirring constantly. Pour the tomatoes and their juice into the skillet and increase the heat to bring mixture to a boil. Using the back of the cooking spoon, mash the tomatoes to break them up. Stir in the tomato paste and season well with black pepper. Continue to cook on medium-high heat 40 to 45 minutes, or until most of the juice has evaporated and the sauce resembles a thick purée. Avoid scorching sauce. Pour the sauce into a food mill and purée. Do not use a blender because the end product would liquefy too much. Press the sauce through a sieve, returning the sauce to the pan. Discard contents of sieve. Bring sauce to a simmer over low heat; add anchovies and red pepper flakes. Cook until sauce has been reduced to 2 cups, stirring frequently. Sprinkle with salt.

GREEN AND WHITE LASAGNE

My high school colors were green and white. Whenever I prepare this lasagne, part of me is still cheering for the "Mighty Lions." Do you remember your own high school colors?

2 tablespoons butter	¼ cup chopped black olives
1 small onion, chopped (½ cup)	15 ounces ricotta cheese
1 tablespoon dried parsley flakes	2 eggs, lightly beaten
1 teaspoon dried basil	8 ounces mozzarella cheese, shredded (2 cups)
¼ teaspoon granulated garlic Pinch of ground nutmeg	½ cup freshly grated Parmesan cheese
2 tablespoons cornstarch	6 lasagne noodles, cooked al dente
2 cups milk	
1 package (10-ounce) frozen chopped spinach, thawed and squeezed dry	

Preheat oven to 350°F. Heat butter in a medium saucepan. Add onion and cook until tender. Stir in parsley, basil, garlic and nutmeg. Dissolve cornstarch in cold milk and add all at once to saucepan. Cook and stir until thickened and bubbly. Stir in spinach and olives. Combine ricotta and eggs in a separate bowl. Add mozzarella and half of the Parmesan cheese to the ricotta mixture; stir to blend well. Arrange three of the lasagne noodles in the bottom of a greased baking dish. Top with half the spinach mixture and half the ricotta mixture. Repeat layers. Top with remaining Parmesan cheese. Bake 40 to 45 minutes or until mixture is bubbly. Allow to stand 15 minutes before cutting into squares.

ALOTTA RICOTTA LASAGNE

Named by the young child of a neighbor of mine, this recipe is as appetite whetting as it is attractive. My neighbor was telling me about this recipe as I was writing it down, when her little girl overheard the conversation. That's when the child said, "That's a lotta ricotta!"

4	tablespoons butter (½ stick)	½	cup vegetable stock (chicken stock may be used)
2	(10-ounce) packages frozen chopped spinach, thawed and squeezed dry	1	teaspoon soy sauce
1	teaspoon dried marjoram	9	lasagne noodles, cooked al dente
15	ounces ricotta cheese Salt and freshly ground pepper	2	ounces cheddar cheese, shredded (½ cup)
8	ounces fresh mushrooms, coarsely chopped	2	ounces mozzarella cheese, shredded (½ cup)

Preheat oven to 400°F. Melt 2 tablespoons of the butter in a medium saucepan. Add spinach and marjoram; simmer over low heat 10 minutes. Remove saucepan from heat and allow mixture to cool. Add ricotta cheese; season with salt and pepper. Heat remaining butter in a skillet; add mushrooms. Cover and simmer, 10 minutes, to extract moisture from mushrooms, but do not drain. Add the vegetable stock and simmer 5 minutes. Transfer the mixture to a blender and purée for a few seconds. Add soy sauce. Lightly grease a baking dish and spread a small amount of the spinach mixture on the bottom. Place three lasagne noodles on top of spinach layer, topped with a layer of mushroom sauce. Continue layers until all sauce and noodles have been used, ending with the mushroom sauce. Sprinkle the cheddar cheese and mozzarella cheese on top. Bake 35 to 45 minutes until bubbly and heated through. Allow to stand 15 minutes before cutting.

CHICKEN AND CHEESE LASAGNE

*The addition of chicken, cheese, spinach and herbs
makes this lasagne both filling and delicious.*

¼	pound butter (1 stick)
1	medium onion, chopped (¾ cup)
1	garlic clove, minced
½	cup unbleached all-purpose flour
1	teaspoon salt
2	cups chicken stock (preferably home made)
1½	cups milk
1	pound mozzarella cheese, shredded (4 cups)
1	cup freshly grated Parmesan cheese
1	teaspoon dried basil
1	teaspoon dried oregano
½	teaspoon white pepper
15	ounces ricotta cheese
2	tablespoons dried parsley
9	lasagne noodles, cooked al dente
2	(10-ounce) packages frozen chopped spinach, thawed and squeezed dry
1	large boneless, skinless chicken breast, cooked and cubed (2 cups)

Preheat oven to 350°F. Melt butter in a large saucepan. Add onion and sauté until tender. Add garlic and cook 3 minutes. Stir in flour and salt; cook until bubbly, stirring constantly. Slowly pour in chicken stock and milk; stir well. Bring to a boil and cook 1 minute. Stir in 2 cups of the mozzarella cheese and ½ cup of the Parmesan cheese. Season with basil, oregano and white pepper; set aside. In a medium mixing bowl, combine ricotta cheese, parsley and remaining mozzarella cheese; set aside. Spread a small amount of the cheese sauce in the bottom of a large greased baking dish. Arrange a single layer of noodles on the bottom of the dish; top with some of the ricotta mixture, some of the spinach and some of the chicken. Pour some of the cheese sauce over the chicken. Repeat layers, ending with cheese sauce on top. Sprinkle remaining Parmesan cheese over cheese sauce. Bake, uncovered, 35 to 40 minutes. Allow to stand 15 minutes before cutting.

Quiches,
Soufflés
and
Eggs

i love spinach

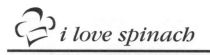
QUICHES, SOUFFLÉS & EGGS

FETA CHEESE AND SPINACH QUICHE

The Greek philosopher Socrates thought that 'hunger is the best appetizer.' That is why perhaps certain recipes from ancient times have been cherished. This feta and spinach quiche is good enough to start a legend of its own.

4 eggs, beaten	1 package (10-ounce) frozen
¾ cup cream (20% butterfat)	chopped spinach, thawed
1 ¼ cup milk	and squeezed dry
Salt and white pepper	4 ounces feta cheese, crumbled
2 tablespoons fresh lemon juice	¼ cup freshly grated Parmesan
2 tablespoons chopped fresh	and/or Romano cheese
parsley	Large pie crust (homemade or purchased)

Preheat oven to 375°F. Mix the eggs, cream and milk. Add the salt, pepper, lemon juice and parsley. Stir in the spinach and feta cheese. Pour mixture into crust and sprinkle Parmesan cheese on top. Bake 30 to 40 minutes, or until knife inserted near the center comes out dry. When done, remove from oven and cool 10 minutes before cutting into wedges.

CRUSTLESS SPINACH-MUSHROOM QUICHE

You won't miss the crust in this healthy and delicious recipe.

10	ounces fresh spinach, thoroughly washed and stems removed	½	cup freshly grated Parmesan cheese
6	ounces fresh mushrooms, sliced	½	cup skim milk
2	eggs, beaten	½	teaspoon dried tarragon
8	ounces cholesterol-free egg substitute, defrosted		Freshly ground pepper
		½	teaspoon salt
			Vegetable cooking spray

Preheat oven to 375°F. Cook spinach in a large saucepan until wilted, using only the water that clings to the leaves. Remove spinach from saucepan using a slotted spoon, leaving liquid in pan. Drain spinach and thoroughly squeeze out excess moisture; chop and set aside. Add mushrooms to liquid and cook until softened, about 3 minutes. Drain mushrooms and discard liquid. Combine spinach and mushrooms and set aside. In a mixing bowl, whisk eggs and egg substitute. Stir in Parmesan cheese, milk, tarragon, pepper and salt. Add mushrooms and spinach and blend well. Lightly coat the pie pan with cooking spray. Pour the mixture into the pan and bake 30 to 35 minutes, or until center is set. Remove from oven and let stand 10 minutes before cutting into wedges.

10 oz ~~mushrooms~~ Spinach, Fresh

6 oz mushrooms

2 eggs

8 oz Egg substitute

1/2 freshly grated Parmesan

1/2 cup skim milk

1/2 tsp Tarragon

Pepper

Salt

Cooking Spray

BACON AND SPINACH SOUFFLÉ QUICHE

A family favorite of ours, this quiche is often prepared for weekend guests. Many weary travelers refer to it as their "comfort food." It goes well with a fresh-squeezed orange juice and champagne cocktail.

1	unbaked pie shell		White pepper
1	medium onion, finely chopped (¾ cup)	1	small package fresh spinach leaves, chopped (3 lightly packed cups)
8	slices chopped lean bacon, uncooked	2	ounces mozzarella cheese, shredded (½ cup)
8	eggs		
4	ounces dairy sour cream (½ cup)	2	ounces Swiss cheese, shredded (½ cup)
½	cup whole milk or light cream		Dash of ground nutmeg
¼	teaspoon salt		

Preheat oven to 450°F. Prepare pastry by making a high fluted edge all the way around the rim. Line pastry shell with double thickness of foil. Bake 8 minutes; remove foil. Bake another 5 minutes. Remove from oven and set on a wire rack. Reduce oven to 300°F; allow at least 10 minutes for heat to adjust. Meanwhile, cook onion and bacon in a skillet, until onion is tender and bacon is crisp. Remove from skillet and drain on paper towels. In a medium bowl, beat eggs with a fork. Add sour cream and milk; stirring to blend. Season with salt and pepper. Stir in onion mixture, spinach, mozzarella cheese and Swiss cheese. Pour into pastry shell and sprinkle lightly with nutmeg. Cover edges with foil collar to prevent over-browning. Bake 45 to 50 minutes, or until knife inserted near center comes out clean. Let stand 10 minutes before cutting into wedges.

CRUSTLESS CHICKEN QUICHE FLORENTINE

One mixing bowl is all it takes to assemble the filling for this crustless pie. Just pour mixture into a baking dish and in less than an hour you can say, "Dinner is served."

1	large chicken breast cooked, deboned and cut into small cubes	1½	cups milk
1	package (10-ounce) frozen chopped spinach, thawed and squeezed dry	1	cup ricotta cheese
		¾	cup biscuit baking mix
		3	eggs
8	ounces sharp cheddar cheese, shredded (2 cups)	¼	cup freshly grated Parmesan cheese
1	small onion, finely chopped (½ cup)	1	teaspoon salt
			Freshly ground pepper

Preheat oven to 350°F. In a large mixing bowl, combine chicken, spinach, cheddar cheese and onion. Spoon mixture into greased medium-sized baking dish. Combine milk, ricotta cheese, baking mix, eggs, Parmesan cheese, salt and pepper using an electric mixer. Pour milk mixture over chicken mixture. Bake 50 to 55 minutes, or until knife inserted near center comes out clean. Let stand 5 minutes before serving.

BEEFY QUICHE

*If the cowboys in your family like a meal they can
sink their teeth into, try this great-tasting pie.*

½	pound extra-lean ground beef	½	cup milk
1	small onion, finely chopped	2	eggs
	(½ cup)	1	tablespoon cornstarch
1	package (10-ounce) frozen	6	ounces cheddar cheese,
	chopped spinach, thawed		shredded (1 ½ cups)
	and squeezed dry		Salt and freshly ground pepper
½	cup mayonnaise	1	unbaked (9-inch) pie shell

Preheat oven to 350°F. Cook beef and onion is heavy skillet; drain thoroughly. In a large mixing bowl, combine spinach, mayonnaise, milk, eggs and cornstarch; blend until smooth. Stir in meat mixture, cheddar cheese, salt and pepper. Pour into pie shell and bake 50 minutes to an hour, or until knife inserted near center comes out dry. Allow to stand 10 minutes before cutting into wedges.

HAM AND CREAMED SPINACH QUICHE

Leftover holiday ham is perfect for this recipe.

1	large pie shell, unbaked	4	eggs, beaten
2	tablespoons freshly grated	4	ounces cooked ham, chopped
	Parmesan cheese		(1 cup)
4	tablespoons butter, melted	3	tablespoons chopped onion
	(½ stick)	3	tablespoons all-purpose flour
1	package (9-ounce) frozen	4	ounces Swiss cheese,
	creamed spinach, defrosted		shredded (1 cup)
1	cup half-and-half		Salt and freshly ground pepper

Preheat oven to 375°F. Press Parmesan cheese onto bottom of pie shell. Stir butter into creamed spinach; add cream, eggs, ham, onion and flour. Blend in Swiss cheese, a little at a time, until thoroughly incorporated. Season with salt and pepper. Pour ingredients into pie shell and bake 35 to 45 minutes, or until knife inserted near center comes out clean. Let stand 5 minutes before serving.

211

SPINACH CRUST

For a different twist on things, bake the spinach inside the crust,
and then fill with your favorite quiche filling.

2   tablespoons extra virgin olive
    oil
1 ½ teaspoons minced onion
12 ounces fresh, finely chopped
    spinach leaves, thoroughly
    washed and patted dry

½   teaspoon salt
¾   cup unbleached all-purpose
    flour
¾   cup Italian bread crumbs
    Pinch of ground nutmeg

Preheat oven to 350°F. Heat olive oil in a large skillet. Sauté onion until tender; increase heat and add spinach, cooking until wilted. Season with salt and remove from heat. Transfer to a large mixing bowl. Stir in flour, bread crumbs and nutmeg. Press firmly into a greased pie pan. Bake 15 minutes.

ITALIAN SAUSAGE QUICHES

For a crowd-pleasing and appetite-satisfying meal,
try these quiches that are packed with alluring ingredients.

1   pound Italian sausage
6   eggs
2   (10-ounce) packages frozen
    chopped spinach, thawed
    and squeezed dry
16 ounces mozzarella cheese,
    shredded (4 cups)

⅔   cup ricotta cheese
½   teaspoon salt
    Freshly ground pepper
    Pinch of garlic powder
4   pie crusts, unbaked
1   tablespoon water

Preheat oven to 350°F. Remove sausage from casing and cook until browned; drain well on paper towels. Reserve 1 egg yolk. Combine egg white and remaining eggs with sausage, spinach, mozzarella cheese, ricotta cheese, salt, pepper and garlic powder. Pour filling into one pie crust. Place second crust on top. Repeat with remaining crusts. Trim edges and seal. Cut slit in top half of the crusts to allow steam to vent. Combine reserved egg yolk with water and brush on top crusts. Bake 1 hour and 15 minutes, or until crust is deep golden brown. Let stand 10 minutes before cutting into wedges.

RICOTTA-FETA-SPINACH TART

Simple ingredients come together to create this charming pie.
For variety, try using different herbs, like marjoram, chives or thyme.

1	Make-Ahead Tart Pastry (recipe follows)	2	ounces feta cheese, crumbled
2	eggs	¼	cup milk
1	cup fresh chopped spinach leaves	1	teaspoon dried oregano
1	cup ricotta cheese	2	tablespoons freshly grated Parmesan cheese

Preheat oven to 325°F. Beat eggs in a mixing bowl. Stir in spinach, ricotta cheese, feta cheese, milk and oregano. Sprinkle Parmesan cheese over tart pastry; fill with egg mixture. Bake 20 to 25 minutes, or until knife inserted near center comes out clean. Let stand 5 minutes before serving.

MAKE-AHEAD TART PASTRY

1 ¼	cups all-purpose flour	¼	cup cold water
¼	teaspoon salt	1	(10-inch) tart pan with removable bottom
⅓	cup vegetable shortening		

Preheat oven to 450°F. In a mixing bowl, combine flour and salt. Cut in shortening until pieces are the size of small peas. Sprinkle 1 tablespoon of the cold water over one side of the mixture, and gently toss with fork to blend. Repeat with small amounts of cold water until the dough is moistened. Shape dough into a ball. Prepare work surface by lightly sprinkling with flour. Flatten dough with hands; roll from center to outer edge, making a 12-inch circle. Loosely wrap tart pastry around a rolling pin. Unroll dough onto a 10-inch tart pan with a removable bottom. Trim pastry even with top of pan rim. Do not prick the crust. Line pastry with a double layer of heavy-duty foil. Bake 8 minutes. Remove foil and continue baking another 5 to 7 minutes, or until golden. Remove from oven and reduce oven temperature to 325°F if you will be preparing filling at this point. If preparing the crust a day ahead, allow to come to room temperature after removing from oven and store in a cool, dry place.

ITALIAN SPINACH TORTA WITH PINE NUTS

The crunchy pine nuts and moist golden raisins
complement each other in this spinach tart.

Torta Pastry Dough

2	cups all-purpose flour (extra for kneading dough)	1	egg yolk
½	teaspoon salt	3	tablespoons milk
¼	pound unsalted butter (1 stick)		Butter for preparing tart pan

Filling

1 tablespoon butter, melted (for preparing pan)
Flour (for dusting pan)
1 package (10-ounce) frozen chopped spinach, thawed and squeezed dry
¼ cup golden raisins, soaked in water 30 minutes; thoroughly drained

3 eggs
¾ cup heavy cream
½ cup freshly grated Parmesan cheese
Salt and freshly ground pepper
3 tablespoons pine nuts

To make dough by hand, pour flour into a large mixing bowl. Add salt and butter. Use a pastry blender to work the butter, until a crumbly dough forms. Work in the egg yolk and milk; knead dough into a ball. Wrap in plastic wrap and refrigerate 1 hour. To prepare the filling, preheat oven to 350°F. Brush about 1 tablespoon melted butter in a tart pan with a removable bottom; dust with flour. Sprinkle flour on a work surface and roll out the dough into a round shape, 2 inches larger than the size of the pan. Line the pan with the pastry dough and trim along rim. In a mixing bowl, combine spinach, golden raisins, eggs, cream and Parmesan cheese. Mix well and season with salt and pepper. Pour mixture into pastry-lined pan and top with pine nuts. Bake 40 minutes, or until top is golden. Remove from oven and allow to stand 10 minutes before transferring torta to a serving dish.

"HERB FEST OF LOUISIANA" MORNING TART

When I created the "Herb Fest of Louisiana", it opened the door for many new friends to come into my life. With those precious friendships come tantalizing recipes using fresh herbs. Among the most commonly used herbs in Italian blends are basil, oregano, parsley, thyme and garlic. If you are lucky enough to have your own culinary herb garden, remember that the general rule of thumb is one part dried herbs to three parts fresh.

1   deep dish (9-inch) frozen pie
     shell, thawed
4   eggs
1½ cups low-fat milk
1   teaspoon dried Italian herb
     mixture, or 1 tablespoon
     fresh
     Dash of salt

     Freshly ground pepper
1   package (10-ounce) frozen
     chopped spinach, thawed
     and squeezed dry
8   ounces low-fat mozzarella
     cheese, shredded (2 cups)
2   small tomatoes, cored and
     thinly sliced

Preheat oven to 450°F. Prick pie shell with fork. Bake 8 to 10 minutes, or until golden color. Remove from oven to cool. Reduce oven to 350°F. In a mixing bowl, combine eggs, milk, Italian herb mixture, salt and pepper. Add spinach and half of the mozzarella cheese; blend well. Pour mixture into a cooled pie shell. Arrange tomato slices on top in a circle, overlapping as necessary. Sprinkle with remaining mozzarella cheese. Bake 45 to 55 minutes, or until a knife inserted near the center comes out clean. Let stand 10 minutes before serving.

ONION TART WITH SPINACH AND PINE NUTS

An old friend of mine claims he eats anything but onions.
He would probably change his mind after one bite of this luscious tart.

Pastry dough for 9-inch tart
  pan (frozen pie crust,
  thawed)
Dried beans (to serve as
  weight for pastry)
3   tablespoons unsalted butter
3   onions, thinly sliced
  (not chopped)
6   cups fresh spinach, stems
  removed and leaves coarsely
  chopped

4   eggs
12 ounces half-and-half
1   teaspoon salt
  Freshly ground pepper
¼   teaspoon freshly grated
  nutmeg
2   tablespoons toasted pine nuts
2   tablespoons freshly grated
  Parmesan cheese

Preheat oven to 400°F. Lightly grease and flour tart pan. Line tart pan with pastry dough. Prick pastry with fork and line with double thickness of heavy foil. Pour dried beans onto foil to weigh it down. Place tart pan on baking sheet and bake 10 minutes. Remove from oven, discard foil and beans, and return to oven. Bake shell another 5 to 10 minutes, or until golden color. Remove from oven and cool on rack. Reduce oven temperature to 350°F. Melt butter in a large skillet. Add onion slices and sauté until transparent and soft, about 15 minutes. Remove skillet from heat. Add spinach and stir until wilted. In a medium bowl, whisk eggs, half-and-half, salt, pepper and nutmeg. Pour onion mixture into pastry shell and level with back of spoon. Pour egg mixture over filling. Bake on a baking sheet 30 minutes. Sprinkle Parmesan cheese on top and bake another 10 to 15 minutes, or until knife inserted near center comes out clean. Let stand 10 minutes before serving.

CREAM-OF-CHICKEN-SOUP SPINACH SOUFFLÉ

Your family will be anxiously awaiting the sound of the
buzzer on the stove when this soufflé is in the oven.

1	can (10 ¾-ounce) condensed cream of chicken soup (full strength)
2	ounces Monterey Jack cheese, shredded (½ cup)
2	ounces cheddar cheese, shredded (½ cup)
1	teaspoon dry mustard
¼	teaspoon ground nutmeg

6	eggs, separated
1	package (10-ounce) frozen chopped spinach, thawed and squeezed dry
4	scallions, finely chopped (¼ cup)
2	teaspoons fresh lemon juice
	Butter for preparing soufflé dish

Preheat oven to 375°F. Combine soup, Monterey Jack cheese, cheddar cheese, dry mustard and nutmeg in a saucepan and cook over low heat, stirring until cheeses melt. Remove from heat and allow to cool about 10 minutes. Beat egg yolks 2 at a time into soup mixture. Add spinach, scallions and lemon juice to soup mixture; stir. In a large mixing bowl, beat egg whites until stiff, but not dry. Gently fold ¼ of the beaten whites into the soup mixture; then pour the soup-spinach mixture over the remaining beaten egg whites and carefully fold together. Pour into a well-buttered 2-quart soufflé dish. Bake 30 to 35 minutes, or until center jiggles only slightly when shaken gently. Serve immediately.

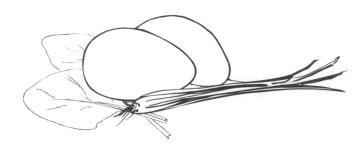

HAM AND SPINACH SOUFFLÉ

Soufflés are simple to prepare, as well as elegant in appearance. Top with a rich Hollandaise Sauce and you will undoubtedly get rave reviews from your dining guests. This combination makes an impressive luncheon dish.

½ cup dry bread crumbs Milk (enough to just cover the crumbs) 3 tablespoons butter 1 cup chopped cooked spinach 1 tablespoon minced onion 1 scallion, finely chopped 4 fresh button mushrooms, chopped	4 ounces cooked ham, diced (1 cup) Freshly ground pepper Salt 3 eggs, separated Hollandaise Sauce (recipe follows)

Preheat oven to 350°F. Soak bread crumbs in milk until soft. Drain off milk. In a saucepan, mix crumbs and butter, stirring until smooth. Add spinach, onion, scallion, mushrooms, ham, pepper, and salt. Beat egg yolks until thick and add to saucepan. Whip egg whites until stiff but not dry and gently fold into spinach mixture. Spoon mixture into unbuttered soufflé dish. Place soufflé dish in baking pan and fill baking pan with water 1-inch deep. Bake 40 to 45 minutes, or until firm. Serve with Hollandaise Sauce.

HOLLANDAISE SAUCE

4 egg yolks 2 tablespoons fresh lemon juice ½ pound unsalted butter, melted (2 sticks)	¼ teaspoon salt Dash of cayenne

In top of double boiler, beat egg yolks and stir in lemon juice. Stir slowly using a wooden spoon over low heat, not allowing water in bottom pan to come to a boil. Add butter to yolk mixture a little at a time. Stir constantly. Season with salt and cayenne. Continue cooking slowly until thickened. Remove from heat and serve immediately.

SUNDAY BRUNCH SOUFFLÉ WITH HAM, SPINACH AND GRITS

When asked what I like best about being raised in the South,
I just smile and answer, "Grits!"

	Vegetable cooking spray	4	ounces reduced-fat sharp
¼	pound lean country ham, diced		cheddar cheese, shredded
1 ½	cups milk		(1 cup)
1	can (10 ½-ounce) low-sodium		Dash of granulated garlic
	chicken broth		Freshly ground pepper
¾	cup quick-cooking grits,	1	can (14-ounce) chopped
	uncooked (do not use		spinach, drained and
	instant)		squeezed dry
		4	egg whites, room temperature

Preheat oven to 375°F. Spray bottom of large saucepan with cooking spray. Sauté ham over medium-high heat until lightly browned. Remove ham from pan and set aside. Pour milk and broth into same saucepan and bring to a boil, stirring constantly. Add grits; reduce heat and simmer until thick, stirring frequently. Combine the ham, cheddar cheese, garlic, pepper and spinach in a large bowl and set aside. Beat egg whites at high speed of mixer until stiff but not dry. Fold small amount of egg whites into the grits mixture. Add remaining egg whites and continue to fold gently until blended. Coat inside of soufflé dish with cooking spray and spoon in soufflé mixture. Bake 40 minutes, or until set and lightly browned.

COTTAGE CHEESE AND SPINACH SOUFFLÉ

If you don't tell your dining guests that there's cottage cheese in this dish, they certainly won't be able to tell by the taste. I've watched people that claim they "never" eat cottage cheese, gobble up this soufflé.

2	(10-ounce) packages frozen chopped spinach	¼	pound butter, softened (1 stick)
1	medium onion, minced (¾ cup)	4	egg yolks
1	tablespoon Worcestershire sauce	1	can (2-ounce) chopped mushrooms, well-drained and patted dry
16	ounces cottage cheese		
6	ounces cheddar cheese, shredded (1 ½ cups)	4	egg whites Dash of ground nutmeg Vegetable cooking spray

Preheat oven to 350°F. Cook spinach according to package instructions and squeeze out excess moisture. Combine spinach, onion, Worcestershire sauce, cottage cheese, cheddar cheese, and softened butter in a large mixing bowl. In a separate bowl, beat egg yolks; add to spinach mixture along with mushrooms. Beat egg whites until stiff but not dry and gently fold them into spinach mixture. Sprinkle lightly with ground nutmeg. Pour contents into soufflé dish sprayed with vegetable cooking spray. Bake 50 to 60 minutes, or until center jiggles only slightly when gently shaken.

EASY SOUFFLÉ WITH CREAM OF MUSHROOM SOUP

Here's a surprisingly flavorful dish that belies the simplicity of its preparation.

2 (10-ounce) packages frozen chopped spinach, thawed and squeezed dry	¾ cup mayonnaise
	2 egg yolks, beaten
	2 egg whites, beaten stiff but not dry
1 can (10¾-ounce) cream of mushroom soup (full strength)	Salt and freshly ground pepper
	¼ cup freshly grated Parmesan cheese, more as needed
2 tablespoons dried onion soup mix	Bacon bits for topping

Preheat oven to 350°F. In a large mixing bowl, combine spinach, soup, onion soup mix, mayonnaise, egg yolks, beaten egg whites, salt, pepper and Parmesan cheese. Pour into prepared soufflé dish. Sprinkle bacon bits on top and more Parmesan cheese, if desired. Bake 30 to 40 minutes, or until knife inserted near center comes out clean.

EGGS SARDOU

Story has it that Antoine Alciatore, proprietor of the world famous Antoine's Restaurant in the New Orleans French Quarter, created this enchanting dish. In 1908, French playwright Victorien Sardou was a guest at a dinner hosted in his honor. This recipe has remained quite popular throughout the years. One taste and you will live the legend.

1 recipe Creamed Spinach (see recipe on page 223)	4 ounces baked ham, minced (½ cup)
4 tablespoons unsalted butter (½ stick)	4 poached eggs
4 large artichoke bottoms	2 cups Hollandaise Sauce (see recipe on page 218)
8 anchovy fillets	Orange slices

In a large skillet, melt butter over medium heat. Add artichoke bottoms; sauté until heated through. Remove from skillet and set aside. Add anchovy fillets to skillet and cook 3 minutes. Remove from skillet and set aside. Add ham to skillet and heat through. To assemble, place a mound of creamed spinach in the center of four serving plates. Place 1 artichoke bottom on each mound. Crisscross 2 anchovies on top of each artichoke bottom. Top with a poached egg. Top each egg with Hollandaise Sauce. Sprinkle with ham and garnish plates with orange slices. Serve immediately.

CREAMED SPINACH FOR EGGS SARDOU

1	package (10-ounce) frozen chopped spinach	2	teaspoons Herbsaint liqueur
3	tablespoons unsalted butter	½	teaspoon granulated sugar
4	scallions, finely chopped (¼ cup)	½	teaspoon salt
2	tablespoons all-purpose flour		Freshly ground pepper
⅔	cup whipping cream	¼	teaspoon freshly grated nutmeg

Prepare spinach according to package instructions; drain and squeeze out excess moisture. Set aside. Melt butter in a large skillet over medium heat. Add scallions and sauté 4 minutes. Add flour all at one time and continue stirring to blend, about 3 minutes. Add whipping cream, cooking and stirring until thickened. Stir in Herbsaint, sugar, salt, pepper and nutmeg. Add cooked spinach, stirring until well blended. Remove from heat.

EGGS AND SPINACH FOR BREAKFAST

Eggs and spinach harmonize with each other to produce a most palatable meal.

1	package (10-ounce) frozen chopped spinach		Salt
3	tablespoons extra virgin olive oil	3	tablespoons freshly grated Parmesan cheese
1	small garlic clove, minced	4	eggs, beaten
	Freshly ground pepper	2	slices lean bacon, cooked crisp and crumbled

Cook spinach according to package instructions. Drain well, squeezing out as much liquid as possible. Heat olive oil in a heavy skillet over low heat. Add garlic and sauté gently to prevent scorched taste. Mix in spinach, pepper, and salt; turn up heat under skillet. Spread spinach mixture over bottom of skillet and sprinkle with 1 tablespoon of the Parmesan cheese. Cook, turning spinach over, until very hot. Add eggs and continue turning mixture until eggs cook through. Add bacon to mixture. Drain any excess oil from skillet. Turn spinach mixture onto warmed serving plate and sprinkle with remaining Parmesan cheese. Serve immediately.

EGG CUPS WITH SPINACH AND CHIVE SAUCE

Snip chives fresh from your herb garden in order to achieve the maximum flavor from this enticing recipe.

Eggs

1	pound fresh spinach leaves, thoroughly washed	1	ounce cheddar cheese, shredded
¼	cup whole wheat bread crumbs	4	eggs
3	scallions, finely chopped		Butter for preparing custard cups or ramekins
1	tablespoon butter		

Sauce

2	teaspoons herb vinegar, or white wine vinegar	¼	cup snipped chives
1	tablespoon lemon juice	4	halves whole wheat English muffins, toasted
4	tablespoons cold butter (½ stick)		

Preheat oven to 350°F. Cook spinach in a large saucepan with only the water that clings to the leaves. Once spinach is wilted, remove the pan from the heat and pour spinach in a sieve to drain and cool. When the spinach is cool enough to handle, squeeze out as much liquid as possible; chop fine. Add bread crumbs to the spinach. Cook the scallions in a small pan with 1 tablespoon butter until tender. Add the spinach. Heavily butter 4 (½-cup each) custard cups. Using the back of a spoon, pack one-fourth of the spinach mixture into each cup, making an even layer on the sides and bottom. Sprinkle 1 tablespoon of cheddar cheese into each cup, then break an egg over the cheese. Using a rubber spatula, push the spinach down below the surface of the egg to prevent burning during baking. Transfer the cups to a baking sheet and bake 20 minutes, or until the whites of the eggs are set and the yolks are just slightly runny, as in poached eggs. Make the sauce in a small pan by combining the vinegar and lemon juice and cooking over medium heat until they have reduced in volume to about 1 teaspoon. Remove the pan from the heat and whisk in the cold butter, about 1 teaspoon at a time. Stir constantly. The butter must form a creamy emulsion rather than melt and become liquid. If the pan cools too quickly, return it to the heat for a few seconds. When all the butter is incorporated, stir in the chives. Loosen each egg and spinach cup from its container using a rubber spatula. Turn each one out onto an English muffin half and spoon a tablespoon of butter sauce over each. Serve immediately.

EGGS FLORENTINE WITH CREAMY SAUCE

After an evening in a romantic Bed and Breakfast, my husband and I awakened to a hot breakfast befitting royalty. Our hostess truly outdid herself. I can still close my eyes and picture the stunning antiques, the century-old china, and her great-grandmother's crystal that lent so much character and charm to the home. One can only dream as to what tales could be told..."if only the walls could talk."

Florentine
1	package (10-ounce) frozen chopped spinach	2	tablespoons freshly grated Parmesan cheese
		1	tablespoon dry bread crumbs

Poached Eggs
	Water	4	eggs

Creamy Sauce
2	teaspoons butter		Dash of ground nutmeg
2	teaspoons all-purpose flour		Dash of cayenne
½	teaspoon instant chicken bouillon	¾	cup half-and-half
		1	ounce Swiss cheese, shredded

Cook spinach according to package instructions; drain and squeeze out excess moisture. Place spinach in ungreased shallow 1-quart baking dish; keep warm. Prepare Creamy Sauce and Poached Eggs. Place eggs on spinach. Cover with Creamy Sauce; sprinkle with Parmesan cheese and bread crumbs. Set oven to broil and place pan about 5 inches from heat. Heat until lightly brown, about 1 minute. To prepare sauce, heat butter in small saucepan; blend in flour, bouillon, nutmeg and cayenne. Cook over low heat until mixture is smooth and bubbly, stirring constantly. Add half-and-half. Heat to boiling, stirring constantly. Boil and stir another minute. Add Swiss cheese; stir until cheese melts. To poach eggs, heat about 2 inches water in a deep skillet or saucepan; bring to a boil then reduce to a simmer. Break eggs, one at a time, into a saucer. Hold saucer close to water's surface and gently slip the egg into the water. Cook until desired doneness, 3 to 5 minutes. Remove eggs from water with slotted spoon.

TIMBALES WITH BUTTER SAUCE

The crowning touch to this recipe is the rich wine and butter sauce.

3	large bunches fresh spinach, thoroughly washed	2	egg yolks
4	tablespoons butter (½ stick)		Pinch of ground nutmeg
1	cup heavy cream		Pinch of cayenne
4	eggs		Salt and freshly ground pepper

Butter Sauce

3	tablespoons white wine vinegar	2	scallions, finely chopped
3	tablespoons dry white wine	½	pound butter, cubed (2 sticks)

Preheat oven to 375°F. Blanch 30 spinach leaves for 30 seconds, then quickly dip them in ice water. Drain well and use them to line ten ½-cup molds. Do this by placing one end of the spinach leaf across the bottom of the greased mold, and draping the other end over the top of the rim, gently pressing leaf against inside of mold. Repeat with other two leaves, overlapping as necessary. Cook remaining spinach in a saucepan using only the water that clings to the leaves, about 2 minutes; drain and chop. Melt the 4 tablespoons of butter in a pan. Add spinach and cook 3 minutes. Stir in cream and let cool. Add eggs, yolks and seasoning; stir to blend. Spoon mixture into molds and cover with buttered foil. Place in a deep pan half-filled with boiling water. Bake 12 to 15 minutes. To prepare the Butter Sauce, boil the vinegar, wine and scallions. Whisk in butter gradually; bring to a boil, still whisking, then strain. Serve timbales unmolded onto a warm plate or platter, and serve with Butter Sauce.

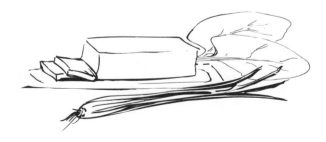

THE STORY OF THE GIANT OMELETTE

Delicious food, lively music, street dancing and a vast assortment of vendors are all things you would expect to see at a festival. Yet in order to keep the crowds returning year after year, each festival must develop a theme that's both appealing and unique. Of all the festivals I've had the pleasure of attending, the "Giant Omelette Celebration" was the most delightful...hands down. First, let's start with the history:

"According to legend, Napoleon and his army were traveling through the south of France when they decided to rest for the night near the town of Bessieres. The next morning, Napoleon feasted on an omelette prepared by a local innkeeper. It was such a culinary delight that Napoleon ordered the townspeople to gather all the eggs in the village. The following day, a huge omelette was prepared for his army.

"From this beginning, the omelette became a tradition of feeding the poor in the village at Easter time. The omelette has also become the symbol of a world-wide fraternity rich in friendship, tradition and cultural exchange, known as the Confrerie."

Because of this long-standing tradition, Abbeville, Louisiana now celebrates its French heritage by hosting this international festival each year on the first Sunday in November. Following a weekend of food and fun, the "Knighted Chef's" begin the parade. Baskets filled with eggs, along with maidens carrying bundles of baguettes, are marched around the town square. The parade ends when they reach the twelve-foot wide skillet positioned over a huge fire in the middle of the street. Yes, a twelve-foot wide black skillet!

The chefs stand on small ladders in order to reach the skillet while using wooden boat oars as cooking utensils. The omelette ingredients are dumped in the skillet and the cooking begins. When finished, the omelette is served up to all in attendance, along with sliced baguettes, free of charge. This is truly the "Omelette of Friendship."

5,000-Egg Giant Omelette

5,000 eggs
50 pounds onions
75 bell peppers
4 gallons scallions
2 gallons parsley
1 ½ gallons vegetable oil
6 ½ gallons milk
52 pounds butter
3 boxes salt
2 boxes black pepper
Crawfish tails
Tabasco Pepper Sauce

Now if I could just convince them to add 25 or 30 pounds of spinach to their recipe, the "Confrerie d'Abbeville" would have the perfect omelette!

GRUYERE AND SPINACH OMELET

Gruyere cheese and Dijon mustard enhance the spinach flavor in this omelet.

1 tablespoon butter
½ small onion, chopped (¼ cup)
1 package (10-ounce) frozen
    chopped spinach, thawed
    and squeezed dry
2 tablespoons Dijon mustard

Salt and freshly ground pepper
4 eggs
¼ teaspoon ground nutmeg
4 ounces Gruyere cheese,
    shredded (1 cup)

Heat ovenproof skillet over medium heat and melt 2 teaspoons of the butter. Add onion and sauté until tender, 10 to 12 minutes. Stir in spinach and mustard; season with salt and pepper. Preheat broiler. Beat eggs in a medium bowl; add nutmeg. Fold in half the Gruyere cheese. Melt the remaining 1 teaspoon butter in nonstick skillet; add egg mixture. Cook until center is almost set, about 5 minutes, using spatula to lift edges, allowing uncooked egg to roll over to skillet bottom. Spoon spinach filling onto one half of omelet. Using spatula, fold other half of eggs onto spinach filling; sprinkle with remaining cheese. Place skillet under broiler 1 minute to melt cheese. Serve immediately.

MUSHROOM-SPINACH OMELET

In a hurry? Whip up this easy omelet in almost no time at all.

1	tablespoon butter	1	cup fresh spinach leaves, thoroughly washed and chopped
1	small garlic clove, minced		Salt and freshly ground pepper
1	can (4-ounce) mushroom stems and pieces, drained	3	eggs, well beaten
		1	teaspoon dried basil

Melt butter in skillet and gently sauté garlic 5 to 8 minutes; add mushrooms and cook another 3 minutes. Stir in spinach, salt and pepper; cook until spinach wilts. Stir in eggs and basil. Using spatula, move egg mixture around, allowing uncooked egg to reach skillet bottom. Flip omelet to finish cooking. Serve hot.

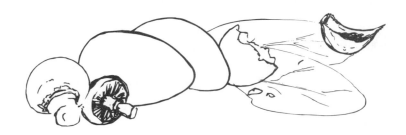

GREEK OMELET WITH SPINACH, FETA AND DILL

My husband and I really enjoy "armchair traveling." We visit our local library and select videos, books, maps and music, all pertaining to a country we want to "visit." I research the foods and customs and plan our meals accordingly. Of all the countries we've visited from our favorite chairs, Greece is by far my favorite. After an evening of learning about Greece, it's a real treat to wake up and prepare this omelet, using many of that country's favorite ingredients.

Sauce

1	large tomato, seeded and chopped (1 cup)	1	teaspoon minced fresh chives
1	teaspoon chopped fresh dill	¼	teaspoon salt

Omelet

	Vegetable nonstick spray	2	teaspoons minced fresh chives
½	small red onion, chopped (¼ cup)	3	egg yolks
2	cups chopped fresh spinach leaves, thoroughly washed	1	tablespoon milk
		3	egg whites (at room temperature)
¾	cup hot cooked rice, unsalted		Dash of salt
1	ounce feta cheese, crumbled	1	tablespoon all-purpose flour
2	teaspoons chopped fresh dill		Freshly ground pepper

To prepare sauce, combine tomato, dill, chives and salt; set aside. Spray a nonstick skillet and place over medium-high heat. Sauté onion until tender; add spinach and continue to cook until spinach wilts. Stir in rice, feta cheese, 1 teaspoon of the dill and 1 teaspoon of the chives; set aside. Beat egg yolks until thick and pale; add milk and beat to blend; set aside. In a separate bowl, beat egg whites and salt until soft peaks form. Add remaining dill and chives, along with flour and pepper. Gently fold egg white mixture into egg yolk mixture. Coat a medium-size nonstick skillet with cooking spray and place over medium heat until hot. Using spatula, spread egg mixture evenly in skillet; top with spinach mixture. Cover and reduce heat to medium-low; cook 6 to 8 minutes or until center is nearly set. Carefully loosen omelet on one side and flip in half. Slide omelet onto warmed serving plate and spoon sauce over top. Serve immediately.

FRITTATA WITH CREOLE SAUCE

Whether you're using egg-substitute or fresh eggs, this frittata comes out a winner.

Creole Sauce (recipe follows)
½ small onion, chopped (¼ cup)
2 teaspoons butter
3 cups coarsely chopped fresh spinach leaves, thoroughly washed
12 ounces cholesterol-free frozen egg product, thawed, or 6 fresh eggs
½ teaspoon fresh thyme or ¼ teaspoon dried
Salt
Freshly ground pepper
2 tablespoons shredded mozzarella cheese

Prepare Creole Sauce; keep warm. Cook onion in butter in large nonstick skillet over medium heat until transparent. Add spinach leaves and stir until spinach wilts. Beat in egg substitute, thyme, salt and pepper; pour over spinach in skillet. Lower heat, cover and cook 5 minutes or until eggs are set and light brown on bottom. Sprinkle with mozzarella cheese before cutting into wedges. Serve with Creole Sauce.

CREOLE SAUCE

1 large tomato, coarsely chopped (1 cup)
½ small onion, chopped (¼ cup)
2 tablespoons minced celery
¼ teaspoon Hungarian paprika
Freshly ground pepper
4 drops Tabasco

Heat tomato, onion, and celery in a small saucepan; bring to a boil stirring occasionally; reduce heat. Season with paprika, pepper and Tabasco. Simmer, uncovered, 10 minutes, stirring until thickened.

BAKED HAM AND SPINACH FRITTATA

Here's a hearty frittata plentiful enough to feed a family of four!

8	eggs	1	package (10-ounce) frozen chopped spinach, thawed and squeezed dry
¼	teaspoon dried basil		
	Freshly ground pepper		
½	small onion, chopped (¼ cup)	4	ounces cooked ham, minced (½ cup)
1	tablespoon butter	1	tablespoon freshly grated Parmesan cheese

Preheat oven to 350°F. Beat eggs, basil and pepper in a mixing bowl; set aside. In a large ovenproof skillet, sauté onion in butter until tender but not browned. Remove from heat. Stir in spinach, ham and egg mixture. Bake, in uncovered skillet, 12 to 15 minutes or until knife inserted near center comes out clean. Sprinkle with Parmesan cheese. Put cover on skillet and allow to stand 5 minutes before cutting into wedges.

MUSHROOM-SPINACH FRITTATA

Lots of fresh mushrooms, tender spinach leaves and creamy butter makes this dish irresistible.

3	tablespoons butter	8	eggs, well beaten
½	small onion, minced (¼ cup)		Salt
8	ounces fresh mushrooms, sliced		Freshly ground pepper
1 ½	cups fresh spinach leaves, thoroughly washed and chopped	¼	cup freshly grated Parmesan cheese

Melt butter in a large cast iron or ovenproof skillet over medium-low heat. Add onions and cook 3 minutes. Stir in mushrooms and cook until limp. Add spinach and cook another 2 minutes. Pour eggs on top of spinach in skillet; cook over low heat until eggs are set, 6 to 8 minutes. Sprinkle with salt and pepper. Place skillet under broiler about 6 inches from heat source for 2 to 3 minutes. Remove from oven. Sprinkle top with Parmesan cheese; cover and allow to stand 2 minutes before serving.

Pies,
Pizzas,
Pastries
and
Breads

i love spinach

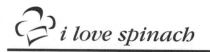

PIES, PIZZAS, PASTRIES & BREADS

SPANIKOPITA

One of the most widely recognized Greek dishes, spanikopita is a legend that lives on generation after generation. Layered between crispy layers of phyllo are spinach, cheeses and eggs. To sum it all up, "It just doesn't get any better than this."

1	package (10-ounce) frozen chopped spinach, thawed	1	teaspoon dried dill
4	ounces feta cheese, crumbled	½	teaspoon dried oregano
1	cup cottage cheese	½	teaspoon salt
3	eggs, lightly beaten		Dash of ground nutmeg
1	medium onion, chopped (¾ cup)	¼	pound butter (1 stick)
2	tablespoons chopped fresh parsley	12	sheets frozen phyllo dough, thawed

Preheat oven to 350°F. Cook spinach according to package instructions; squeeze out moisture. In a large mixing bowl, combine spinach, feta cheese, cottage cheese, eggs, onion, parsley, dill, oregano, salt and nutmeg; set aside. Brush bottom of a shallow baking pan with butter; reserve remainder of melted butter for phyllo. Cut phyllo sheets in half crosswise. Gently separate a half sheet of phyllo and place it in the bottom of the baking pan, folding edges over to fit the bottom. Brush lightly with melted butter and repeat with 11 more half-sheets. Cover unused phyllo with a damp cloth or plastic wrap to keep it from drying. Spread spinach mixture over phyllo dough in the pan. Place remaining 12 half sheets of phyllo, buttering each; tuck in edges over filling. Cover with foil and bake 25 minutes. Uncover and continue to bake 5 to 10 minutes, or until golden brown. Let stand 10 minutes before cutting into squares for serving.

ONION AND SPINACH PIE

With or without the sour cream topping, this pie is excellent! This wonderful mix of herbs, spices and cheeses accent the onion and spinach flavors.

1	medium onion, chopped (¾ cup)
¼	cup chopped fresh parsley
½	teaspoon ground nutmeg
½	teaspoon freshly ground pepper
2	tablespoons extra virgin olive oil
1 ½	teaspoons dried dill
5	eggs
½	cup milk

2	(10-ounce) packages frozen chopped spinach, thawed and squeezed dry
1	pound feta cheese, crumbled
¼	pound unsalted butter, melted (1 stick)
12	sheets frozen phyllo dough, thawed
	Dairy sour cream (optional)
	Snipped fresh dill (optional)

Preheat oven to 375°F. In a large skillet or saucepan, cook onion, parsley, nutmeg and pepper in olive oil. Cover and continue cooking over low heat until onions are very tender, about 20 minutes, stirring occasionally. Stir in the dill; set mixture aside. In a medium mixing bowl, combine eggs and milk, beating well until smooth. Stir in onion mixture, spinach and feta cheese. Brush the bottom of a rectangular baking dish with some of the melted butter. Unfold phyllo sheets and cut in half crosswise, forming 24 half-sheets. To prevent the phyllo from drying out while you are working, cover the stack of sheets with plastic wrap or a damp cloth. Place one half-sheet of phyllo in the bottom of the baking pan and brush it with melted butter. Repeat this process with additional 11 half-sheets. Evenly spread the spinach filling over the 12th layer of buttered phyllo. Layer the remaining half-sheets, alternating with brushed-on melted butter between each sheet. Use a sharp knife to score the phyllo into serving sizes. Bake, uncovered, 30 to 35 minutes, or until golden brown. Let stand 10 minutes before cutting along scored lines. If desired, top each serving with a dollop of sour cream and fresh dill.

GREEK CROUSTADE

Fashioned in a "spoke pattern" and baked until crispy, this croustade will fill the room with an enticing aroma. I can still remember seeing people in the Athens, Greece airport restaurant biting into phyllo pastries. The crusts were so flaky and the fillings were moist and succulent. You'll enjoy this recipe.

1	package (10-ounce) frozen chopped spinach	1	cup milk
½	small onion, chopped (¼ cup)	2	eggs, beaten
¼	pound plus 4 tablespoons butter, melted (1 ½ sticks)	1	cup cream-style cottage cheese
¼	cup all-purpose flour	2	ounces feta cheese, crumbled
¼	teaspoon dried tarragon Freshly ground pepper	12	sheets frozen phyllo dough, thawed

Preheat oven to 375°F. To prepare filling, cook spinach according to package directions; squeeze dry. In a medium saucepan, cook onion in 4 tablespoons of the butter until tender. Stir in flour, tarragon, and pepper. Add milk and cook until mixture starts to bubble and thicken. Combine eggs and half the milk mixture in a mixing bowl. Pour contents of mixing bowl into remaining milk mixture in saucepan. Stir in spinach, cottage cheese and feta cheese. Remove from heat and set aside. Unfold phyllo dough and carefully remove 1 sheet. Cover remaining phyllo with plastic wrap or a damp cloth while working. Lightly brush the phyllo sheet with melted butter, using a soft pastry brush. Fold in thirds lengthwise, brushing top with melted butter. Place one end of folded phyllo sheet in the center of a 12-inch pizza pan, extending the other end over the side of the pan. Repeat this procedure, overlapping sheets at the center of the pizza pan, until all the phyllo sheets have been used, with the end result arranged in an equally-spaced spoke fashion. Spoon the spinach filling in the center of the pizza pan, spreading it out to form an 8-inch circle. Beginning with the last phyllo sheet placed on the pan, lift the end of the strip that is extended over the pan, and twist it several times to form a crinkled look. Fold the crinkled strip in half toward the center, coiling and tucking the end. Lightly press the coiled end into the spinach filling, leaving the center of the filling exposed to allow to vent. Repeat with the remaining phyllo strips in the reverse order in which they were placed on the pan. Drizzle any remaining butter on top. Bake 35 to 45 minutes, or until light golden in color. Use a pizza cutter or sharp knife to cut into wedges for serving.

GOAT CHEESE AND SPINACH TURNOVERS

An old friend of mine who taught me so much about cooking, often said, "Quality in equals quality out." These turnovers are filled with fresh, quality ingredients, making the end result magnificent.

1 tablespoon extra virgin olive oil
1 small red onion, minced (½ cup)
2 garlic cloves, minced
2 bunches fresh spinach, thoroughly washed, stemmed and chopped
2 ounces mild goat cheese (such as Montrachet)
½ cup pine nuts, toasted
3 tablespoons freshly grated Parmesan cheese
½ teaspoon minced fresh rosemary
½ teaspoon fresh lemon zest
   Salt and freshly ground pepper
4 sheets frozen phyllo dough, thawed
¼ pound butter, melted (1 stick)

Preheat oven to 375°F. In a heavy skillet, heat olive oil; add onion and garlic and sauté until onions are tender, but now brown. Add spinach and sauté until wilted, about 5 minutes. Pour contents of skillet in a colander and press out moisture, using the back of a large spoon. Transfer drained spinach mixture to a bowl and allow to cool. Add goat cheese, pine nuts, Parmesan cheese, rosemary and lemon zest. Season with salt and pepper. Place 1 phyllo sheet on work surface. Cut lengthwise into 3 equal strips. Using a soft pastry brush, lightly coat with melted butter. Place 1 heaping tablespoon of spinach filling at 1 end of phyllo strip. Starting at 1 corner, fold phyllo over filling, forming a triangle. Repeat folding up entire length of phyllo, forming a triangle with each fold. Brush with butter. Continue procedure with remaining phyllo sheets. Transfer turnovers to baking sheet. Bake 11 to 13 minutes. Cool slightly before serving.

GREEK STRUDEL

Ricotta and Jarlsberg cheeses create a great-tasting strudel,
especially when paired with spinach.

	Butter-flavored vegetable cooking spray	½	teaspoon dried oregano
			Freshly ground pepper
1	medium onion, chopped (¾ cup)	¼	teaspoon salt
		¼	teaspoon dried basil
2	garlic cloves, minced	15	ounces nonfat ricotta cheese
1	package (10-ounce) frozen chopped spinach, thawed and squeezed dry	3	egg whites
		8	sheets frozen phyllo dough, thawed
8	ounces Jarlsberg cheese, shredded (2 cups)	¼	cup dry bread crumbs

Preheat oven to 375°F. Spray a small non-stick skillet with cooking spray. Cook onion and garlic until tender, about 5 minutes. In a large mixing bowl, combine skillet contents, spinach, Jarlsberg cheese, oregano, pepper, salt, basil, ricotta cheese and egg whites; stir to blend. Place 1 sheet of phyllo onto a slightly damp towel and spray with cooking spray. Sprinkle 2 teaspoons breadcrumbs evenly on top. Place another sheet of phyllo on top of the first and continue layering with cooking spray and breadcrumbs, until all phyllo has been used. Spoon spinach mixture along longer edge of top sheet of phyllo, staying 3 inches from the edges. Fold the longer border over the spinach. Fold the short edges of the phyllo stack inward 1 inch. Starting with the long folded edge of the phyllo, roll into a jelly-roll shaped log. Remember to keep folding in the shorter sides of the strudel as you roll, to prevent filling from falling out. Spray a large baking sheet with cooking spray. Place the strudel seam side down in the center. Use a sharp knife to score along the top of the strudel; lightly spray it with cooking spray. Bake 30 minutes, or until golden brown. Allow to stand 10 minutes before slicing.

CHEESE-STUFFED CHICKEN IN PHYLLO

*Truly a cheese-lover's "dream come true", these chicken,
spinach and cheese-filled bundles will melt in your mouth.*

8 skinless and boneless chicken breast halves	2 ounces feta cheese, crumbled
Salt and freshly ground pepper	2 ounces cheddar cheese, shredded (½ cup)
3 tablespoons extra virgin olive oil	1 egg yolk, beaten
1 medium onion, chopped (¾ cup)	1 tablespoon all-purpose flour
	½ teaspoon ground nutmeg
4 cups fresh spinach, thoroughly washed and chopped	½ teaspoon ground cumin
	16 sheets frozen phyllo dough, thawed
4 ounces cream cheese, cubed and softened	¼ pound butter, melted (1 stick)
4 ounces mozzarella cheese, shredded (1 cup)	

Preheat oven to 350°F. Place each chicken breast half between a double thickness of plastic wrap and pound with the flat side of a meat mallet, until very thin (¼-inch). Season with salt and pepper; set aside. Using a large skillet, heat olive oil; cook onion until tender; add spinach and sauté 3 minutes. Remove from heat. Add cream cheese and stir until blended. Stir in mozzarella cheese, feta cheese and cheddar cheese. Add egg yolk, flour, nutmeg and cumin. Spoon ¼ cup of the spinach filling on each chicken breast half. Roll each jelly-roll style. Place 1 sheet of phyllo dough onto work surface, keeping remaining sheets covered with plastic wrap or a damp cloth. Brush phyllo lightly with melted butter. Place a second sheet of phyllo on top of the first sheet and brush it with butter. Place one chicken roll near a short side of the chicken roll together once. Fold the long the rolled chicken. Continue rolling from have a phyllo package with the chicken insi chicken and phyllo. Place each bundle i butter. Bake, uncovered, 35 to 40 minutes

For

CHICKEN AND SPINACH BUNDLES IN PHYLLO

The herbs in this recipe enhance the spinach and chicken flavors to create a savory meal. For variety, refer to the Herb Guide in the back of this cookbook for ideas on trying different herbs in this recipe.

¼ pound fresh mushrooms, sliced (¾ cup)	¼ teaspoon dried mint
1 garlic clove, minced	¼ teaspoon dried thyme
1 tablespoon extra virgin olive oil	¼ teaspoon dried sage
	8 sheets frozen phyllo dough, thawed
½ (10-ounce) package frozen chopped spinach, thawed and squeezed dry	4 tablespoons butter, melted (½ stick)
3 ounces feta cheese, crumbled	4 skinless and boneless chicken breast halves

Preheat oven to 375°F. Sauté mushrooms and garlic in olive oil until tender. Set aside. In a mixing bowl, combine mushroom mixture, spinach, feta cheese, mint, thyme and sage. Cut phyllo sheets in half crosswise, making 16 half-sheets. Keep phyllo covered with plastic wrap or a damp cloth while you work. Place one phyllo half-sheet on work surface and lightly brush with butter, using a soft pastry brush. Repeat until four half-sheets have been stacked, brushing butter on each layer. Place one chicken piece at one of the short ends of each stack. Divide filling into four equal amounts and spoon onto each piece of chicken. Roll phyllo and chicken over once, then fold long sides toward center, overlapping on the chicken. Continue rolling until phyllo is completely wrapped around chicken and spinach. Brush ends and sides of phyllo with melted butter. Place seam side down on a large baking sheet, making sure bundles do not touch one another. Bake 30 to 35 minutes, or until chicken is tender and phyllo is golden. Let stand 10 minutes before serving.

"OLD WORLD" SPANIKOPITA

One of my friends married a man from Greece who graciously shared his mother's favorite recipe with me. I prepared this recipe using the feta cheese I bought at a festival hosted by a Greek Orthodox Church in Biloxi, Mississippi. Whenever I see this recipe, I'm reminded of the young Greek women in authentic outfits, performing the traditional dances to the music that exemplifies their rich culture.

1 large onion, finely chopped (1 cup)	2 cups cottage cheese
¼ cup extra virgin olive oil	1 tablespoon chopped fresh parsley
2 garlic cloves, crushed	1 tablespoon chopped fresh dill
2 (10-ounce) packages frozen chopped spinach, thawed and squeezed dry	Salt and freshly ground pepper
	½ pound butter, melted (2 sticks)
2 eggs, beaten	1 package (1-pound) frozen phyllo dough, thawed
8 ounces feta cheese, crumbled	

Preheat oven to 350°F. In a medium skillet, sauté onion in olive oil until tender. Add garlic and sauté another 2 minutes. Stir spinach into onion mixture until heated through. Set aside. In a large mixing bowl, combine eggs, feta cheese, cottage cheese, parsley and dill. Season with salt and pepper. Add the spinach mixture and stir to blend thoroughly. Brush the bottom of a large baking pan with melted butter. Carefully unfold the phyllo sheets onto a work surface and keep covered with plastic wrap or a damp cloth while you work. Start layering phyllo, one sheet at a time, brushing each lightly with melted butter. Layer up to 12 sheets and then spread spinach filling evenly on top. Top with remaining phyllo sheets, one at a time, brushing each with butter. Use a sharp knife to score squares into the top layers of phyllo. Bake 45 to 50 minutes, or until golden brown. Let stand 10 minutes. Cut all the way through the scores before serving.

CRAWFISH SPINACH PIES

Southwest Louisiana is famous for its rich heritage filled with good-tasting food, toe-tapping music and lively festivals. Crawfish is almost always associated with Cajun cuisine and this recipe showcases both crawfish and spinach. Two of my favorites.

2 (16-ounce) packages fresh spinach, stems removed	1 pound crawfish tail meat
½ cup extra virgin olive oil	2 teaspoons salt
8 scallions, finely chopped (½ cup)	Tabasco sauce
	4 eggs
½ bell pepper, finely chopped (¼ cup)	1 pound feta cheese, crumbled
	½ pound butter, melted (2 sticks)
4 garlic cloves, minced	1 package (1-pound) frozen
¼ cup finely chopped parsley	phyllo dough, thawed

Preheat oven to 350°F. Thoroughly wash spinach and pat dry with paper towels. Tear spinach leaves into bite-size pieces. Set aside. Heat olive oil in a large pot; add scallions and bell pepper, cooking until tender. Add garlic and parsley and cook another 3 minutes over medium-low heat. Stir in crawfish tails, salt and Tabasco. Mix with spinach and set aside. In a mixing bowl, beat eggs; stir in feta cheese. Combine spinach mixture with egg mixture, stirring to blend. Grease a shallow baking dish with melted butter and line with half the phyllo sheets, brushing butter between each layer. Pour the filling on top and spread evenly. Continue layering phyllo leaves, brushing each with butter before adding the next. Brush the top layer with butter. Use a sharp knife to score squares through the top layers of phyllo. Bake 50 to 60 minutes. Let stand 10 minutes before cutting through the score lines.

IMPOSSIBLE GREEK SPINACH PIE

Even the most inexperienced cook will find this recipe easy to prepare, as well as flavorful. Packages of pre-washed spinach are readily available, making this recipe even easier.

1	tablespoon butter	1	cup milk
8	scallions, finely chopped (½ cup)	½	cup biscuit baking mix
		3	eggs
1	bag (10-ounce) fresh spinach leaves, thoroughly washed and patted dry	1	teaspoon fresh lemon juice
			Freshly ground pepper
1	teaspoon Greek seasoning	3	tablespoons freshly grated Parmesan cheese
1	cup cottage cheese	¼	teaspoon ground nutmeg

Preheat oven to 350°F. Melt butter in a skillet and add scallions. Add spinach and Greek seasoning. Cook over medium heat until spinach wilts, about 5 minutes. In a greased baking dish, layer spinach mixture and cottage cheese. In a blender, combine milk, baking mix, eggs, lemon juice, pepper, Parmesan cheese and nutmeg; mix well. Slowly pour contents of blender over cottage cheese layer. Bake 35 to 40 minutes. Cut into squares and serve.

HASH BROWN POTATOES SKILLET PIE

One of the most delicious recipes in this cookbook, this skillet pie is so easy that it almost prepares itself.

4	eggs, beaten	1	package (10-ounce) frozen chopped spinach, thawed and squeezed dry
1	tablespoon milk		
¼	teaspoon granulated garlic		
	Salt and white pepper	2	ounces Swiss cheese, shredded (½ cup)
1 ½	cups frozen hash brown potatoes with onions and peppers, thawed		

Mix eggs, milk, garlic, salt and pepper in a mixing bowl. Add hash brown potatoes, spinach and cheese. Stir to blend. Set aside. Heat a well-greased skillet and slowly add mixture. Cook, uncovered, over medium heat until soft-set, about 10 minutes. Remove from heat and allow to stand 5 minutes before cutting into wedges for serving.

244

NO-CRUST SPINACH PIE

Looking for a recipe that doesn't use flour? This is it!

1	cup cottage cheese	1	small bunch fresh spinach
¼	cup milk		leaves, thoroughly washed
3	eggs		and chopped
¼	teaspoon Dijon mustard	1 ½	teaspoons dried dill
1	teaspoon canola oil		Vegetable cooking spray
4	scallions, finely chopped	⅛	teaspoon ground nutmeg

Preheat oven to 350°F. In a blender, combine cottage cheese, milk, eggs and mustard. Process at medium-low speed until smooth. Set aside. Pour oil in a large skillet and cook scallions over low heat until tender. Add spinach, cooking until wilted. Stir in dill. Spray a pie plate with cooking spray. Spread spinach mixture in pie plate, patting down lightly with back of spoon. Slowly pour the contents of the blender over the spinach. Sprinkle with nutmeg and bake 40 to 45 minutes. Let stand 10 minutes before serving.

ORZO-CRUSTED SPINACH PIE

Orzo is a rice-shaped pasta, which makes a unique crust for this spinach pie. Purchased spaghetti sauce cuts down on the preparation time.

1 ½	cups uncooked orzo	1	package (10-ounce) frozen
2	eggs, beaten		chopped spinach
1	jar (15 ½-ounce) chunky	½	cup ricotta cheese
	spaghetti sauce	¼	teaspoon ground nutmeg
⅓	cup freshly grated Parmesan	2	ounces mozzarella cheese,
	cheese		shredded (½ cup)

Preheat oven to 350°F. Cook orzo according to package directions, yielding 3 cups cooked orzo. Combine cooked orzo, eggs, ½ cup of the spaghetti sauce and Parmesan cheese. Spread mixture in greased pie plate, pressing it up the sides to form a shell. Cook spinach according to package directions; squeeze out as much moisture as possible. In a large mixing bowl, combine spinach, ricotta cheese and nutmeg. Pour spinach mixture into pie plate, topping with remaining spaghetti sauce. Cover rim of pie with foil and bake for 30 minutes. Remove from oven and top with mozzarella cheese. Return pie to oven and continue baking for 5 minutes, or until cheese is melted. Remove from oven, discard foil collar, and transfer to a wire rack. Let stand 5 minutes before serving.

PEPPERONI PIZZA POCKETS

There's nothing like homemade pizza pockets to satisfy those after-school "hungries." Your kids will gobble up these treats as soon as they get home and throw their book sack on the floor. Serve with a big glass of ice-cold milk for a nutritious and satisfying snack.

Dough

2 cups all-purpose flour	¼ cup vegetable shortening
4 teaspoons baking powder	1 cup low-fat milk
½ teaspoon salt	

Filling

½ (10-ounce) package frozen chopped spinach	2 ounces mozzarella cheese, shredded (½ cup)
½ cup bottled pizza sauce	1 ounce cheddar cheese, shredded (¼ cup)
⅓ cup chopped pepperoni	½ teaspoon dried oregano
½ small onion, finely chopped (¼ cup)	½ teaspoon basil
1 can (4-ounce) chopped mushrooms, drained	Salt and freshly ground pepper

Preheat oven to 400°F. In a medium bowl, combine flour, baking powder and salt. Cut in vegetable shortening. Add milk and stir until soft dough forms. Knead gently on a floured work surface until dough is pliable. Roll out dough to ¼-inch thickness. Using a 4-inch biscuit cutter, cut into circles. Set aside. Cook spinach according to package instructions; squeeze dry. Mix spinach, pizza sauce, pepperoni, onion, mushrooms, mozzarella cheese, cheddar cheese, oregano, basil, salt and pepper in a large bowl. Place 1 ½ tablespoons of the filling in center of each circle. Fold dough over to form a semi-circle. Pinch edges to seal. Press edges with tines of fork. Bake 15 to 20 minutes, or until puffed and golden brown. Pizza pockets may also be deep-fat fried and drained on a wire rack or paper towels.

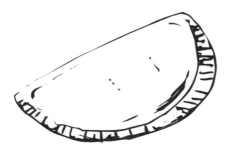

STUFFED PIZZA

Got a hungry crowd to feed? A pizza stuffed with pepperoni, spinach, mushrooms and lots of mozzarella cheese, piping hot from the oven, will definitely do the trick.

Flour (for dusting work surface)

2 (1-pound) loaves frozen bread dough, thawed

1 bottle (15-ounce) pizza sauce

1 package (3 ½-ounce) pepperoni, chopped

1 package (10-ounce) frozen chopped spinach, thawed and squeezed dry

4 ounces mozzarella cheese, shredded (1 cup)

1 cup ricotta cheese

1 cup plus 2 tablespoons freshly grated Parmesan cheese

1 can (4-ounce) mushroom stems and pieces, drained

1 can (3.8-ounce) sliced ripe olives, well drained

1 tablespoon extra virgin olive oil

Preheat oven to 350°F. Sprinkle flour on work surface. Roll each bread dough into a 12-inch circle. Place one circle on a greased baking sheet or large pizza pan. Spread ¼ cup of the pizza sauce on bread dough, leaving a 1-inch border around the edge. In a large bowl, combine pepperoni, spinach, mozzarella, ricotta, 1 cup Parmesan cheese, mushrooms and olives. Stir until thoroughly blended. Spread spinach mixture over pizza sauce. Spread ¼ cup of the pizza sauce evenly over spinach topping. Dampen outside edge of dough with fingertips dipped in water. Place remaining dough circle on top and pinch edge to seal tightly. Cut 8 slits in top dough to allow steam to vent. Bake on lowest rack of oven 20 minutes. Remove from oven and brush with olive oil; sprinkle with remaining 2 tablespoons of the Parmesan cheese. Return to oven and continue baking 15 to 20 minutes, or until deep golden brown. Allow to stand 10 to 15 minutes before cutting into wedges. Warm remaining pizza sauce, spoon into small bowls and serve with pizza wedges.

SAUSAGE AND SPINACH PIZZA PIE

For a touch of Italy at your own dinner table, try this winning pizza. One year I gave "dinner feasts" as holiday gifts. I filled canvas bags with things like a pizza pan, pizza cutter, jars of mushrooms, olives, Parmesan cheese and even included some recipes. After the food items were gone, they still had the "goodies" to use over and over again.

1 ½ cups all-purpose flour	1 package (10-ounce) frozen chopped spinach, thawed and squeezed dry
¼ teaspoon plus ½ teaspoon salt	
¼ pound firm butter (1 stick)	
1 egg, lightly beaten	1 teaspoon fresh lemon juice
1 pound mild Italian sausage, casings removed	⅛ teaspoon ground nutmeg
	8 ounces Monterey Jack cheese, shredded (2 cups)
1 medium onion, finely chopped (¾ cup)	2 fresh tomatoes, sliced ¼-inch thick
½ pound fresh mushrooms, thinly sliced	

Preheat oven to 450°F. Combine flour and ¼ teaspoon salt. Thoroughly cut in cold butter using a pastry blender or two knives. Stir egg into flour mixture. Shape dough into a compact ball, then place it on a lightly floured work surface. Roll dough into a circle to fit a large pizza pan or jelly-roll baking sheet. Press edges against pan sides or crimp to form shallow lip; set aside. Crumble sausage meat and cook, uncovered, in a large skillet until browned. Add onion and cook until tender. Add mushrooms and cook until all liquid evaporates. Remove skillet from heat and add spinach, lemon juice, the remaining ½ teaspoon salt, and nutmeg. Stir to blend. Spread sausage filling evenly over pastry. Sprinkle with 1 ½ cups of the Monterey Jack cheese. Bake 15 minutes. Remove pizza from oven and top with tomato slices and remaining cheese. Return to oven and continue baking 5 to 8 minutes, or until cheese is bubbly and crust is lightly browned. Let stand 5 minutes before cutting into wedges.

GREEK SPINACH PIZZA WITH FETA CHEESE AND ROSEMARY

All the flavors of Greece make this pizza a feast to remember. I get my Kalamata olives at a international food market and I simply make my own flavored oils so they are always fresh. By planting a few culinary herbs near your kitchen door, you can have easy access to the freshest herbs possible. Just step outside and snip what you need.

1	large pizza crust, purchased or homemade	1	teaspoon minced lemon zest
1	tablespoon extra virgin olive oil, (more for preparing pan)		Garlic-flavored olive oil (optional)
1	small red onion, thinly sliced	8	Kalamata olives, pitted and coarsely chopped
1	teaspoon salt	4	ounces feta cheese, crumbled
½	teaspoon freshly ground pepper	4	ounces mozzarella cheese, shredded (1 cup)
1	garlic clove, minced	3	tablespoons freshly grated Parmesan cheese
1	pound fresh spinach leaves, stems removed, thoroughly washed (8 to 10 cups)	1	teaspoon chopped fresh rosemary

Preheat oven to temperature indicated on purchased pizza crust package or homemade recipe. Heat 2 teaspoons of the olive oil in a skillet. Add the onion, ½ teaspoon of the salt and ¼ teaspoon of the pepper. Sauté until tender, about 5 minutes. Stir in half the garlic and sauté gently for another 2 minutes. Pour contents of skillet into a bowl; set aside. Heat the remaining olive oil in the same skillet, adding the fresh spinach, remainder of the salt, pepper and garlic. After 1 minute, remove spinach from the skillet and place it in a strainer. When cool to the touch, squeeze out the excess moisture using your hands. Chop spinach and add lemon zest. Place pizza dough on a large, lightly oiled pizza pan, and brush with garlic-flavored olive oil, if desired. Arrange the onion slices evenly on the dough, and spoon the spinach over that. Sprinkle the olives next, followed with the feta cheese and finally the mozzarella. Bake 10 to 15 minutes, or until the crust is lightly browned and crisp. Remove the pizza from the oven and sprinkle with the Parmesan cheese and fresh rosemary.

BREAKFAST PIZZAS

Overnight guests in your home will be delighted when you prepare these quick and easy breakfast pizzas. Organize the ingredients the night before for added ease the next morning. Serve them with hot coffee, fresh fruit and the morning newspaper!

Olive oil (for preparing baking pan)	6 fresh button mushrooms, coarsely chopped
2 cups all-purpose baking mix	½ cup prepared spaghetti sauce
⅔ cup milk	½ teaspoon dried oregano
¼ pound bulk breakfast sausage	½ teaspoon dried basil
1 cup fresh spinach leaves, stems removed, thoroughly washed	2 ounces mozzarella cheese, shredded (½ cup)
	4 eggs

Preheat oven to 425°F. Lightly oil baking sheet. In a mixing bowl, combine baking mix and milk, blending until soft dough forms. Lightly flour a work surface and gently knead dough a few times. Evenly divide dough into 4 pieces and place on prepared baking sheet. Press each piece into a circle, pinching the outer rim to form a lip. Brown the sausage in a skillet; drain well. Add spinach and mushrooms to sausage Stir in spaghetti sauce, oregano and basil. Pour ¼ of the sauce mixture onto each pizza circle, spreading it to the rim. Carefully place 2 tablespoons of mozzarella cheese around the rim, and crack an egg in the center of each pizza. Bake 10 to 15 minutes, or until crust is a golden brown and the egg white is cooked.

FRENCH BREAD PIZZAS

No time to prepare a traditional pizza crust? Use French bread instead for an unexpected treat. Just split the bread in two lengthwise, spread with spinach topping and pop in the oven.

2 cups chopped fresh spinach, thoroughly washed	⅛ teaspoon garlic powder
Salt and freshly ground pepper	French bread, cut into six ½-inch thick diagonal slices
¼ cup mayonnaise	6 slices (⅛-inch thick) Canadian bacon
½ teaspoon dried herb of choice, such as thyme, basil or oregano	2 small tomatoes, thinly sliced
	4 ounces Swiss or mozzarella cheese, shredded (1 cup)

Preheat oven broiler. Cook spinach in a saucepan with just the water clinging to the leaves, 5 minutes. Season lightly with salt and pepper. Allow to cool. Mix together mayonnaise, herbs of choice, and garlic powder. Toss with spinach. Spread spinach mixture on one side of each bread slice. Place bread slices, spinach side up, on the unheated rack of a broiler pan. Arrange Canadian bacon and tomato slices atop spinach mixture. Broil 4 inches from heat source until heated through, 3 to 5 minutes. Remove from oven, top with cheese and broil another minute, or until cheese melts and starts to bubble.

WORLD'S GREATEST SPINACH AND ARTICHOKE PIZZA

The name of this pizza says it all! You can use any combination of your favorite toppings to create your own signature pizza.

Pizza

3	tablespoons extra virgin olive oil
1	garlic clove, roasted and pressed
2	(16-ounce) bags fresh spinach leaves, chopped
½	teaspoon lemon-pepper seasoning
2	pizza crusts, pre-baked
1	can (14-ounce) artichoke hearts, coarsely chopped

2	teaspoons fresh Italian herbs (such as oregano, basil, thyme, and/or rosemary)
1	can (3.8-ounce) sliced black olives, well drained
12	sun-dried tomato halves (oil-packed), julienned
1	small red onion, thinly sliced
8	ounces feta cheese, crumbled
1	cup freshly grated Parmesan cheese

Garlic-Butter Dipping Sauce

¼	pound butter (1 stick)
2	garlic cloves, pressed or puréed

¼	cup chopped fresh Italian parsley (flat-leaf)
1	tablespoon fresh lemon juice

Preheat oven to 425°F. Heat olive oil in a large skillet. Add garlic and sauté gently. Add spinach, a handful at a time; cover and sauté until completely wilted. Season with lemon-pepper. Drain spinach and set aside; use the olive oil from the skillet to drizzle over the pizza crusts. Spread spinach evenly over pizza crusts, stopping just short of the outer edge. Arrange artichoke heart pieces over spinach; season with herbs. Top with olives, tomato strips, and onion rings. Sprinkle feta cheese over toppings and press down using the back of a large serving spoon. Sprinkle with Parmesan cheese and bake 10 to 12 minutes, or until heated through. Meanwhile, prepare sauce by mixing butter, garlic, parsley and lemon juice in a small saucepan. Simmer on low heat while pizza is baking. Serve in small bowls alongside serving plates so guests can dip their pizza slices, or simply drizzle sauce on top of pizza.

OYSTERS, HAM AND SPINACH IN PUFF PASTRY

A succulent medley of flavors makes this recipe a favorite. Served with white wine or champagne, these delicate little jewels make for an enticing and romantic midnight dinner.

2	tablespoons unsalted butter	1	package (17.3-ounce) frozen
4	scallions, finely chopped		puff pastry, thawed
1	garlic clove, minced		(2 sheets)
1	pound fresh spinach leaves,	3	ounces shaved ham slices
	thoroughly washed	8	shucked oysters, drained
	Salt and freshly ground pepper	1	egg, lightly beaten
1	cup whipping cream	1	tablespoon cold water
2	tablespoons Pernod (or other		
	licorice-flavored liqueur)		

Heat butter in a large skillet. Add scallions and sauté 3 minutes. Add garlic and cook gently another 2 minutes. Add spinach and season with salt and pepper. Cook until moisture evaporates, stirring occasionally, 5 to 6 minutes. Add whipping cream and liqueur; simmer 8 minutes, or until liquid is reduced by half. Remove from heat and allow to come to room temperature. Preheat oven to 425°F. Lightly flour work surface and roll 1 sheet of puff pastry to ⅛-inch thick. Cut into four 4-inch squares; trim. Repeat procedure with second puff pastry sheet. Divide ham equally among the eight pastry squares, trimming to fit shape of pastry. Place 1 oyster on top of each piece of ham; top with ⅛ of spinach mixture. Gather four corners of pastry and pinch together in the center above oyster. Continue pinching until packet is closed. Repeat procedure until all eight packets are pinched closed. Place pastries on a large baking sheet, spacing so they do not touch one another. Gently brush egg, beaten with water to make egg wash, on tops of pastries. Bake 15 to 20 minutes, or until golden brown.

TURKEY, SPINACH AND HAM IN PUFF PASTRY

For a filling yet light meal, serve this pastry along with a fresh fruit salad.

½ (17.3-ounce) package frozen
   puff pastry (1 sheet)
2 scallions, finely chopped
2 tablespoons chopped pimiento
½ teaspoon dried oregano
8 ounces cooked ham, sliced
8 ounces cooked turkey, sliced

1 cup fresh spinach leaves,
   thoroughly washed and
   chopped
4 ounces Swiss cheese, sliced
1 egg
1 tablespoon cold water

Thaw pastry sheet at room temperature 30 minutes. Preheat oven to 400°F. Mix scallions, pimiento and oregano in a bowl and set aside. Unfold pastry onto lightly floured surface. Roll into a 12 x 16-inch rectangle. Layer ham, turkey, spinach and cheese down center of pastry, stopping 1 inch from edges. Sprinkle with scallion mixture. Starting with short end, roll up like a jelly-roll. Place seam side down on baking sheet. Tuck ends under to seal. Mix egg and water to make egg wash; brush pastry with egg wash. Bake about 25 minutes, or until golden brown.

POACHED EGGS, SMOKED HAM AND SPINACH TURNOVERS

The hardest thing about this recipe is deciding whether to serve these turnovers for brunch time, lunch time or munch time!

½ (17.3-ounce) package frozen
   puff pastry (1 sheet)
1 package (10-ounce) frozen
   chopped spinach, thawed
   and squeezed dry

4 slices fully cooked smoked
   ham
4 teaspoons Dijon mustard
4 poached eggs, cooked only
   3 minutes and drained
4 slices Swiss cheese

Preheat oven to 425°F. Prepare work surface by lightly dusting with flour. Roll pastry into a rectangle, 18 x 10 inches. Cut into 4 rectangles, 10 x 4½ inches. Spoon spinach on one end of each rectangle. Top spinach with ham, mustard, poached egg and cheese. Fold each pastry over cheese. Fold pastry edges, pinching firmly to form seal. Bake on cooking sheet until pastry is puffed and deep golden, 20 to 25 minutes.

CLASSIC FRENCH CRÊPES

These crêpes may be prepared and used in any
crêpe recipe called for in this cookbook.

2 eggs	½ teaspoon salt
2 egg yolks	2 tablespoons unsalted butter,
1 ¼ cups milk	clarified (see note)
1 cup unbleached all-purpose	
flour	

Beat eggs and egg yolks in a mixing bowl. Whisk in milk. Add flour and salt, beating until smooth. Pour clarified butter into batter. Let stand 30 minutes to an hour. To prepare crêpes, preheat round flat griddle pan, which has been lightly greased. Batter should be thick as heavy cream, kept in a pitcher for easy pouring. If batter thickens upon standing, stir in a teaspoon of water or milk. Holding the handle of the pan in one hand, slowly pour 2 tablespoons batter into the center of the pan. Tilt the pan in a rotating motion to rapidly spread the batter evenly over the bottom. Place the pan directly over the heat source. Cook about 30 seconds, or until the top surface appears set and the bottom is just dry enough to come away from the pan with ease. Pick up the edge of the crêpe with your finger to loosen from the bottom. Avoid using a spatula, as this will tear the crêpe. While holding the handle in one hand, remove it from the heat and thrust it forward and upward with a short, quick motion. Quickly pull it back forward to catch the crêpe, bottom side up. Cook another 15 to 20 seconds. Slide the crêpe off the pan onto a flat plate. Wipe the pan with a fat-saturated paper towel before cooking each crêpe.

Note: Clarify butter by placing in a small, deep pan and bringing quickly to a boil. Let butter stand 1 minute for foam to settle. Use a spoon to skim foam from surface. Pour off clear, golden clarified butter, leaving the milk solids that settle on the bottom.

LAYERED SPINACH CRÊPES

Mornay Sauce is poured over these stacks of crêpes and spinach,
which are then crowned with Swiss cheese and baked in an oven.

12	Classic French Crêpes (see recipe on page 297)		Dash of ground nutmeg Pinch of salt
2	(10-ounce) packages frozen chopped spinach		Freshly ground pepper
1	tablespoon unsalted butter	1	cup Mornay Sauce (recipe follows)
1	tablespoon all-purpose flour	1	ounce Swiss cheese, finely
3	tablespoons half-and-half		grated (¼ cup)
1	teaspoon sugar		

Preheat oven to 400°F. Cook spinach as directed on package. Squeeze out excess moisture by hand and chop in food processor. Melt butter in a skillet; add flour and stir. Add spinach, half-and-half, sugar, nutmeg, salt and pepper. Stack the crêpes on a buttered baking dish, layering spinach filling between each. Cover with Mornay Sauce; top with Swiss cheese. Bake until cheese melts and spinach is heated through, 10 to 15 minutes.

MORNAY SAUCE

2	tablespoons unsalted butter	½	teaspoon salt
3	tablespoons unbleached all-purpose flour	⅛	teaspoon white pepper
1⅔	cups milk (not skim)	⅓	cup freshly grated Parmesan cheese

In a small saucepan, melt butter over low heat. Add flour. Gradually add milk and stir, cooking at medium temperature. Stir constantly until mixture boils and thickens. Add salt, pepper and Parmesan cheese. Continue to stir until cheese melts.

BAKED CRÊPES WITH SPINACH AND MARINARA SAUCE

The combination of ricotta cheese and spinach can't be beat in this rich and delicious filled-crêpe recipe. The marinara sauce adds a touch of excellence sure to bring rave reviews to the cook.

Filling

1   package (10-ounce) frozen chopped spinach, thawed and squeezed dry
 Salt and freshly ground pepper
2   cups ricotta cheese

½   cup freshly grated Parmesan cheese, more for serving suggestion
1   tablespoon chopped fresh parsley

Crêpes

3   egg whites
1   cup all-purpose flour
1 ⅓ cups water

Olive oil for preparing crêpe pan

Topping

2   cups marinara sauce (recipe follows), or use purchased spaghetti sauce

Preheat oven to 325°F. Season spinach with salt and pepper; set aside. In a separate bowl, mix ricotta cheese, Parmesan cheese and parsley; set side. Prepare crêpes by mixing egg whites, flour and water; beat with a wire whisk to smooth out lumps. Prepare crêpe pan or small skillet, with olive oil, and heat to medium temperature. Ladle 2 to 3 tablespoons crêpe batter into heated pan, tilting pan to spread batter evenly. When edges of crêpe start to turn brown, gently flip crêpe over. Cook another 15 seconds and slide crêpe onto plate. Continue until all batter is used. To assemble, spoon 2 to 3 tablespoons of ricotta cheese mixture onto each crêpe, topped with 1 tablespoon spinach mixture. Fold each crêpe to seal in fillings. Place crêpes in greased rectangular baking pan and cover with marinara sauce. Bake 15 to 20 minutes. Remove from oven and serve with extra Parmesan cheese, if desired.

MARINARA SAUCE

2 tablespoons extra virgin olive oil	4 cups canned Italian plum tomatoes, undrained
2 tablespoons unsalted butter	1 tablespoon tomato paste
1 large onion, finely chopped (1 cup)	Freshly ground pepper
1 cup finely chopped carrot	3 flat anchovy fillets, drained, rinsed in ice water and finely chopped (1 teaspoon)
1 tablespoon dried basil	Dash of red pepper flakes
2 tablespoons minced Italian (flat leaf) parsley	Sea salt (regular table salt may be used)
1 bay leaf	

Place olive oil and butter in a large, heavy skillet on low heat. Add the onion and cook until tender. Stir in the carrot and cook another 5 minutes. Add the basil, parsley and bay leaf. Simmer 2 more minutes, stirring constantly. Pour the tomatoes and their juice into the skillet and increase the heat to bring mixture to a boil. Using the back of the cooking spoon, mash the tomatoes to break them up. Stir in the tomato paste and season well with pepper. Continue to cook on medium-high heat 40 to 45 minutes, or until most of the juice has evaporated and the sauce resembles a thick purée. Avoid scorching sauce. Remove and discard bay leaf. Pour the sauce into a food mill and purée. Do not use a blender because the end product would liquefy too much. Press the sauce through a sieve, returning the sauce to the pan. Discard contents of sieve. Bring sauce to a simmer over low heat; add anchovies and red pepper flakes. Cook until sauce has been reduced to 2 cups, stirring frequently. Sprinkle with salt.

Quick Spinach-Topped French Bread

Busy people enjoy this recipe not only because it's so easy,
but also because it's so delicious.

¼ pound butter, melted (1 stick)	1 package (10-ounce) frozen chopped spinach, thawed and squeezed dry
8 ounces cheddar cheese, shredded (2 cups)	
8 ounces mozzarella cheese, shredded (2 cups)	½ teaspoon granulated garlic
	1 loaf French bread, cut lengthwise

Preheat oven to 350°F. Mix together butter, cheddar cheese, mozzarella cheese, spinach and granulated garlic. Spread mixture evenly on cut surface of bread. Place on a baking sheet and bake at 350°F 10 to 15 minutes.

Note: May be wrapped in foil and frozen before baking.

Feta and Spinach Bread

My first taste of feta cheese was in Athens, Greece at a little restaurant near the Parthenon. Whenever I prepare a recipe using feta, I'm immediately taken back to that lovely country. Greeks are beautiful people very passionate about love of country, love of family and love of good food.

1 small onion, chopped (½ cup)	8 ounces cheddar cheese, shredded (2 cups)
1 small garlic clove, minced	
¼ pound butter (1 stick)	2 tablespoons chopped black olives
1 package (10-ounce) frozen chopped spinach, thawed and squeezed dry	
	¼ teaspoon freshly ground pepper
4 slices lean bacon, cooked crisp and crumbled	2 loaves French bread, cut lengthwise
4 ounces feta cheese, crumbled	Extra butter for bread

Preheat oven to 350°F. Sauté onion and garlic in butter. Add spinach and sauté another 3 to 5 minutes. Add bacon and cheeses. Stir gently until melted. Add olives and pepper. Spread butter on both cut sides of bread. Spread spinach mixture on one half of each loaf, topping with remaining halves. Wrap loaves in foil. Place in oven until heated through. Slice before serving.

GREEK SALAD PITA SANDWICHES

Light and nutritious, these pita sandwiches make this the perfect lunch.

12	ounces small tomatoes, cored, halved and thinly sliced	16	large, fresh basil leaves, shredded
6	cups small spinach leaves, stemmed, thoroughly washed and patted dry	¼	cup extra virgin olive oil
		1 ½	tablespoons fresh lemon juice
1 ½	cups thinly sliced cucumber	1	garlic clove, minced
4	ounces feta cheese, crumbled		Salt and freshly ground pepper
⅓	cup coarsely chopped Kalamata olives	4	round wheat pita breads, toasted

Place tomato slices in strainer; drain 20 minutes. Combine drained tomato, spinach, cucumber, feta cheese, olives and basil in large bowl. Whisk olive oil, lemon juice and garlic in a small bowl to blend. Season olive oil mixture with salt and pepper. Pour over salad and toss to coat. Cut pita bread in half crosswise. Divide salad mixture among pita halves and serve.

SAUSAGE CALZONES WITH SPINACH

Hot Italian sausage adds a robust flavor to these calzones.

1	box (16-ounce) hot roll mix	1	pound hot Italian sausage, casing removed, cooked, and drained
2	tablespoons extra virgin olive oil		
1	package (9-ounce) frozen creamed spinach, defrosted	⅓	cup freshly grated Parmesan cheese
8	ounces mozzarella cheese, shredded (2 cups)		

Preheat oven to 425°F. Prepare hot roll mix according to package directions, omitting egg and margarine, and adding 1 ¼ cups hot water and 2 tablespoons olive oil to flour and yeast mixture. Knead dough 5 minutes. Divide dough into 8 pieces; set aside 10 minutes. Mix together creamed spinach, mozzarella cheese, sausage, and Parmesan cheese. Roll each piece of dough onto lightly floured work surface, forming 6-inch circles. Spoon ½ cup spinach mixture onto each circle. Fold dough over filling to form half circle; press edges together with fork to seal. Place calzones on 2 greased baking sheets. Prick tops with fork. Bake 12 to 15 minutes, or until golden brown. Serve warm.

SPINACH AND FETA CHEESE STRATA

Assemble this dish the night before and place it in the refrigerator.
The next morning, all you need to do is pop it in the oven.

6	croissants, split in half lengthwise	½	teaspoon salt
6	eggs, beaten	¼	teaspoon freshly ground pepper
1 ½	cups milk	¼	teaspoon ground nutmeg
1	package (10-ounce) frozen chopped spinach, thawed and squeezed dry	6	ounces Monterey Jack cheese, grated (1 ½ cups)
		8	ounces feta cheese, crumbled

Preheat oven to 350°F. Arrange croissant halves on a greased baking pan, with sides overlapping. In a medium bowl, combine eggs, milk, spinach, salt, pepper and nutmeg. Spread spinach mixture over croissants. Sprinkle cheeses over spinach mixture. Cover and refrigerate 8 hours or overnight. Uncover and bake 40 to 45 minutes, or until lightly browned. Serve immediately.

EASY SPINACH CROISSANTS

Need a quick sandwich? These are so easy to prepare
that you can fix them on your lunch break.

1	package (10-ounce) frozen chopped spinach, thawed and squeezed dry	6	croissants, split in half lengthwise
4	ounces feta cheese, crumbled	3	slices Swiss cheese, cut in half diagonally

Preheat oven to 425°F. In a medium mixing bowl, stir together the spinach and feta cheese. Lay the bottom halves of the croissants on a large baking sheet. Spoon the spinach mixture onto the croissant bottoms. Place a piece of Swiss cheese on top. Bake until the cheese is bubbly. Remove from oven and immediately cover with the top halves of the croissants. Serve warm.

WEEKEND BREAKFAST-IN-BREAD

For a most enjoyable brunch, prepare these stuffed loaves ahead of time. Your overnight guests will savour the pleasure of your company as you join them in relaxed conversation. Sausage, spinach, cheese and scrambled eggs create the colorful layers inside round bread loaves. Wrapped in foil and kept warm in the oven, this captivating and gratifying meal can be cut into generous wedges and served alongside fresh fruit and hot coffee.

2 loaves round bread (about 6 inches high)	8 eggs
1 pound top-quality bulk sausage	¼ cup evaporated milk, or whole milk
1 medium onion, finely chopped (¾ cup)	1 teaspoon chopped fresh basil leaves
½ bell pepper, finely chopped (½ cup)	Salt and white pepper
1 can (10-ounce) Rotel tomatoes, chopped and undrained	4 ounces mozzarella or Monterey Jack cheese, shredded (1 cup)
Tabasco (optional)	1 package (10-ounce) frozen chopped spinach, cooked and squeezed dry
1 tablespoon butter	

Preheat oven to 375°F. Cut a slice off tops of both bread loaves; set aside. Carefully remove inside of loaves, forming hollow bowls; set aside. In a heavy skillet, brown sausage; drain well. Add onion and bell pepper and cook until tender. Add Rotel tomatoes; simmer until liquid has evaporated. Meanwhile, melt butter in a medium skillet. Beat eggs along with evaporated milk, basil, salt and pepper. Scramble egg mixture in skillet, but do not overcook. Eggs should still be moist; keep warm. Sprinkle a little cheese on the inside bottom of the bread bowls. Divide fillings in half and fill each bread loaf. First, spoon a layer of sausage, a thin layer of cheese, a layer of eggs (using all the eggs), then spinach. Repeat with another layer of cheese, sausage, cheese, spinach; end with a layer of cheese on top. Sprinkle a little bit of cheese along the rim of the bread bowl and replace the slice that was removed. (As the cheese melts, the top will stay attached.) Wrap each bread loaf in extra-heavy foil. Place on baking sheet and bake 20 to 30 minutes. If the loaves need to be kept warm for an hour or two before serving, turn oven to warm setting after 15 minutes of baking. To serve, remove foil and cut into thick wedges.

STUFFED ITALIAN CALZONE

Served with a bottle of Chianti, these calzones
will take you back in time to romantic Italy.

1	can (14 ½-ounce) tomatoes, well drained	½	cup chopped pimiento-stuffed green olives
1	package (10-ounce) frozen chopped spinach, thawed and squeezed dry	⅓	cup freshly grated Parmesan cheese
1	package (3 ½-ounce) thinly sliced pepperoni, chopped (¾ cup)	1 ½	teaspoons garlic powder
		1 ½	teaspoons dried basil leaves
		1 ½	teaspoons dried oregano leaves
3	ounces thinly sliced salami, chopped (¾ cup)	1	teaspoon freshly ground pepper
4	ounces mozzarella cheese, shredded (1 cup)	2	(1-pound) loaves frozen bread dough, thawed
1	cup ricotta cheese	2	tablespoons extra virgin olive oil

Preheat oven to 350°F. Using a large bowl, combine tomatoes, spinach, pepperoni, salami, mozzarella cheese, ricotta cheese, olives, Parmesan cheese, garlic powder, basil, oregano and pepper. Set aside. Cut each bread loaf in half. On a lightly floured work surface, roll one bread dough in a 12-inch circle. Place circle on pizza pan. Spread 1 ⅓ cups of filling on one half of dough circle, stopping ½ inch from edge. Fold dough over filling forming a half circle. Press along edges with fork to form seal. Cut 3 or 4 slits in dough to allow steam to escape. Repeat process making 3 more calzones. Bake 20 minutes. Brush with olive oil and bake another 5 to 10 minutes, or until tops are golden brown. Allow to stand 10 minutes before cutting.

CRAB AND SPINACH TORTA

Both wholesome and bountiful, this recipe produces a generous meal. If fresh crabmeat isn't available, try using canned. Just rinse canned crabmeat in ice water first and drain well.

2 (1-pound) loaves frozen bread dough, thawed
1 tablespoon chopped fresh thyme, or 1 teaspoon dried
1 medium red onion, chopped (¾ cup)
1 garlic clove, minced
3 cups fresh sliced mushrooms (¾ pound)
   Salt and freshly ground pepper
3 tablespoons extra virgin olive oil
2 tablespoons chopped fresh dill

4 small zucchini, sliced ¼-inch thick
½ bunch fresh spinach leaves, thoroughly washed and patted dry
3 ounces Monterey Jack cheese, shredded (¾ cup)
3 ounces mozzarella cheese, shredded (¾ cup)
8 ounces crabmeat, cooked and flaked (1 ½ cups)
1 egg, lightly beaten

Preheat oven to 375°F. Combine both loaves of bread dough and allow to rise until doubled in size. On a floured work surface, sprinkle dough with thyme and roll dough into a 18-inch circle. Transfer dough circle to a greased, 10-inch springform pan, letting the edges drape over the sides. Sauté onion, garlic, mushrooms, salt and pepper in 2 tablespoons of the olive oil until tender, about 7 minutes. Stir in dill and set aside. Sauté zucchini in remaining oil until tender. Layer half of the mushroom mixture into the dough-lined pan, continuing with layers of half the zucchini, half the spinach leaves, half the cheeses and half the crabmeat. Repeat. Bring dough together over top of fillings, leaving a small vent for steam to escape. Brush lightly with beaten egg. Bake 45 to 55 minutes, or until golden and crusty. Cut into wedges to serve.

EASY SPINACH BREAD

The smooth and creamy spinach filling of this bread provides a nice snack for all to enjoy. And speaking of "bread"...an old friend of mine told me a story about his early scouting days. The boys went on a camping trip and used their new canvas tent. It poured down rain that night so one of the boys decided to rub his hand on the inside roof of the tent, just to see what would happen. Well sure enough, the rain came pouring in. My friend ran and jumped into the back seat of the Scout Master's car and slept like a baby. The next morning he crawled back into the tent, thinking nobody would know. At breakfast, the Scout Master said they would not be able to have toast or even sandwiches all weekend because "someone" had totally flattened all the loaves of bread he had laid across the back seat of his car!

2	(1-pound) loaves frozen bread dough, thawed	2	tablespoons extra virgin olive oil
8	ounces cream cheese	2	garlic cloves, finely minced
1	package (10-ounce) frozen chopped spinach, thawed and squeezed dry		

Roll out one loaf of bread dough 9 x 12 inches and place on a baking sheet. Spread cream cheese onto dough, leaving ¾-inch along edges uncovered. Spread spinach lightly over cream cheese. In a small bowl, mix olive oil and garlic. Spread evenly over spinach. Using about ¾ of the second bread dough, roll out into a rectangle and place on top of first rectangle. Dampen the edges slightly with a little water and bring up the sides from the bottom and seal by crimping. Remaining dough may be cut into shapes using a cookie cutter and arranged in a pattern on top of the bread. Allow to stand while preheating oven to 350°F. Bake until golden brown.

STUFFED BREAD WITH TOMATO MUSTARD

Whenever I see this stuffed bread roll, it reminds me of the jellyrolls my grandmother used to bake. One taste will make this spinach and feta cheese-stuffed bread one of your favorite recipes. The Tomato Mustard is my all-time number one choice for spreading on any spinach bread.

1   medium onion, chopped
    (¾ cup)
1   garlic clove, minced
2   tablespoons extra virgin olive
    oil
2   (10-ounce) packages fresh
    spinach leaves, chopped
    Juice from one lemon

1 ½   pounds pizza dough
8   ounces feta cheese, crumbled
1   egg
1   tablespoon cold water
1   tablespoon poppy seeds or
    sesame seeds (optional)
    Tomato Mustard
    (recipe follows)

Preheat oven to 350°F. In a large skillet, sauté onion and garlic in olive oil. Add spinach and allow to wilt. Remove spinach mixture from skillet and spoon into a large sieve, pressing with the back of a spoon to remove moisture. Place spinach mixture and lemon juice in a bowl. Roll out the pizza dough into rectangle shape. Spread a layer of spinach mixture on dough, smoothing with a spatula. Top with a layer of feta cheese, pressing it down with a spatula. Roll the dough from one end to another, like a jellyroll. Pinch seams together. Cover the bottom of a large baking sheet with parchment paper sprayed with non-stick cooking spray, if desired. Carefully place spinach roll on parchment paper. Prepare egg wash by lightly beating egg with water; brush roll with egg wash using a pastry brush. Sprinkle seeds on top. Cut diagonal slits into the dough to expose spinach filling. Bake 40 to 50 minutes, or until golden brown.

TOMATO MUSTARD

⅓   cup dry white wine
¼   cup dry mustard
¼   cup top-quality white wine
    vinegar
1   tablespoon sugar
½   teaspoon salt

3   egg yolks
¼   cup tomato paste
2   tablespoons diced pimiento,
    drained
1   teaspoon Hungarian paprika

In top of a double boiler, combine white wine, dry mustard, white wine vinegar, sugar and salt. Allow to stand two hours. Whisk in egg yolks. Add tomato paste, pimiento and paprika, whisking constantly. Cook over hot water (not boiling) 5 minutes. Transfer mixture to a small glass jar and allow to cool; cover and refrigerate up to 3 weeks. May also be used as a sandwich spread, or served with shrimp, fish or even baked ham.

SPINACH MUFFINS

Need a new and refreshing idea for a side dish? Bake a batch of these muffins and even your kids will gobble them up. (Tomato Mustard also tastes yummy with these muffins.)

⅔ cup milk
1 tablespoon vegetable oil
1 egg
½ cup coarsely chopped fresh spinach
2 ounces Swiss cheese, shredded (½ cup)

¼ cup freshly grated Parmesan cheese
2 large scallions, chopped
2 cups buttermilk biscuit baking mix

Preheat oven to 400°F. Grease the bottom and sides of 12 medium muffin pans. In a medium mixing bowl, beat the milk, oil and egg until well blended. Stir in spinach, cheeses, scallions and baking mix, just until moistened. Divide the batter evenly among the muffin cups. Bake 15 to 17 minutes, or until golden brown. Cool slightly before removing from pan.

STUFFED CORNBREAD

As a child, we often had cornbread and milk on Sunday evenings for dinner, especially on days when we had a big Sunday lunch. This cornbread is so good, you won't be able to wait for Sunday.

3	cups yellow cornmeal	4	ounces cheddar cheese, shredded (1 cup)
¼	cup all-purpose flour		
4	tablespoons baking powder	12	ounces lean bacon, cooked and crumbled (1 cup)
1	teaspoon salt		
2	eggs, lightly beaten	1	package (10-ounce) frozen chopped spinach, thawed and squeezed dry
¼	cup vegetable oil		
1	cup milk		

Preheat oven to 350°F. Place a large cast iron skillet into oven to heat. In a large bowl, combine cornmeal, flour, baking powder and salt. Add eggs, oil and milk to cornmeal mixture. Remove hot skillet from oven. Pour ⅓ of cornbread mixture into skillet. Alternate with layers of cheese, bacon, spinach and cornmeal mixture, ending with cornmeal mixture on top. Return skillet to oven and bake 45 to 50 minutes.

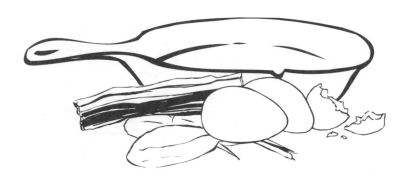

STUFFED PISTOLETTES

Pistolettes are French Style enriched brown-and-serve rolls. They are hard-crusted, about the size of a fist and are lightly covered with cornmeal. Once filled, they can be baked in the oven, or deep-fried until golden brown, which takes only a minute or two. This is definitely a "must try" recipe.

1	package (10-ounce) frozen chopped spinach, cooked and squeezed dry	1	tablespoon butter
1	tablespoon bacon drippings	1	tablespoon all-purpose flour
½	small onion, chopped (¼ cup)	¼	cup half-and-half (milk may be substituted)
1	small garlic clove, minced	3	slices lean bacon, cooked crisp and crumbled
2	tablespoons toasted pine nuts	12	Pistolettes (hard-crusted dinner rolls dusted with cornmeal)
2	ounces feta cheese, crumbled (or cheese of your choice)		Flour and water "paste"
	Dash of salt		Vegetable oil for deep-frying (optional)
	Dash of white pepper		
	Dash of cayenne		

Chop spinach in food processor; set aside. Heat bacon drippings in heavy skillet and sauté onion until tender; add garlic and cook 2 minutes. Add spinach, pine nuts and feta cheese. Season with salt, white pepper and cayenne. Stir well and heat through. In a separate skillet, melt butter over medium heat. Gradually add flour, stirring constantly. Slowly add half-and-half and continue cooking until bubbly; do not allow mixture to brown. Add spinach mixture, stir and heat until well blended. Add bacon pieces and remove from heat. To prepare Pistolettes, cut off one end, about ½-inch thick, and set aside. Poke a hole in the cut end of the roll using the handle of a wooden spoon. Be careful not to push the handle through the far side, causing a hole in the roll because the filling will fall out. Slowly and gently rotate the handle, pushing the inside walls of the bread toward the outside, forming a hollow shell for the filling. Spoon the spinach mixture into the opening, gently pushing down with the wooden handle. Mix a little flour and water until a soft paste-like consistency forms. Use this "paste" to reattach the end slice to the filled Pistolette. Stuffed Pistolettes may now be baked at 400°F until golden brown, or dropped into heated cooking oil until browned. Drain fried pistolettes on paper towels; serve hot.

HERB GUIDE

Basil

Fresh basil has a sweet clove-like spiciness. Dried basil has a flavor that leans more toward anise and lemon. It is good with tomatoes, pasta, pesto, shrimp and fish, most vegetables, beans, soups and salad dressings.

Chives

Chives have a slightly sweet, light onion flavor and lift many foods above the mundane. They are best fresh. Chives go well with soft cheeses, vegetables, salad dressings, potatoes, egg dishes such as omelets, soup and fish. They also taste great in herb butters.

Dill

Fresh dill has a sweet, full aroma. The seeds are delicious fresh or dried. The leaves are best used fresh, but may be used dry. Dill is great in pickled cucumbers, breads, pasta, coleslaw, scrambled eggs, potato salad, and cream soups.

Fennel

Fennel has a pronounced aniseed flavor, with its seeds having the strongest flavor; dried fennel loses most of its flavor. The seeds, leaves and bulbs are all used in cooking. Mix with thyme and parsley to create an herb butter for fish, or mix with rosemary and garlic for roasted pork. Great in breads, sauces and soups. Seeds are a main seasoning in Italian sausage.

Garlic

Fresh garlic is strongest when first cut or mashed and used raw. Roasted garlic has a more mellow taste. Use with sauces, dressings, meats, fish, poultry, and tomato dishes. Cut a clove in half and rub cut side on inner surface of salad bowl before adding fresh salad for just a hint of flavor.

Marjoram

Fresh and dried marjoram are both delicious, possessing a distinctive savory flavor. A cousin to the stronger oregano, marjoram is good with any robust-flavored food. Use in butter sauces for fish, with cheese, chopped meats, soups, stews, potatoes, pasta, rice and most vegetables.

Mint

Mint has a clean, sharp flavor and is best used fresh, with peppermint being the most popular choice. Use fresh leaves in both fruit and vegetable salads, creamy fruit soups and when making mint jelly. Rub fresh leaves on poultry before baking.

Oregano

Oregano is a very popular herb, especially in Italian cooking. Use in pizzas, meats, beans, sauces, soups and fresh mushrooms. It couples well with tomatoes, eggs and cheeses, and can be used fresh, dried or frozen.

Parsley

Flat-leaf (Italian) parsley is known for its flavor, whereas curly parsley is most often used for plate garnishing. Add parsley toward the end of the cooking time to soups, sauces, egg dishes, salads, creamed potatoes and marinades. Sprinkle over vegetables, hot cooked rice, pasta and potatoes. Combine with bay and thyme for a bouquet garni.

Rosemary

Rosemary is an aromatic resinous leaf which aids the digestion of fats in foods such as lamb and pork. It is delicious in breads and biscuits, soups, egg dishes, baked fish, meats, basting sauces and poultry. Dried rosemary retains its flavor well.

Sage

Sage has a strong, pungent flavor that's best when used lightly in foods. It's a classic in turkey stuffing and in poultry seasoning blends. Mix sage with fennel and use with fish, veal and sausage.

Tarragon

Tarragon is an aristocratic herb with a mild flavor and a hidden tang. It is excellent used in salad dressings and flavored vinegars. Add to poached fish, cooked vegetables, mustards, sautéed meats and even sugar cookies. Tarragon is indispensable for hollandaise and Béarnaise sauces.

Thyme

Thyme is a strong herb with a sweet fragrance. It adds a fine flavor to marinades, eggs, tomato sauces, chowders, meats and poultry, pasta, rice dishes, and especially mushrooms, tomatoes and potatoes. Use lemon thyme in fish and poultry dishes.

acidulated water: [a-SIHD-yoo-lay-ted] water to which a small amount of lemon juice, lime juice or vinegar has been added. Fruits and vegetables that darken quickly (such as apples) when their cut surfaces are exposed to air, are dipped in this water to prevent discoloration.

al dente: [al-DEN-tay] pasta cooked just enough to retain a somewhat firm texture; an Italian phrase meaning "to the tooth," used to describe food that is cooked only until it offers a slight resistance when bitten into.

andouille sausage: [ahn-DOO-ee] a heavily smoked sausage made from tripe and pork chitterlings; French in origin, andouille is a spicy, specialty sausage of Cajun/Creole cooking. It's traditionally used in jambalaya and gumbo.

balsamic: [bal-SAH-mihk] vinegar that is made from unfermented grape juice and aged in wooden casks.

Béchamel sauce: [BEH-shah-mehl] a basic French white sauce made by stirring milk into a butter-flour roux. The thickness of the sauce depends on the proportion of flour and butter to milk. Béchamel, the base of many other sauces, was named after its inventor, Louis XIV's steward Louis de Béchamel.

calzone: [kal-ZOH-nay] a stuffed pizza that resembles a large turnover, which is then deep-fried or brushed with olive oil and baked. Usually made as an individual serving, the fillings can be various vegetables, meats, or cheeses; mozzarella is the cheese used most frequently.

caper: [KAY-per] a pickled flower bud from the caper shrub (from the Mediterranean region), pickled and used as a seasoning, condiment or garnish.

caramelized: [KA-rah-mah-lyzd] to convert (as sugar) into caramel.

cilantro: [sih-LAHN-troh] the parsley-like leaves of coriander used as a flavoring or garnish.

crepe: [KREHP] a very thin pancake, often rolled around a filling, like a cigar.

croustade: [kroo-STAHD] an edible container made from a deep-fried or toasted pastry, a hollowed-out bread loaf, or puréed potatoes or pasta, that have been shaped to form a casing for food.

crudités: [kroo-dee-TAYZ] raw vegetables, such as celery sticks, carrot sticks, radishes, and bell pepper strips, often served with a dip.

feta: [FEHT-uh] a white, moderately hard and crumbly Greek cheese made from ewe's or goat's milk, which has been preserved in brine.

florentine: [FLOHR-uhn-teen] served, prepared or dressed with spinach.

frittata: [frih-TAH-tuh] an unfolded omelet, sometimes baked in a skillet in the oven, often containing chopped vegetables or meats.

Herbsaint: [EHRB-saint] an anise-flavored liqueur developed and made primarily in New Orleans; used in such specialties as Oysters Rockefeller.

herbes de Provence: [EHRBZ duh proh-VAWNS] an assortment of dried herbs most commonly used in southern France; commonly contains basil, lavender, fennel seed, rosemary, marjoram, sage, summer savory and thyme.

hors d'oeuvres: [or DERVZ] small appetizers, usually finger foods, that are served before a meal.

Kalamata: [kahl-uh-MAH-tuh] a Greek almond-shaped olive, ½ to 1 inch in size; they're a dark aubergine color and have a flavor that can be rich and fruity; slit to allow the wine vinegar marinade to penetrate the flesh.

manicotti: [man-uh-KOT-tee] pasta shaped like tubes, that may be stuffed with a ricotta cheese or meat mixture.

marinara: [mah-ree-NAHR-uh] an Italian sauce made with tomatoes, onions, garlic, and spices.

Montrachet: [mohn-truh-SHAY] a soft, mild cheese made from goat's milk.

Mornay: [mohr-NAY] a white sauce to which Parmesan cheese or Swiss cheese, has been added; served with eggs, fish, shellfish, vegetables or chicken.

orzo: [OHR-zoh] a rice-shaped pasta; also referred to as "rosamarina."

Pernod: [pehr-NOH] a yellowish, licorice-flavored liqueur very popular in France; usually mixed with water, which turns it whitish and cloudy; similar in taste to Absinthe. (Absinthe is a potent, bitter liqueur distilled from wormwood and flavored with a variety of herbs. It has a distinct anise flavor and is 68 percent alcohol [136 proof]. Absinthe is usually diluted with water, which changes the color of the liqueur from green to milky white. Because it's considered habit forming and hazardous to health, Absinthe is prohibited in many countries and was banned in the United States in the early 1900's.)

pesto: [PEH-stoh] a sauce made with fresh basil, garlic, olive oil, pine nuts, butter and grated cheese (usually Parmesan and/or Romano); usually used to coat hot cooked angel hair pasta.

phyllo: [FEE-loh] an extremely thin pastry dough that is layered, producing a flaky pastry.

portobello: [por-toh-BEHL-loh] a very large cultivated mushroom belonging to a dark meaty variety of the button mushroom.

prosciutto: [proh-SHOO-toh] a dry-cured spiced Italian ham, usually sliced very thin.

puff pastry: a pastry dough made of many alternating layers of dough and butter, or the light flaky pastry made from it.

quiche: [KEESH] an unsweetened egg and cheese custard pie, usually having a savory filling (such as spinach, mushrooms, bacon or ham).

ricotta: [rih-KAHT-tuh] a white unripened whey cheese of Italy, that resembles cottage cheese.

Rockefeller: [RAH-kah-feh-ler] a mixture of chopped spinach, butter, bread crumbs and seasonings often served over oysters on the half shell, either baked or broiled.

roulade: [roo-LAHD] a soufflé-type mixture that's spread on a jelly roll pan and baked until firm but still moist, then spread with a savory or sweet filling and rolled up in a jelly-roll fashion; a slice of meat rolled around a filling and cooked.

saffron: [SAF-ruhn] a pungent, aromatic spice of yellow-orange stigmas from a small purple crocus. Saffron is the world's most expensive spice.

scallion: [SKAL-yuhn] a green onion; a member of the onion family; immature onions which have a white base that has not fully developed into a bulb and green leaves that are long and straight.

soufflé: [soo-FLAY] a dish that is made from a sauce, egg yolks, stiffly-beaten egg whites, and a flavoring or purée (such as seafood, fruit, or vegetables) and baked until puffed up.

spanakopita: [span-uh-KOH-pih-tuh] originating in Greece, this traditional savory pie consists of top and bottom phyllo-dough crusts with a filling of spinach, onions, feta cheese, eggs and seasonings.

strata: [STRAH-tuh] horizontal layers arranged one on top of another.

stromboli: [strahm-BOH-lee] a calzone-like enclosed sandwich wrapped in a pizza dough and baked.

tasso: [TAH-soh] a lean chunk of cured meat (most often pork, but sometimes turkey or beef) that has been richly seasoned with ingredients such as cayenne, garlic, filé powder and any of several other herbs or spices. It is then smoked for about two days. The result is a firm, smoky and highly-flavored meat that is principally used for seasoning.

tofu: [TOH-foo] soybean curd sometimes used in Oriental cooking.

tomatillo: [tohm-ah-TEE-oh] the small round pale green, yellow or purplish edible viscid fruit of a Mexican ground-cherry.

torta: [TOHR-tuh] the Italian word for tart; the Spanish word for cake, loaf or sandwich.

zest: outer peel of lemons, limes and oranges, which contains a strong fruit flavor; the grated peeling, without the white pith.

Index

 *Index*

Index

Index

285

Burgundy L. Olivier
"i love SPINACH"
P.O. Box 61952 • Lafayette, LA 70596

Please send _____ copy(ies)   @ \$19.95 each _____
    Postage and handling   @ \$ 4.95 each _____
    Louisiana residents add sales tax   @ \$ 1.50 each _____
                           Total _____

Name _____
Address _____
City _____ State _____ Zip _____

Make checks payable to: **Burgundy L. Olivier**

Burgundy L. Olivier
"i love SPINACH"
P.O. Box 61952 • Lafayette, LA 70596

Please send _____ copy(ies)   @ \$19.95 each _____
    Postage and handling   @ \$ 4.95 each _____
    Louisiana residents add sales tax   @ \$ 1.50 each _____
                           Total _____

Name _____
Address _____
City _____ State _____ Zip _____

Make checks payable to: **Burgundy L. Olivier**

Burgundy L. Olivier
"i love SPINACH"
P.O. Box 61952 • Lafayette, LA 70596

Please send _____ copy(ies)   @ \$19.95 each _____
    Postage and handling   @ \$ 4.95 each _____
    Louisiana residents add sales tax   @ \$ 1.50 each _____
                           Total _____

Name _____
Address _____
City _____ State _____ Zip _____

Make checks payable to: **Burgundy L. Olivier**